D1526636

BOXING IN AMERICA

BOXING IN AMERICA

An Autopsy

David L. Hudson, Jr.

 PRAEGER

AN IMPRINT OF ABC-CLIO, LLC
Santa Barbara, California • Denver, Colorado • Oxford, England

Library of Congress Cataloging-in-Publication Data

Hudson, David L., 1969–
    Boxing in America : an autopsy / David L. Hudson, Jr.
        p. cm.
    Includes index.
    ISBN 978-0-313-37972-7 (hardback) — ISBN 978-0-313-37973-4 (ebook)
1. Boxing—United States—History.   2. Boxing—Social aspects—
United States.   I. Title.
    GV1125.H84   2012
    796.83—dc23   2012005007

ISBN: 978-0-313-37972-7
EISBN: 978-0-313-37973-4

16   15   14   13   12   1   2   3   4   5

This book is also available on the World Wide Web as an eBook.
Visit www.abc-clio.com for details.

Praeger
An Imprint of ABC-CLIO, LLC

ABC-CLIO, LLC
130 Cremona Drive, P.O. Box 1911
Santa Barbara, California 93116-1911

This book is printed on acid-free paper ∞

Manufactured in the United States of America

To Harold Lederman—the best person in boxing

CONTENTS

INTRODUCTION

The sport of boxing possesses a primal power that seeps into one's soul. Perhaps it appeals to innate violent instincts. Perhaps it compels attention because of its naked drama. Two men—or women—attempt to batter each other senseless, to render the opponent unconscious. For whatever reason, it creates addicts out of its aficionados, who crave another high.

Think of the epic "Thrilla in Manila"—the fatalistic, fistic encounter between Muhammad Ali and Joe Frazier that concluded their trilogy. Consider "Irish" Micky Ward and the late Arturo Gatti, who waged their own trilogy—albeit on a lesser plane. Think of Jose Luis Castillo and the late warrior Diego Corrales, who beat each other senseless.

No doubt, boxing suffers from certain woes. Some wish that it would be abolished as barbaric baseness. The medical community and others urge its abolition, the underworld has seized it as its own, and the greedy have sought to exploit its participants.

For all its warts, boxing remains a beautiful art when practiced at its finest. There remains no more superbly conditioned athlete than a top-flight professional boxer. The best boxers—those who have mastered the science of pugilism—possess an uncanny, almost unnatural power over others. But, at its heart, the sport of boxing attracts—or demands—attention because of its brutal simplicity.

It has inspired the best of writers to tap deep into their creativity. Consider that Ernest Hemingway, Jack London, Norman Mailer, and Joyce Carol Oates have committed their considerable literary talents to writing about the sport.

Boxing in America: An Autopsy takes a panoramic view of the sport of boxing by covering different fighters, different eras, and different subjects. Much of the book focuses on the dominant heavyweight champions of certain time periods. There are many great fighters in the lighter weight classes, but the heavyweight champions have garnered the most attention and the most acclaim. Just as the United States Supreme Court is known by the last name of the Chief Justice—the Warren Court after Chief Justice Earl Warren—boxing often is known by the holder of the heavyweight crown. We speak of the age of Louis, the age of Ali, or the age of Tyson.

John L. Sullivan—the last bare-knuckle heavyweight champion—dominates the discussion in chapter 1. The bravado, charisma, and natural punching power catapulted the "Boston Strong Boy" to fame and fortune. He became a bona fide American sports hero.

Chapter 2 focuses on as compelling and divisive a subject that the United States of America ever has grappled with—the specter of race and racism. For many years, an abject color bar prevented the top black fighters from receiving their "just due"[1]—to quote former heavyweight champion Larry Holmes. The centerpiece of chapter 2 focuses on the life of Jack Johnson, the colorful, controversial champion who inspired visceral hatred from white America.

Johnson cast a long shadow over the sport of boxing, long enough that it took years for another African American to receive a shot at the heavyweight crown. Chapter 3 looks at a man who became a genuine American hero—Joseph Louis Barrow, better known as Joe Louis. The "Brown Bomber" held the heavyweight championship for more than a decade, defending his title an astonishing 25 times.

Louis started a trend that continued for many years—of African Americans dominating boxing in the heavyweight division. A prominent exception was an Italian American from Brockton, Massachusetts, named Rocky Marciano (covered in chapter 4). "The Rock" never lost a professional fight, compiling a record of 49–0. He personified the 1950s, when America felt good about itself, a golden age of sorts.

The 1960s were a different, more volatile time in U.S. history. The civil rights movement and the Vietnam War created a vortex of social activism unmatched in modern U.S. history. Out of this mix came a loquacious lightning rod named at birth as Cassius Marcellus Clay, covered in chapter 5. He converted to Islam, changed his name to Muhammad Ali, and became a vilified figure. This hated figure later became the most recognizable—and perhaps most beloved—figure on the planet. He truly was incomparable.

Turning from the incomparable to the improbable, there perhaps is no greater comeback in the sport of boxing than that of a former champion in the 1970s who returned to the ring amid cries of ridicule in the late 1980s as an overweight preacher. This former sullen monster of a man literally transformed himself into a different person and regained the heavyweight title in the most improbable fashion at age 45. Chapter 6 tells the inspiring story of "Big" George Foreman. Chapter 7 then tells the incredible story of "Iron" Mike Tyson—a compelling if tragic figure in the sport of boxing.

After examining several ages of boxing through the prism of heavyweight greats, the book turns to other serious topics. Much of the book focuses on dominant champions and top contenders. But the lifeblood of the sport, the club fighters who ply their trade without fanfare, are called journeymen. They travel to other fighters' hometowns on short notice against long odds. Most of the time, journeymen lose either legitimately or by hometown decisions. But sometimes they reach up and grab the brass ring. Prospects and champions start their career by facing these fighters. Chapter 8 highlights some of the more unusual journeymen of recent vintage in American boxing.

Chapter 9 focuses on the most controversial aspect of boxing: death in the ring. Boxing inflicts punishment on its combatants in most brutal fashion. While a precious few boxers have become nonagenarians—former champion Max Schmeling lived to age 99—many have not survived brutal ring encounters. The images of a beaten Benny "Kid" Paret slumped in the corner still horrify those who saw it. Too other pugilists have met the same tragic end.

Boxing and prison have had a unique relationship for many years. In prison, an inmate literally must fight to survive; the same stark phenomenon takes place in the boxing ring. Many prominent fighters learned boxing behind bars. A few even fought professionally as prison inmates. Chapter 10 focuses on one of the most mystifying characters in all of boxing history—Charles "Sonny" Liston.

Finally, the book concludes with chapter 11, "The Future of Boxing and the Threat of Mixed Martial Arts." Boxing has taken a beating in recent years, while another sport—mixed martial arts—has attracted greater crowds and generated more fight cards. Mixed martial arts—particularly at the highest level in the Ultimate Fighting Championship (UFC)—have mastered the art of putting on competitive cards, matching the best fighters against each other, and avoiding the promotional tug-of-wars that sometimes afflict boxing.

I am one of those souls addicted to the sport of boxing, loving it with every sinew in my body. Whether writing books about the sport or judging professional boxing bouts, I believe there is no more compelling drama in all of sports than a competitive boxing match.

Chapter 1

JOHN L. SULLIVAN: BOXING HERO AND CULTURAL ICON

Boxing's home for many years was Great Britain, the country where James Figg set up a decorated school and tutored members of the royal family in the art of pugilism. Great Britain was home to Jack Broughton, who developed the sport's first set of rules—such as the use of padded gloves and the introduction of timed rounds. Great Britain also was home to John Shoto Chambers, who, with the blessing of the Marquis of Queensbury, introduced a more modern set of rules to govern what later became known as the "Sweet Science." Great Britain was home to the great Daniel Mendoza, a Jewish man known for his remarkable skill in the ring.

The most notable U.S. boxers in the early 19th century, ironically, were two African American fighters named Bill "the Terror" Richmond and Tom Molineaux. These men were so gifted with fistic prowess that they earned their freedom, Molineaux for his bravery during battles royale—where slave owners often placed numerous slaves in combat with one another. Both men traveled overseas to challenge the great English champion Tom Cribb. Both lost to Cribb, though Molineaux was robbed in the first fight, in part because of rank racial prejudice.

But these two great fighters were, as historian Michael Isenberg writes, "were dimly seen black flashes before the dawn of American prizefighting."[1] The United States lacked a compelling boxing figure who brought popularity to the sport on its own soil. Part of that was because boxing was considered a sport for the dregs of humanity, a brutal, violent sport that most jurisdictions outlawed. "By 1880, then, professional boxing was moribund," writes Isenberg. "Many boxers were, indeed, no better than criminals."[2]

That changed with a charismatic young man from Boston named John L. Sullivan. Known as the "Boston Strong Boy," Sullivan packed not only a powerful punch but also presented compelling charisma. Reputedly, he would saunter into local bars and taverns, boasting loudly: "I can lick any son-of-bitch-in the house"—and he often did.

Nat Fleischer, publisher of *The Ring* magazine, explained: "Sullivan was something more than the greatest figure in boxing. He was the man, who, more than any other, made boxing reputable. This he succeeded in doing, largely through accident, because he was a great popular hero."[3] Sullivan rose from relative obscurity to become the nation's first genuine sports celebrity and a man of mythic proportion. He dined with presidents and earned obnoxious amounts of money because of his fistic prowess and charismatic personality.

Born on October 15, 1858, Sullivan walked at 10 months, talked at 14 months, and even delivered his first black eye as a toddler to a doting, unsuspecting aunt. Sullivan's father Michael stood only 5' 3" and weighed no more than 130 pounds. Sullivan's mother, however, outweighed her husband by 50 pounds. Sullivan had uncles and other relatives from Ireland who were large men, sometimes known as the "big Sullivans."[4]

Young John L. attended the Primary School on Concord Street, then Dwight Grammar School, where he graduated. During his early years, he played baseball and other sports. But he also found himself in a number of scraps, where he usually prevailed. "I had many a fracas with the other fellows, and I always came out on top," Sullivan said with his typical immodesty.[5]

Sullivan attended Comer Commercial School for a year and then spent 16 months at Boston College. His parents hoped that he would become a priest, but John L. had designs on more worldly pursuits. "It was the desire of my parents to have me study for the priesthood, but it was not mine."[6] Instead, Sullivan worked as an apprentice, learning the plumbing trade. Unfortunately, John L. had a disagreement with a journeyman—a supervisor—that led to fisticuffs. The young Boston lad won the fight but left the job.

He then took a stint as a tinsmith, which lasted a year and a half. Once again he had a disagreement with a superior. "It was odd the way the journeyman disagreed with this apprentice," Fleischer writes.[7]

Sullivan turned to his athletic prowess, playing baseball for a minor league team. He caught the attention of a local scout who offered him $1,300 to join a team in Cincinnati. But during his youth, Sullivan discovered he had a knack for winning fights. In 1877, he attended a benefit performance at the Dudley Street Opera House in the Boston Highlands. A local brawler named Tom Scannel—a tough man of some renown—came to the stage and loudly boasted that he could beat any man in a fistfight.

Scannel appeared to be staring a hole through Sullivan, as people had talked of the powerful young athlete. Sullivan accepted the challenge. He extended his right glove to signify respect to his opponent, but the ruffian Scannel responded with a left hook that staggered Sullivan. An enraged

Sullivan threw a right cross that smashed Scannel's face, knocking him sense-less into the orchestra.[8]

Apparently, some Harvard students who were taking boxing lessons wit-nessed the beating. Impressed with Sullivan's natural power, they told their classmate Ramon Guiteras, who boxed regularly. A few days later, Sullivan and Guiteras sparred. Guiteras used his superior speed and experience to keep the stronger man at bay, though Sullivan's strength and power were evident.[9]

BECOMING A PROFESSIONAL FIGHTER

This was a private sparring session. In 1878, Sullivan had his first public sparring session with a man named Johnny Woods, a veteran of several pro-fessional prizefights. "I soon disposed of him," Sullivan says.[10] The knockout over Woods landed Sullivan a match with Dan Dwyer, a man known as the "Terror of Boston." Sullivan writes that "I had the best of the encounter."[11] He then defeated Tommy Chandler, a fighter of some renown in the Northeast.

Sullivan then engaged in a public sparring session with "Professor" Mike Donovan, a world middleweight champion. Sullivan showed good speed for a bigger man and even dropped Donovan in the third round. Donovan's wily ring skills saved him from a knockout in the fourth and final round, but the middleweight knew that he was facing a future champion. For his part, Sul-livan told Donovan after their encounter: "If I had landed, it would have been all day with you."[12]

Sullivan learned from the experience and became a better fighter. He also continued to win, dispatching a Providence-based opponent named Jack Hogan. People began thinking of Sullivan as more than a prodigy with a strong punch. People began to believe that he may be among the best pugi-lists of the day. He didn't dissuade that line of thinking when he flattened Joe Goss of England relatively easily.

He further heightened expectations when he traveled to Cincinnati in De-cember to square off against John Donaldson, a smaller but effective fighter known as the "Champion of the West." Sullivan and Donaldson did battle on Christmas Eve. Donaldson's elusiveness made him an effective foil to his larger, stronger foe for several rounds. Eventually, however, Sullivan landed a patented bomb and kayoed his opponent in the 10th round. Sullivan wrote that his experienced opponent "hugged the floor the greater part of the time."[13]

Sullivan faced arrest for participating in a boxing match, which was il-legal at that time in Ohio. Authorities arrested both Donaldson and Sul-livan. Fortunately for the two men, the presiding judge, Judge Moriarty, was an avid fight fan. During the trial, Johnny Moran—brother-in-law of English featherweight champion Peter Morris—testified as to what he saw as a spectator. Judge Moriarty asked Moran if he had seen the prizefight in question. Moran replied, "Oh, no Your Honor. I saw a foot race." Moran then described Donaldson as a sprinter and that Sullivan pursued him diligently. Judge Moriarty later delivered his verdict of not guilty: "It is plain that these men merely engaged in a foot race, which cannot be listed as a violation of the law. The defendants are discharged."[14] Isenberg reports that "the defense lawyer, the judge, and the boxers promptly adjourned to a neighboring bar."[15]

It was during this time that Sullivan realized another important fact that would contribute greatly to his career—the power of self-promotion. He and his manager Billy Madden also realized that place was important in boxing—that where the event took place dictated public appeal. Sullivan and Madden arranged a match in New York City against John Mahan, whose ring name was Steve Taylor. The bout took place at Henry Hill's, a popular nightspot in the city.

Sullivan trounced Taylor in two rounds. The press took notice of the strong man from Boston. One reporter commented: "He didn't possess much science. But what a wallop he packed."[16] Another spectator at the bout was none other than Richard Kyle Fox, the wealthy owner of the *National Police Gazette,* considered the most important sports journal of the day. Legend has it that Fox, desirous of meeting Sullivan, had minions go tell Sullivan to come visit his table. Sullivan allegedly responded: "If Fox wants to see me, tell him to come to my table."[17] Fox later had a high-profile feud with Sullivan, fanning the flames of some of the sport's earliest rivalries. Fox would tout various challengers to Sullivan's supremacy through the years. While Sullivan would win in the ring, Fox would fatten his wallet.

Sullivan's next major bout was against John Flood, the "Bull's Head Terror." Flood had acquired a reputation as a local tough in Five Points, a rough-and-tumble neighborhood known for its prevalence of crime. Police authorities learned of an impending boxing match, causing promoter Harry Hill to seek an alternate location. He cleverly came up with a match on a barge along the Hudson River, avoiding the reaches of the law.

In May 1881, Sullivan faced Flood on the barge. The winner would receive $750. Most spectators actively cheered for their local New York tough rather than the outsider from Boston. But the beauty of boxing is that, in the ring, it is one fighter against another. Sullivan pounded Flood with a heavy right cross that felled the New Yorker. He dropped Flood seven times, stopping him in the eighth round. Sullivan had to redouble his efforts later in the bout, as the police were approaching the barge.

BECOMING THE CHAMPION

A most interested spectator was Paddy Ryan, the heavyweight champion in some people's minds at that time. Ryan acknowledged that Sullivan looked good in the ring but publicly claimed that the young man was no match for him. Ryan ducked Sullivan for the time being. Sullivan had to take on other comers to increase his public persona. He defeated Flood again in a rematch.

Publisher Fox stoked the sporting public's passions by proposing a match between his man Ryan and the cocky John L. Sullivan. Each side would put up $5,000, and the winner would win the heavyweight championship. The fight was scheduled to take place in New Orleans, but legal ramifications forced the bout to Mississippi. However, the Mississippi legislature then hurried through a bill that banned prizefighting in its borders.[18] The promoters eventually chose a remote location in Mississippi City, Mississippi, for the contest.

Sullivan entered the ring and had to wait 15 minutes for his opponent Ryan. The two battled, and it did not take long for Sullivan to draw first blood. He dropped Ryan in the first round, but Ryan rose to his feet. These early bouts did not feature standard three-minute rounds. A round often ended when one fighter hit the ground. That fighter would then have up to 30 seconds to rise to his feet. For example, the third round lasted only four seconds, because Sullivan dropped Ryan with the first punch he threw.[19]

Sullivan dominated the contest, stopping Ryan in the ninth round after only 11 minutes of total action. The *New York Times* captured the essence of the one-sided affair: "The fighting was short, sharp and decisive on Sullivan's part throughout, Ryan showing weariness after the first round."[20]

Sullivan quickly left the ring and hurried back to his hotel. He wanted to get out of Dodge before law enforcement officials in Mississippi caught up with him.[21] Ryan admitted that his opponent possessed formidable power. "I thought a telegraph pole had been shoved up against me endways."[22] Sullivan received $4,500 for his victory, after expenses. He traveled a hero's welcome to New York City, Chicago, and other cities. Sullivan recalled that the "journey from New Orleans was an ovation."[23] In New York, he was the talk of the town. Mobs of people swarmed him as he toured the cities. Newspapers across the country reported on the new champion.

Sullivan indulged his many appetites—particularly food and drink—for several weeks. He also issued a public challenge to any pugilist to face him for $5,000. He dispatched a series of nondescript opponents in what the *New York Sun* called a "series of picnics."[24] In July 1882, he faced Tug Wilson at Madison Square Garden—the first time that venue hosted a prizefight. Sullivan, perhaps affected by his partying, failed to knock out Wilson, who came to survive. Sullivan dropped Wilson 27 times during the four-round bout, but each time Wilson scrambled to his feet within the allotted 30-second time limit.[25] For his part, Sullivan said that Wilson went the distance because of "floor crawling and hugging."[26]

Sullivan faced a tough challenge in English fighter Charley Mitchell—a skilled veteran who fought at middleweight but who regularly defeated much larger men. The two fought an exhibition in New York City, where official prizefights were banned. Sullivan dropped Mitchell twice in the early going, but then the unexpected happened—Mitchell returned the favor and dropped Sullivan. He rose quickly and chased Mitchell around the ring for the remainder of the fight. Sullivan was incensed at the outcome of the bout—both Mitchell's tactics and his own performance.

Sullivan began to train with more vigor. The result was bad news for his subsequent opponents, who faced a powerful and in-shape Sullivan. He dispatched Herbert A. Slade, a large New Zealander trained by former champion Jem Mace. He then ran through a series of exhibitions that Nat Fleischer called "one of the truly great feats in the history of athletic endeavor."[27] Sullivan faced 59 men in a series of exhibitions; he knocked them all out. Opponent James McCoy exclaimed: "I never thought any man could knock me out with gloves; but holy murder! I never thought any man could hit as hard as he does."[28] Another opponent, Morris Hefey from Minnesota, proclaimed: "If you want to know what it is to be struck by lightning, just face Sullivan one second."[29]

Sullivan proclaimed that he wanted to give any stout young man a chance to prove his reputation against the champion. "I never had any objection to meeting with gloves any strong, healthy young men who wanted to contest for boxing honors, for I appreciate their position as one in which I found myself on starting out," he wrote. "I know full well that reputation does not make the man."[30]

Even though his exhibitions were popular, there was always the fear of law enforcement intervening and arresting the participants. In November 1884, Sullivan and Alf Greenfield were questioned for preparing to engage in a prizefight in New York City. When queried by his attorney, Colonel Charles Spencer, about planning a prizefight, Sullivan calmly responded: "I merely made an engagement to give with Greenfield a scientific exhibition of the art of self-defense."[31] Sullivan and Greenfield fought on November 18, 1884. Sullivan nearly kayoed Greenfield but was prevented from doing so as the police stopped the bout and arrested both participants.[32]

The public knockout tour certainly solidified Sullivan's reputation as the toughest man on the block, as the true boxing champion. He then took to working for a weekly salary of $500 for the Lester and Allen's Minstrels, where he played himself to doting crowds. "Fighting well or fighting badly, sober or drunk, benign or evil tempered, John L. was always the hero," writes Fleischer.[33]

During the apex of his powers, Sullivan apparently would face anyone. He even agreed to cross the color line and fight the formidable black boxer George Godfrey in Boston in 1881, before the police called off the fight. Sullivan said that he would fight Godfrey or the great Peter Jackson, a great black boxer from Australia, if the price was right.[34] In 1890, Sullivan's manager made a formal offer to Jackson about a three-round bout. Jackson declined the bout, viewing the pay as paltry.[35] It was many years later that Sullivan issued his infamous proclamation that he would never fight "a Negro."[36]

In November 1886, Sullivan dispatched Ryan in three rounds before a sizeable audience in San Francisco. He paraded around the country, fighting and winning other exhibitions. In Boston, he received a gaudy belt studded with nearly 400 diamonds with the inscription: "Presented to the Champion of Champions, John L. Sullivan, by the People of the United States."[37]

In 1887, publisher Richard Kyle Fox declared that the real boxing champion was Jake Kilrain, a tough customer. Fox awarded Kilrain a championship belt from the *Police Gazette*. Kilrain even traveled to England to defend his title against Jem Smith—a fight that was declared a draw after 106 rounds.

Sullivan generally paid little attention to Fox, dismissing Kilrain as a mediocre contender rather than any champion. Sullivan instead met with the president of the United States and then later traveled to England to face the toughest challengers from across the Atlantic. In April 1887, Sullivan traveled to the White House and met face-to-face with President Grover Cleveland.[38] After meeting the president, Sullivan later in the year set his sights on others whom he wished to meet. He certainly wanted another crack at Charley Mitchell, and he wanted to silence Jem Smith, who had repeatedly called out Sullivan.

Before his bouts, Sullivan toured England and even met with British royalty. He charmed them with his personal charisma and bravado. On one instance, he told the Prince of Wales: "Well, Prince, next to Jem Smith, your champion, who I'm so anxious to whip, the Prince of Wales is the man I most wanted to see when I came to England."[39]

In March 1888, Sullivan finally met Charley Mitchell again—this time in France. Sullivan wanted a smaller ring, but Mitchell successfully petitioned for a large 24-foot ring. He also strategically took a knee whenever Sullivan landed any serious blows. By this strategy, he could take 30-second rests, recover himself, and hopefully tire out the larger Sullivan. During the bout, which was conducted in cold temperatures, Sullivan dropped Mitchell 38 times. In modern boxing, Sullivan would have been seen as dominating the action. But under the London Prize Ring Rule of the day, the only way a boxer could lose was by knockout. After 39 rounds, the bout was declared a draw.

Unfortunately, Sullivan and Mitchell were jailed for their 39 rounds by French authorities.[40] They posted bond and traveled as fast as they could to England. When he returned home to the United States, Sullivan needed to make some money. He joined forces with several showmen who sponsored a circus.[41]

Sullivan then suffered a series of physical maladies that precluded a return to the ring. He claimed he had typhoid fever, gastric fever, inflammation of the bowels, and liver trouble. At one point, he thought he would die. His physicians claimed—perhaps with some hyperbole—that Sullivan's maladies would have killed a hundred other men.[42] Meanwhile, Fox and Kilrain publicly questioned Sullivan's claims to the American heavyweight championship. Sullivan agreed to face Kilrain in New Orleans in July 1889. The problem was that he was in disastrous physical condition.

Sullivan and his handlers enlisted the services of William Muldoon to serve as his chief trainer. Muldoon was obsessive in his training methods and forbade Sullivan from any drinking or partying. Instead, it was all work, healthy eating, and physical exercise. John L. Sullivan trained like he had never trained in his life. Arguably past his prime, he needed the extra training, as he had ballooned to over 240 pounds.

The fighters descended on New Orleans for the bare-knuckle bout and then had to take trains 100 miles north to Richburg, Mississippi, where wealthy lumber magnate Charles Rich had constructed a ring especially for the title bout. Kilrain entered the ring with his trainer, Charley Mitchell—the same Mitchell who had fought Sullivan twice. Sullivan and Kilrain each wagered $1,000 of their own money on the outcome. Kilrain entered the ring a fit and trim 195 pounds.

Some expected Sullivan to enter the contest in flabby condition. They didn't know of the Spartan-like existence that the champion had led under the circumspect eye of Muldoon. The final result of the obsessive trainer's efforts was a 207-pound John L. Sullivan. In the first round, Kilrain surprised the champion by throwing him to the ground. Sullivan returned the favor in the second round. He began to impose his dominance in the third round, landing a blow to Kilrain's heart that Sullivan later said turned the bout in his favor.

As the bout progressed, Kilrain would hit the canvas to obtain respites from the fighting action. "During this fight it was Kilrain's intentions, through the advice of his seconds, to keep in the ring by repeatedly falling or being knocked down, it being the only resort or hope he had of winning this fight," Sullivan reflected.[43] At times, Kilrain would go to the ground without suffering the effects of a significant blow.

In the 45th round, Sullivan vomited, perhaps from heat exhaustion. But he clearly won nearly every round. In the 68th round, Sullivan landed a right uppercut that felled Kilrain. The courageous challenger rose to his feet, but he was clearly the worse for the wear. In the 75th round, Kilrain went down, and one of his cornermen called a halt to the bout, throwing a sponge in the ring.

The fight lasted two and a quarter hours. Mississippi officials sought to arrest Sullivan and Kilrain for their participation in an illegal prizefighting competition. In Nashville, Tennessee, a squad of police officers boarded the train with search warrants looking for Sullivan. The police arrested Sullivan and took him to jail. With the assistance of legal counsel, Sullivan was released.

A Judge Allison, whom Sullivan described as a "very liberal minded man,"[44] released him. Newspaper accounts accused Sullivan of bribing the judge. Perhaps the judge was simply an avid fight fan. Whatever the case, Sullivan managed to extricate himself from the situation.

Mississippi governor Robert Lowry maintained a $1,000 reward for anyone facilitating the arrest and extradition of Sullivan and Kilrain to the state of Mississippi. Through his lawyers, Sullivan consented to travel to Mississippi to resolve the matter. Eventually, a local jury in Purvis, Mississippi, convicted Sullivan. He received a sentence of 12 months in the county jail.[45] The state high court reversed the conviction, finding that Sullivan did not receive a fair trial. Eventually, Sullivan and his lawyers paid a hefty fine and he left the state a free man rather than face a retrial.[46]

Sullivan gladly left the South for his hometown. He seriously considered running for Congress as a Democrat. He wrote a letter explaining his virtues as a political candidate. He mentioned that he had entertained people across the country and been a solid guy to his friends and fans. "But I feel to be more important than all else is the work which I have done to keep up the reputation of America among other nations," he wrote.[47]

But Sullivan turned from politics to the more comfortable venue of the theaters. He became a thespian rather than a pugilist or a politician, starring in *Honest Hearts and Willing Hands*. He played a blacksmith who knocked out the villain in the final act. Sadly for at least one of his colleagues, Sullivan was not good at pulling his punches and knocked out another actor.[48]

LOSING THE CHAMPIONSHIP

Sullivan's boxing skills eroded as he grew older and did not maintain the physical conditioning that he had achieved before the Kilrain fight. A young challenger named James J. Corbett—known as "Gentleman Jim"—had his eyes on the title. Corbett had knocked out Joe Choynski, a tough fighter, and then fought to a draw with Peter Jackson.

In 1892, Sullivan—already past his prime—agreed to face Corbett, a man eight years his junior and a much more technically sound boxer. The fight was to take place in New Orleans. Sullivan did not train with the same arduousness that he did before the Kilrain fight. "Sullivan was his own boss in 1892, and he was never one to be too stern with himself."[49]

The New Orleans bout was a major boxing extravaganza, featuring top-level championship fights on three successive days. On September 5, Jack McAuliffe knocked out Billy Myer to retain his world lightweight championship. The next day, Canadian-born George Dixon won the featherweight championship over opponent Jack Skelly. These two bouts sparked interest, particularly the interracial contest between Dixon (who was black) and Skelly (who was white), but they paled in comparison to the heavyweight battle on September 7 between Sullivan and Corbett.

Sullivan entered the ring at 212 pounds, while Corbett weighed only 178. But Corbett was younger and in much better condition. He also relied on boxing skills more than Sullivan, who often relied on his natural power and stamina. Sullivan's reputation still carried some weight with many boxing experts. Jake Kilrain certainly never forgot Sullivan's power as he explained in print why he felt that Sullivan would win the showdown. "I don't believe Jim will stand punishment," Kilrain said. "If he gets one or two of Sullivan's stiff punches, his science will leave him."[50]

In the first round, Sullivan tried to land one of his patented haymakers, but he couldn't catch the elusive Corbett. In round five, Corbett began to land combinations on the champion. Sullivan continued to fight with courage, even landing a significant blow in the 15th round. But Corbett's accumulation of landed blows began to take their toll. Corbett stopped Sullivan in the 21st round. The *New York Times* summed it up well: "The Californian kept away from the big fellow's blows."[51] The paper also reported that "it was a contest between science and strength."[52] Science prevailed convincingly over strength in the Sullivan–Corbett contest.

After the bout, Sullivan addressed the crowd: "Gentlemen, it's the old, old story. It's the story of an old man going against a young fellow. There are gray hairs in my head and I should have known better."[53] To his credit, Sullivan offered no excuses and accepted Corbett as the better fighter.

But Sullivan still gave Corbett a battle for more than 20 rounds. As historian Isenberg writes, the amazing thing was not that Corbett won. "It is that a prematurely aged, overweight, short-winded man, who had been out of the prize ring for three years, stood in for one solid hour of battle with a man in his physical prime."[54] Sullivan's former manager, Billy Madden, insisted for years after the bout to anyone who would listen that John Sullivan in his prime would have licked James J. Corbett in his prime: "When they tell me that Corbett at his best could have mastered the skill of John L. Sullivan in John's prime, I must take more than a modicum of salt to swallow such a yarn."[55]

Sullivan never again returned to the ring after he lost his championship. Instead, he again acted on the vaudeville circuit, drank too much alcohol, and occasionally fell into legal and financial troubles. He attempted to open saloons and later sold alcohol in the streets. He was not successful at either endeavor, so he returned to the stage and worked on a monologue, where he spoke to crowds about his former championship days and told jokes. Some referred to it as "Sullivan's travelogue."[56] He finally passed away in January 1918. His obituary in the *New York Times* exclaimed: "The prize ring never brought fame to any man as it did John L. Sullivan."[57]

LEGACY

Sullivan had what Isenberg calls a "checkered legacy."[58] On the negative side, he expressed racist sentiments and openly opposed black fighters battling for championships, particularly later in his life. He drank too much, and his alcoholism led to many run-ins with the law. He was not particularly adept at business or in managing his finances.

But on the positive side, John L. Sullivan was an ambassador for the sport of boxing. He talked about the important health benefits of boxing as a form of exercise. "I think it is something that every man should be skilled in," he told reporters. "It is one of the best athletic exercises in the whole endeavor of sports."[59]

Sullivan was a cultural hero who defined the masculine force of the expanding United States. He was, as Nat Fleischer writes, a "champion of champions."[60] He held the boxing championship from February 1882 until losing to Corbett more than a decade later in September 1892.

"Everywhere that Sullivan went he was hailed as a hero," the *New York Times* wrote when he died. "Everywhere his train stopped there were great throngs to cheer him. Men fought with each other to reach him and shake his hand."[61] No sports figure—and perhaps no other American—captured the public's imagination quite like John L. Sullivan.

Chapter 2

RACE AND BOXING: THE INTRACTABLE COLOR LINE AND THE PHENOMENON OF JACK JOHNSON

W.E.B. Du Bois famously wrote that the "problem of the 20th century is the problem of the color line."[1] Harvard professor Cornel West put it more bluntly nearly 100 years later: "Race matters."[2] For many years, race certainly mattered in the sport of boxing, as many African American fighters were denied their shot at a world title. Even those that received a title shot—like the great Jack Johnson—endured continual discrimination from a society not prepared for a champion of a darker hue. But, many early black fighters ran against an impregnable color bar. Australian boxing great Peter Jackson may have been the best fighter of his generation in the late 1880s and 1890s, but he never received a title shot. The great John L. Sullivan—the bare-knuckle boxing great and genuine American sports hero—refused to face Jackson, declaring in 1892 that he would never cross the color line. "Gentleman" Jim Corbett, who dethroned Sullivan, did fight Jackson in 1891 for 61 rounds. Declared a draw, the man known as the "Black Prince" left a lasting impression on Corbett, who declared Jackson to be the finest boxer he ever faced. But, interestingly, Corbett also decided when he was world champion that it was in his best interest to avoid Jackson.

TWO EARLY GREATS

It is ironic given the perniciousness of race discrimination that the first boxers from the United States who achieved any sort of world prominence for their fists were black—Bill Richmond and Tom Molineaux. Born a slave in Staten Island, New York, Richmond learned the fistic arts largely on his own. His skill attracted the attention of Lord Percy, the Duke of Northampton, who witnessed Richmond acquitting himself quite nicely against several

British soldiers. Percy later matched Richmond against several pugilists. In 1777, Percy sent Richmond to England, where Richmond's reputation grew. Richmond defeated several top white fighters, eventually earning a shot at the English champion—Tom Cribb—when he was well past his prime at 42 years old.[3] Richmond's technical skill confounded Cribb for many rounds, but Cribb's superior size eventually wore down Richmond.

The second American to achieve world acclaim was another slave—Tom Molineaux from Virginia. Boxing historian Bill Calogero writes: "Molineaux's is a quintessential American story, an up-from-the-bootstraps tale in which an individual could rise out of abject poverty and, through skill and perseverance, challenge the world's best."[4] Born in March 1874 in Richmond, Virginia, Molineaux toiled in hard, manual labor. But he learned the art of boxing from his father, Zachary, who won many bouts.[5]

Molineaux earned the attention of his master, Algernon Molineaux, by winning several battle royales—notorious contests in which several slaves were thrown together for an all-out brawl. Algernon profited handsomely off Tom's fighting skill and ability to defeat other slaves in bouts. In 1801, a nearby plantation owner named Randolph Peyton boasted that he had a slave named Abe who could beat any other man around in a bare-knuckle boxing match. Algernon Molineaux believed that his slave—17-year-old Tom Molineaux—could make Peyton eat his words. Algernon promised young Tom that he would grant him his freedom if he could defeat Abe. Tom Molineaux dominated Abe over five rounds. Algernon Molineaux proved good to his word, giving Tom $500 and, more importantly, his freedom.[6]

Molineaux moved to New York, where he distinguished himself as the best fighter of his day. Some even called him "Champion of America." But Tom was not satisfied. He kept hearing that the best fighters in the world were from Great Britain, not the United States. He sought to travel across the Atlantic Ocean to beat the best of the best.

Molineaux made the arduous journey to England in 1809, eager to earn a living as a professional boxer. He eventually enlisted the services of Richmond as his manager/trainer. Richmond saw in Molineaux a very raw fighter—but a fighter with physical tools who might be molded into a formidable force.[7]

Molineaux dispatched several fighters, including Jack Burrows, who was trained by none other than the world champion, Tom Cribb. Molineaux then defeated Tom "Tough Tom" Blake, stopping him in the eighth round. Many began to believe that this impressive physical specimen had improved enough to give the great Cribb a good battle.[8]

Molineaux called out Cribb, who was in semiretirement, to determine who was the better fighter. Richmond worked the press to stir up public interest. Eventually Cribb agreed to face Molineaux in December 1810. The historic bout took place in awful weather. The two fighters battered each other for round after round. Cribb showed superior boxing skill, but Molineaux's strength proved to be a problem for the champion. "By the time the nineteenth round began, both fighters were so disfigured and covered in blood that it was virtually impossible to tell them apart."[9] Later in the round, Molineaux had Cribb in a headlock and was pounding him in the face—a legal tactic under the early, primitive rules. A group of people in the crowd—Cribb supporters— stormed the ring and attacked Molineaux. They broke one of his fingers in the process. Calogero called it the "first of two travesties" in the bout.[10]

The 28th round featured another travesty of epic proportions. Molineaux landed a devastating blow that felled Cribb. Under the rules at that time, a downed boxer had 30 seconds to toe the mark and resume the contest. Cribb stayed down much longer than 30 seconds, which meant that Molineaux should have been declared the champion. But the referee probably was terrified at the prospect of awarding the world title to an American—and to make matters worse—a black American. The referee yelled three times for Cribb to continue, but the champion was unable to.

Joe Ward, Cribb's second, leaped into the ring and accused Molineaux of having bullets in his clenched fists. The referee investigated, giving Cribb more crucial time to recover. It became clear that the crowd and the referee were not going to allow Molineaux to win the bout. To his credit, Cribb recovered and managed to drag on in the bout. After the 39th round, Molineaux said he could fight no more. He fell from exhaustion, giving Cribb the disputed victory.[11]

Molineaux issued a public challenge for a rematch with the champion. He published an open letter that indicated the specter of racial prejudice: "I cannot omit the opportunity of expressing a confident hope that the circumstances of my being of a different color to that of a people amongst whom I have sought protection, will not in any way operate to my prejudice."[12]

Finally, Cribb agreed to a rematch set for September 1811. Molineaux trained poorly for the rematch. He dominated the early rounds, but Cribb wisely began to work Molineaux's body. Molineaux's poor conditioning caught up with him, and he fell in the 11th round. Cribb had trained seriously for the return engagement, while Molineaux had partied and drank himself into poor shape.

Molineaux was never the same fighter after the second loss to Cribb. He died broke and beaten a few years later. But the reality is that this former slave became a famous man and arguably the best fighter in the world. "Without the illegal interference of the hostile British crowd, Tom Molineaux would have been recognized as the first black world heavyweight champion, a century before Jack Johnson."[13]

EARLY BLACK CHAMPIONS

Fighters in the lower weight classes fared better, as a special few received title shots. George "Little Chocolate" Dixon became the first black man to win a world boxing title when he defeated Nunc Wallace in 1890 for the bantamweight title. Born in Canada, Dixon later added the featherweight title to his accomplishments. Some members of the press called him "the greatest of them all" and the "fighter without a flaw."[14] Some credit him with inventing shadow boxing—where boxers practice their craft by punching in the air and work on avoiding imaginary punches thrown at them.[15]

Born in 1870 in Africville, Nova Scotia, Dixon's mother was black and his father reportedly a white British soldier.[16] Dixon boxed a little as a teenager but took the sport seriously after his family moved to Boston. Though he stood only 5' 3" and weighed 100 pounds, he showed great skill in the ring at an early age. His manager, Tom O'Rourke, was convinced he had something special in the man that would become known as "Little Chocolate."

Dixon traveled to England to face Nunc Wallace for the world bantamweight title, as the British considered their champion the world champion. Dixon traveled overseas to hostile territory, much as Richmond and Molineaux had done years earlier. Unlike his two worthy predecessors, Dixon won the title. "George Dixon had accomplished a deed that no other American fighter had been able to achieve; he traveled to England and defeated an English boxer for an international title."[17]

Dixon received a hearty welcome when he reached U.S. soil, but he was still regarded as a Negro. In one fight against a white opponent in Providence, Rhode Island, Dixon had to box from the center of the ring to avoid blows from blackjacks and slug shots from racist white fans who desperately wanted the white fighter to win.[18]

In 1892, Dixon defeated Jack Skelly in New Orleans—the first interracial world boxing championship. Many white fans did not take well to Dixon beating up a white man at the Olympia Club. The club forbade any future interracial bouts for more than 50 years after that match. Dixon also faced racist attitudes when he married a white woman named Kitty O'Rourke, sister of his manager Tom. The couple often had to stay in separate hotels in the South.[19]

Dixon continued to perform at a high level in the boxing ring, later adding the featherweight championship to his accomplishments. He finally met his match in 1900 against "Terrible" Terry McGovern—another future Hall of Fame fighter. McGovern was simply too young and strong for the older Dixon, who had passed his prime.

"Little Chocolate" Dixon died at age 37 in New York City. The public did not pay attention, as Dixon had fallen from the headlines. Several boxing people—including his former rival, Terry McGovern—collected monies for the erection of the George Dixon Memorial Fountain in New York City—a fitting tribute to a trailblazing fighter.

The second African American fighter to capture a world title was Joe Gans, who won the world lightweight championship in 1902, defeating Frank Erne. Nicknamed "the Old Master," Gans became the first black man born in the United States to win a world boxing championship. He held the title until 1908 and is considered among the top pound-for-pound boxers in history.

Born in 1874 in Baltimore as Joseph Saifuss Butts, Gans's father—a professional baseball player—gave his child to a foster mother named Maria Jackson Gant.[20] Gant later became Gans. Gans boxed as a young kid. Reportedly he became so skilled that the adults made him fight two other kids at the same time.[21] He turned pro at age 17, after he became acquainted with Baltimore gambler and businessman Lincoln "Al" Hereford, who saw promise in the young fighter.

Gans established himself as the premier black lightweight of his time. Eventually he began to face top-flight white fighters as well. He suffered setbacks against Elbows McFadden and, more significantly, a loss to Frank Erne for the lightweight championship in 1900. After suffering a horrific cut above the eye—caused by a head butt—Gans refused to continue. Though blinded by the cut, many accused Gans of being a quitter and his reputation suffered heavily.[22]

Between 1900 and 1902, Gans won 19 straight bouts, earning a rematch against Erne in Canada. Gans stopped Erne in the very first round to win the crown. Gans held the title for several years, before finally losing in 1908 to Oscar "Battling" Nelson—another future Hall of Fame fighter.

Gans died two years later of tuberculosis, but he left behind a large legacy. Historian Colleen Aycock writes: "For both George Dixon and Gans, despite all of their ring prowess and the science they brought to boxing, their greatest achievement, and perhaps boxing's legacy to American culture, was crossing the color line."[23]

SEGREGATION

It is amazing that George Dixon and Joe Gans captured world titles when they did, in the late 19th and early 20th centuries. The United States had a fully operational caste system—a society segregated rigidly by race. The United States Supreme Court fully sanctioned segregation as a way of life in its 1896 decision in *Plessy v. Ferguson*.[24] Homer Plessy had challenged the constitutionality of an 1890 Louisiana law that provided for separate railway accommodations on the basis of race. Plessy was one-eighth black—derisively called an octoroon. The rule of law in that day was that if you had one drop of black blood, you were black.

Plessy contended that depriving him of the opportunity to ride in the whites-only section of the trains—the best and most comfortable sections—deprived him of his right to equal protection under the Equal Protection Clause of the Fourteenth Amendment, which provides that "no state shall . . . deny any person equal protection of the laws." The U.S. Supreme Court upheld the law by a 7–1 vote (Justice David Brewer did not participate). Justice Henry Billings Brown wrote the majority opinion: "If one race be inferior to the other socially, the constitution of the United States cannot put them upon the same plane."[25]

Justice John Marshall Harlan of Kentucky wrote a famous dissenting opinion. Though he hailed from a former slave-owning family, Harlan had views quite different from his colleagues on matters of race. In one of the most stirring passages in U.S. jurisprudence, Harlan wrote:

> But in view of the constitution, in the eye of the law, there is in this country no superior, dominant, ruling class of citizens. There is no caste here. Our constitution is color-blind, and neither knows nor tolerates classes among citizens. In respect of civil rights, all citizens are equal before the law. The humblest is the peer of the most powerful. The law regards man as man, and takes no account of his surroundings or of his color when his civil rights as guarantied by the supreme law of the land are involved.[26]

Harlan's lone dissent in this case and an earlier civil rights decision in 1883 earned him the moniker "the Great Dissenter." *Plessy v. Ferguson* had an indelible impact on society, as various state and city governments passed a variety of segregation laws—called Jim Crow laws after a minstrel character. Society—particularly Southern society—segregated nearly all aspects of public life. Restaurants, swimming pools, bathrooms, theaters, and prisons were all segregated by race. "Whites only" and "Colored only" signs were prominently displayed and became implanted in the public consciousness. Lynchings took place to ensure that the colored race knew its place.

JACK JOHNSON

Segregation also began to touch sports. Moses Fleetwood Walker had been allowed to play professional baseball with whites in the early 1880s, but baseball became segregated. The inaugural running of the Kentucky Derby in 1875 featured 13 African American jockeys out of 15 in the original "Run for the Roses." But soon horse racing became segregated. The same thing happened in boxing, particularly in the heavyweight division. The color line was strictly enforced. This explains why great black fighters such as George Godfrey and Peter Jackson never received a title shot.

But one man managed to break through the shackles of segregation and challenge white America in way never before seen. He eventually taunted and haunted white America through his ring prowess and his in-your-face lifestyle. He not only managed to win the world heavyweight championship as a black man, but he also lived according to his own set of rules. He openly dated and married white women. He taunted white opponents and the un-ruly crowds who paid dearly to see him lose. He was a unique force of nature with the relatively common name of Jack Johnson.

Legend has it that in 1910, Halley's Comet was scheduled to flash across the sky. The event was much anticipated, as the comet appears only once every 75 years. In San Francisco, someone ran up to the hotel suite of heavy-weight champion Jack Johnson to get out of bed and come outside to view the comet. Johnson replied that there were hundreds of comets, "but there ain't gonna be but one Jack Johnson."[27]

This unique character was born in March 1878 in Galveston, Texas, as John Arthur Johnson to Henry and Tina Johnson. Henry worked as a custo-dian and most likely was a slave before the Civil War. Tina Johnson was an intelligent woman who also worked a blue-collar job to support Jack and her five other children. One of Jack's first jobs was at a livery stable, where he rev-eled in riding the horses. He had to leave the employment after his boss dis-covered that he was riding the horses too often and too hard. He then worked as an apprentice at a bakery. He quickly grew weary of the bakery shop and took a job on the docks.[28] Johnson acquired a reputation as fast with his fists and powerful in his punch.

At some point, Johnson realized that his best path to a better life was in his athletic prowess as a boxer. He traveled around the country, though he returned to Galveston and survived the horrific flood in 1901. Later that year, he faced the most experienced opponent of his young professional career in Joe Choynski, a Polish-born Jew who was a top fighter in his day. Choynski knocked Johnson out in the third round, using his superior boxing skills to defeat the younger, bigger man. A Texas ranger arrested both men for partici-pating in a prizefight.

In jail, Johnson soaked up as much knowledge as he could from Choynski, who allegedly schooled Johnson on the finer points of defense, ring general-ship, and how to throw punches with more leverage. He told Johnson: "A man who can move like you should never have to take a punch. Don't try to block—you're fast enough to get clear out of the way."[29]

After three weeks confinement in jail with Choynski, the warden released the men. Johnson left Texas as quickly as possible and moved to California, where he began to fight more regularly. He knocked out fighters such as Jack Jeffries (brother of future world champion and Johnson foe Jim Jeffries) and Frank Childs. Often, Johnson had to face other talented black fighters, as white fighters began to avoid him. He squared off against Denver Ed Martin, Joe Jeannette, Sam McVey, and the great Sam Langford. Ironically, Johnson never gave any of these black fighters a title shot after he became champion.

In February 1903, he defeated Ed Martin to win the colored heavyweight championship. That year, he publicly claimed that he could defeat the current champion, James J. Jeffries, a mountain of a man who had dominated the division since he kayoed a much smaller Bob Fitzsimmons. The *Los Angeles Times* reported that Johnson was a top challenger for the champion, writing that it "looks black for Jeffries."[30] Unfortunately for Johnson, he dropped a disputed decision to future world champion Marvin Hart in 1905. The *Los Angeles Times* reported that Hart "seemed the beaten man from physical appearances" as his "whole face resembled a large raw steak."[31] However, the referee gave the decision to Hart in part because he pressed forward for much of the bout. Historian Randy Roberts aptly wrote that "the bout was fought along racial rather than pugilistic lines."[32]

Johnson rebounded from the setback and continued to win bout after bout. He attracted public attention after he thrashed former champion Fitzsimmons in two rounds in 1907. Later that year, he easily defeated Jim Flynn, another top white fighter. By this time, Johnson was universally recognized as the top contender to the title. Many considered him the uncrowned champion, even though he was black.

But the world title still belonged to a white fighter—Tommy Burns. The world title had changed hands several times. Jeffries retired from the ring unbeaten. He had captured the title from an aging Fitzsimmons in 1898 and then successfully defended it several times through the years, including a rematch over Fitzsimmons, two victories over former champion Corbett, and others. When Jeffries retired, Marvin Hart and Jack Root squared off in July 1905 to determine who would be Jeffries's successor. In an unusual circumstance, Jeffries served as the referee for the bout. Hart won the bout in the 12th round. However, Hart—known as the "Fightin' Kentuckian"—lost the title in his first defense to Tommy Burns, a short but effective fighter who began his career in the lighter weight divisions. Burns was an active world champion, who defended his title many times. It appeared, though, that Burns avoided Jack Johnson like the plague.

Johnson literally chased Burns all over the globe, hoping for a title shot. Johnson finally received his chance in Sydney, Australia, thanks to the enterprising efforts of promoter Hugh "Huge Deal" McIntosh. In December 1908, Johnson stopped a courageous Burns in the 14th round. Johnson toyed the much shorter and smaller Burns throughout, taunting him. "Who told you I was yellow?" he asked. "You're white Tommy, white as the flag of surrender."[33] Johnson stayed in Australia for several weeks. Before he left, he visited Toowong Cemetery—the grave site of the great Peter Jackson.[34]

Jack Johnson had become the first black heavyweight champion—an accomplishment that rattled much of white America. Author Jack London, who covered boxing for newspapers, hated that a black man had captured the title. He wrote: "But one thing remains. Jeffries must emerge from his alfalfa farm and remove that smile from Johnson's face."[35] Johnson endured the racist backlash of a society that simply could not accept that a black man was heavyweight champion. Consider the language of a *Washington Post* article in February 1909: "Jackson is as black as a hat. . . . His arms are unusually long, like those of a gorilla."[36]

Originally Jeffries declined offers to return to the ring to face Johnson. He turned down a $50,000 offer in January 1909 from John Wren, who sought to hold the bout in Melbourne, Australia. Jeffries simply said that he was retired and would not fight anymore.[37] Former champion James J. Corbett entertained offers to fight Johnson as well. Corbett exhibited the racial prejudice that afflicted so many at the time. He wrote in the *Chicago Daily Tribune:*

> I will consider an offer to fight Johnson if the Australian fight promoters will give a $50,000 purse, such as they offered for Jeffries and Johnson.
>
> I do not say that I will fight, but I am in splendid physical condition and am feeling as well as I ever did. I am sure that I can put up a creditable battle and would like to have the chance to regain the championship for a white American fighter. I am not anxious to fight a negro but it galls me to see a black champion.[38]

In fairness, Corbett exhibited praise for his former ring rival, Peter Jackson, the great black heavyweight fighter from Australia. When asked to compare Jackson to Johnson, Corbett wrote: "I always have thought of Peter Jackson as one of the world's great fighters."[39] Corbett added that, in a bout between the two, "Jackson would have been the winner."[40]

Pressure mounted on Jeffries to come out of retirement and regain the title for white America. In early January 1909, Jeffries began to take serious interest in the bout and resumed training. He claimed that he was still the real champion, as he had retired without losing his title in the ring. But he never officially said he would take the fight. In July 1909, he changed course and said that he would never fight Jack Johnson. Jeffries said that there were other white men who could defeat Johnson: "There are plenty of men who can trim this man Johnson. The fans can count me out, though."[41]

Because of Jeffries's indecision, Johnson defeated other challengers, including Al Kaufman and middleweight champion Stanley Ketchel. Johnson failed to kayo Kaufman and even suffered a knockdown from Ketchel before quickly rallying to knock his opponent senseless. Jeffries must have thought that he saw something in those bouts that made him think he could actually regain his title.

One man who had no doubt that Johnson would win the fight was Jack Earl of Dublin—the former heavyweight champion of Ireland. He wrote to the *New York Times,* criticizing the paper for its racist treatment of the champion. "That the colored man Johnson is the superior man, physically and mentally, no intelligent person can doubt. That he is a real champion is beyond question."[42]

Jeffries finally succumbed to the mounting public pressure and the lure of the ring. He returned and trained with a vengeance. He fully expected to be able to wrest his title back from Johnson. For his part, Johnson expressed his typical confidence in his own abilities. On the eve of the fight, he stated: "I honestly believe that in pugilism I am Jeffries' master and it is my purpose to demonstrate this in the most decisive way possible."[43]

This was the fight of the century—or the fight of the first 10 years of the 20th century. Jim Jeffries, the undefeated former champion, returned from retirement to attempt to lift the title from Johnson. The two squared off on July 4, 1910, in Reno, Nevada. Promoter Tex Rickard refereed the bout. Virtually the entire nation was watching. Johnson was simply too quick and gifted for the slower Jeffries. Johnson put on a boxing exhibition, showcasing his finely tuned defensive skills.

Johnson taunted Jeffries during the bout. He also taunted former champion James J. Corbett, who served as Jeffries's trainer during the contest. The fight was mercifully halted in the 15th round. Jack London could do nothing but write: "The greatest battle of the century was a monologue delivered to twenty thousand spectators by a smiling negro who was never in doubt and who was never serious for more than a moment at a time."[44] John L. Sullivan, the former champion, wrote for the *Chicago Daily Tribune:* "Scarcely ever has there been a championship match that was so one-sided."[45] Sullivan colorfully added that "no sorrier sight ever has gone to make pugilistic history."[46]

Jeffries acknowledged after the bout that Johnson was the better fighter. "I don't think I could have beaten Johnson at my best," he told reporters. "I don't think I could have beaten him in a thousand years."[47]

The fight unleashed a fury of interracial violence around the country. Geoffrey Ward wrote that "no event yielded such widespread racial violence until the assassination of Dr. Martin Luther King, Jr. fifty-eight years later."[48] The riots occurred seemingly everywhere. "Rioting broke out all over the country tonight between whites disappointed and angry that Jeffries had lost the big fight at Reno, and negroes jubilant that Johnson had won," wrote the *Atlanta Constitution.*[49] Race riots erupted in New Orleans, Atlanta, Springfield, Illinois, and other cities across the country. Johnson himself faced an angry mob in Ogden, Utah, when his train stopped there.[50]

Still, Johnson's victory did offer hope for a downtrodden race. An oft-quoted poem circulated in various parts of the country:

> Amazing grace, how sweet it sounds,
> Jack Johnson knocked Jim Jeffries down,
> Jim Jeffries jumped up n hit Jack on the chin,
> And then Jack knocked him down again.
> The Yankees hold the play,
> The white man pulls the trigger,
> But it makes no difference what the white man say,
> The world's champion is still a nigger.[51]

Blacks across the country erupted in genuine celebration. Nat Fleischer recalls: "I shall never forget the sight that greeted us in New York: Thousands of Negroes crowded the streets, parading, shouting, shooting off fireworks, and carrying on in hilarious fashion. They were celebrating a Roman holiday."[52]

Johnson's victory over Jeffries also had an impact on censorship. Politicians across the country, including President Theodore Roosevelt, called for the banning of fight films after the Johnson victory.[53] Numerous cities prohibited the showing of film of the Johnson–Jeffries bout, fearing further race riots.[54] Congress responded in kind, passing a law that criminalized the transportation of moving pictures of boxing across state lines.[55] Congressman Seaborn Roddenberry of Georgia even introduced a measure that would create a federal law outlawing interracial marriages.[56]

Johnson now reigned as world champion—an ugly, hard reality for much of the country. Corbett admitted that "there seems to be at this writing little prospect for the overthrow of the Negro champion."[57]

The public searched in vain for a white hope to lift the crown from Johnson. Graeme Kent explains in his book *The Great White Hopes* that white managers looked everywhere in vain to find someone of white skin who could defeat Johnson. "Managers began to scour the factories, farms, armed services, and even prisons for a behemoth who would be their meal ticket in the lucrative scramble to dethrone the black champion."[58] They were not successful for many years.

The first "white hope" that Johnson faced was a charismatic Englishman named Victor McLaglen. In 1909, Johnson tangled with McLaglen in fight in Vancouver, Canada, officially billed as an exhibition. Johnson reportedly toyed with McLaglen through the bout, as his superior skill was simply too much. Johnson did not sit on his stool between rounds and allegedly carried on a conversation with a friend outside the ring during the fight. Johnson dominated the six-round bout. McLaglen later left the boxing ring, served in World War I, and then achieved notoriety as an actor. In 1935, McLaglen won an Academy Award for Best Actor for his role in *The Informer.* But acting didn't pull at the talented man's soul like boxing. He once said later in life that acting was not his great passion—"the only thing that ever thrilled me was boxing."[59]

Johnson seemed to take a thrill in living his life as he pleased—no matter the cost. His flamboyant lifestyle outraged the police. Johnson's bigger battles were with the legal authorities, who essentially prosecuted Johnson for his involvement with white women. After Johnson's first wife—a black woman named Clara—left him, Johnson almost exclusively dated white women. This touched a nerve in a racist society that regarded interracial relationships as taboo. Interracial marriages were illegal in 30 states. The U.S. Supreme Court did not officially strike down a law banning such unions until its decision in *Loving v. Virginia* in 1967.[60]

Johnson had open relationships with several white women: Hattie Mc-Clay, Belle Schreiber, Etta Duryea, and Lucille Cameron. McClay and Schreiber were prostitutes or "sporting women." Many felt that Johnson taunted white America by flaunting his white companions and wealth. He certainly lived the way he wanted to and resented anyone telling him what to do.

Prosecutors eventually charged Johnson with violating the Mann Act, a federal law known as the White Slave Traffic Act. Named after its sponsor, Congressman Robert Mann of Illinois, it sought to crack down on interstate prostitution. In November 1912, federal prosecutors arrested Johnson and charged him with violating the law, allegedly for transporting Schreiber from Pittsburgh to Chicago in 1910.[61] Schreiber, upset at Johnson for dumping her and replacing her with Duryea, later served as the chief prosecution witness against Johnson. Even in jail, Johnson couldn't escape the color line. When white prisoners learned he was placed in their section of the segregated jail, they caused disruptions, forcing Johnson's relocation to the colored section of the jail.[62]

In May 1913, a federal jury convicted Johnson of violating the Mann Act. Assistant District Attorney Harry Parkin said after the verdict: "This verdict will also go around the world. . . . This negro, in the eyes of many, has been persecuted. But, it was his misfortune to be the foremost example of the evil in permitting the intermarriage of whites and blacks. Now he must bear the consequences."[63] Johnson seemingly accepted his fate: "Oh well. They crucified Christ, why not me?"[64]

Rather than serve time in prison, Johnson fled the United States for France, where he was treated much more hospitably. The *Chicago Defender* blasted the prosecution and persecution of Jack Johnson, saying that it really was for whipping James Jeffries.[65]

Johnson's fight skills dissipated through years of hard living overseas, stress from battling the U.S. government, and advancing age. Johnson was not very active in keeping his skills sharp. Johnson eventually lost his title in 1915 to a hulking 6' 6" giant named Jess Willard in Havana, Cuba. Nat Fleischer had predicted Johnson's demise: "I felt that the easy life he had led, his carousing in France and Argentina, had softened him and that Willard, if in condition, should emerge a winner."[66] Johnson started strong, using his superior boxing skills. Fleischer recalls that, at several points during the first nine rounds, he felt that Johnson would score a knockout.[67] But the intense heat, lack of physical conditioning, and a large, young opponent were too much for the great champion. Willard stopped Johnson in the 26th round.

While Johnson often seemed boastful in victory, he handled defeat with class. He shook Willard's hand and saw him off when Willard left Cuba. He even gave him some advice on how to handle being world champion.[68] However, years later, Johnson claimed that he took a dive in the Willard fight.[69]

After his defeat, Johnson went overseas again to avoid arrest. He finally returned to the United States in July 1920, when he was placed in a Los Angeles jail pending his extradition to Chicago. He then was sentenced to a year and a day at the federal prison in Leavenworth, Kansas. The former number-one fighter in the world became inmate number 15,461.[70] He earned his release in July 1921, after having served 10 months. He sought to fight new world champion, Jack Dempsey, but never received another shot at the world title. Johnson died in 1946 in an automobile accident. His widow told a reporter: "I loved him because of his courage. He faced the world unafraid. There wasn't anybody or anything that he feared."[71]

Johnson remains the subject of conversation even today, particularly as the lens of history views his conviction under the Mann Act as unjust. In 2009 Congress passed a resolution supporting the presidential pardon of Jack Johnson. However, President Barack Obama did not grant a pardon to Johnson. In early 2011, Rep. Peter King of New York and Sen. John McCain of Arizona introduced resolutions in the House and Senate to push for a presidential pardon again. The proposed resolution expresses "the sense of Congress that John Arthur 'Jack' Johnson should receive a posthumous pardon for the racially motivated conviction in 1913 that diminished the athletic, cultural, and historic significance of Jack Johnson and unduly tarnished his reputation."[72]

The measure concludes:

> Resolved by the House of Representatives (the Senate concurring), That it remains the sense of Congress that Jack Johnson should receive a posthumous pardon . . .
>
> (1) To expunge a racially motivated abuse of the prosecutorial authority of the Federal Government from the annals of criminal justice in the United States; and
> (2) In recognition of the athletic and cultural contributions of Jack Johnson to society.[73]

McCain, a former boxer in the armed forces, stated in a news release: "A full pardon would not only shed light on the achievements of an athlete who was forced into the shadows of bigotry and prejudice, but also allow future generations to grasp fully what Jack Johnson accomplished against great odds."[74]

LEGACY

Jack Johnson left an indelible imprint on the sport of boxing—both positive and negative. From a purely pugilistic point of view, he was a defensive master who was one of the greatest heavyweights of all time. Nat Fleischer wrote: "I rank the burly Negro as the best heavyweight of all time. . . . His mastery of ring science, his ability to block, counter, and feint are still unexcelled."[75]

But Johnson left negative marks too, particularly for other black fighters. White America just couldn't stand the thought of another Jack Johnson. Before the Johnson–Willard bout, Ray Pearson wrote presciently for the *Chicago Daily Tribune:* "If this black man is defeated tomorrow, there are many reasons why the honor of holding the title will never go to another man of his color."[76] For many years, no other black man was given a shot at the world heavyweight title. Even a popular champion like Jack Dempsey failed to defend his title against top black contenders such as Harry Wills, Larry Gains, and Sam Langford and never received a world title shot.

In fact, it took 22 years for another black man to receive a shot at the world heavyweight title. His name was Joe Louis.

Chapter 3

JOE LOUIS: HEAVYWEIGHT GREAT AND AMERICAN HERO

White America's hatred of Jack Johnson had profound consequences for black heavyweights, as a generation of skilled pugilists could not fight for the title no matter how deserving they might be. Instead, a succession of white fighters battled for the crown jewel of sports. Johnson's conqueror, Jess Willard, lost the belt in dramatic fashion to a popular slugger known as the "Manassa Mauler." Jack Dempsey packed a mean punch and became a genuine sports hero of the Roaring '20s along with baseball great Babe Ruth. But Dempsey would not defend his title against the leading black fighters of the day, including Harry Wills. The color line had been drawn, and it was intractable.

Dempsey lost his title to a skilled boxer named Gene Tunney—known as "the Fighting Marine." Tunney never lost his title in the ring, but the intelligent man decided to hang up the gloves for greener pastures. This led to a succession of fighters to the top crown—men such as Max Schmeling, Jack Sharkey, Primo Carnero, Max Baer, and James J. Braddock. They weren't bad fighters. In fact, their stories were compelling.

The German Schmeling possessed a powerful right hand and savvy ring skills. He had to cope with world pressures caused by the rabid leader of a rising political force in Germany known as Nazism led by charismatic but troubled leader Adolf Hitler. Sharkey crossed the color line to defeat the talented Wills and gave Dempsey a tough bout. He lived to 91 years of age—a remarkable feat for anyone, much less someone who takes blows to the head for a living.

Primo Carnero—"the Ambling Alp"—was a semitragic figure in boxing history. A gargantuan—yet gentle—man, he destroyed Sharkey for the title but was built more on hype than achievement. He lost badly to the talented

Max Baer—"the Clown Prince of Boxing" whose immense talent sometimes lost out to his playboy lifestyle. Carnera's story inspired Budd Schulberg's famous novel, *The Harder They Fall.* Baer's lackadaisical approach belied his true talent, and he possessed a monster punch that killed a man. Baer lost his title to a 10–1 underdog named James J. Braddock—dubbed "the Cinderella Man" by Damon Runyon. Braddock began his career as a promising light heavyweight but was felled by persistent hand injuries. He suffered badly during the Great Depression, barely able to provide enough sustenance for his family. But his hand healed, and he put together an impressive string of victories that culminated in a surprising victory over Baer.

None of these white champions accomplished nearly as much as their successor. None of them held the championship more than two years. None of them made even as many as five successful defenses of their crown. In comparison, Joe Louis Barrow—shortened to Joe Louis—held the heavyweight title for 12 years and defended his title a record 25 times. "The Brown Bomber" dominated the division like no one before or after.

Humble Beginnings

Joseph Louis Barrow was born on May 13, 1914, to Munroe and Lillie Barrow—the seventh of eight children—near Lafayette, Alabama. Joe would later say there was something lucky about number seven.[1] Munroe—a large man standing six feet tall and weighing more than 200 hundred pounds—worked as a sharecropper while Lillie did everything to keep her family intact. Munroe Barrow was a troubled man who was committed to the Searcy Hospital for the Criminal Insane in Mount Vernon, Alabama, when Joe was only two years old.[2] "The years of strain and hard work was too much for him," Joe said.[3]

Lillie Barrow then married a man named Pat Brooks, who served as Joe's father figure for the rest of his life. The family struggled economically, but Brooks managed to provide well enough for his wife and children. Brooks survived a near-attack by the Ku Klux Klan, and his work and that of others in agriculture took a blow due to the boll weevil, an insect that destroyed crops.

Brooks heard from family members about better economic opportunities up north in Detroit. "There were jobs that didn't depend on the rainfall or the boll weevil," Louis explained years later.[4] Brooks took a job sweeping streets before landing a job at Ford Motor Company. Detroit's population exploded in part due to the opening of its first automobile plant in 1899. Between 1910 and 1920, the black population of the city increased from

5,000 to 41,000.[5] Many blacks lived in a crowded part of the east side of the city known as Black Bottom. This was the place Joe Louis called home when he was 12 years old.

Louis struggled mightily in school, showing little aptitude for any of his classes. "I couldn't keep up with the class," he admitted. "I was bigger than anybody and couldn't seem to get past the sixth grade."[6] A well-meaning teacher suggested that he transfer to an all-boys vocational school where he could learn a trade.[7] Louis learned cabinetry and other woodworking skills. The family struggled to make ends meet during the Great Depression.

Louis ran the streets as a youngster, but he never became a gangster. A black police officer named Henderson "Ben" Turpin kept Louis on the straight and narrow. Once, Turpin chased Louis away from several gang youths and made him go home. "Most of that gang would up in jail."[8] Turpin also encouraged young Joe to come down to a local recreation center run by Leon Wheeler and a former prizefighter named Atler "Kid" Ellis.[9] Louis played baseball, soccer, and boxing. Allegedly, Louis floored the first youngster he ever sparred with in the ring. For a while, Louis's mother had no idea he was boxing. She assumed he was dutifully attending his violin lessons. An amateur boxer named Thurston McKinney told Louis he should drop the violin lessons that his mother encouraged and take up boxing full-time instead. McKinney came to that accurate conclusion after tasting Louis's power in a sparring session.[10] Louis agreed and eagerly took Ellis's boxing classes at the gym.[11] Young Joe wanted to be like Thurston, who had just won a Golden Gloves title in the lightweight (147-pound) division.

Louis learned early on that he could win on size and strength alone. A young bantamweight named Ken Offet beat the tar out of him. Detroit was a good boxing town with an active amateur boxing presence headlined by the Golden Gloves. Louis soaked up knowledge from Ellis and from a talented young fighter named Holman Williams, who boxed professionally for 16 years. Williams owned victories over greats such as Charley Burley and Archie Moore. Louis recalled that Williams was a "beautiful boxer."[12] But Williams's greatest contribution to ring history may have been his instructions to Joe Louis. Williams taught Louis the importance of footwork and combination punching.[13]

Louis benefited from a talented group of young boxers that included not only Williams but also Eddie Futch (who later became a Hall of Fame trainer), Lorenzo Pack, and Curtis Shipp.[14] Louis progressed rapidly, winning the novice division for light heavyweights in 1933. The next year, he won the national Amateur Athletic Union championship in April with an impressive second-round knockout of an overmatched Ario Soldati. Louis won four bouts in three days in easy fashion. A press account noted that the "poker-faced" Louis "seemed to be toying with his opponents."[15]

RISING THROUGH THE PROFESSIONAL RANKS

Louis progressed exponentially in the ring. His style and natural power seemed naturally suited for the professional ranks. He attracted the attention of some well-connected businessmen—including John Roxborough, a wealthy numbers runner. The son of a New Orleans–based lawyer, the shrewd Roxborough originally planned on following in the footsteps of his older brother Charles and becoming a lawyer. Instead he chose a different path—first as a bail bondsman and then in the numbers game.

Roxborough enlisted the help of his friend Julian Black, who had fight connections in Chicago. Black also served as a numbers magnate. Black introduced Roxborough to a former lightweight fighter with a prominent facial scar named Jack Blackburn. The scarred man had a fiery temper and reportedly killed a man, but he was an excellent trainer. Originally, Blackburn didn't want to train Louis. He preferred to train white fighters, who would be given world title shots. "I don't care how good he is," Blackburn told Roxborough and Black. "Bring me a white boy so I can make some money."[16] Blackburn told Louis how to plant his feet and obtain the full power from his punches.

This trio of Roxborough, Black, and Blackburn became the prime movers in Joe Louis's professional boxing career. Roxborough and Black served as the managers, while Blackburn served as Louis's trainer. Louis called his managers Mister, but affectionately referred to Blackburn as "Chappie." In turn, Blackburn also called Louis the same term of endearment.

The trio established a set of strict rules that Louis would adhere to so as not to fall into the same abyss as Jack Johnson. The commandments were to never have your picture taken with a white woman, never enter a nightclub alone, never participate in a fixed fight, never gloat over a fallen opponent, maintain a deadpan expression, and live and fight clean.[17]

Joe Louis adhered to these rules—at least on the surface. He didn't gloat over fallen opponents—particularly white opponents. He kept his dalliances with white movie actresses on the down low—the general public had no idea that Louis was not an ideal husband to his wife Marva. Louis certainly adhered to these rules when he made his pro debut on July 4, 1934, against veteran Jack Kracken. Louis stopped Kracken in the first round. Headlines referred to Louis as "the Poker Face."[18] One reporter compared Louis to the great Joe Gans, writing that "there isn't much to tell about the fight—it was too one-sided."[19]

Only a week later, Louis won his next bout in easy fashion. His fourth opponent, Jack Kranz, proved more durable, lasting the full eight rounds with Louis. But Louis ended Kranz's 12-fight winning streak and won every round.[20] Louis's stepfather, Pat Brooks—originally quite opposed to Joe becoming a professional boxer—became a fan.[21] Louis continued to win fights at an accelerated pace. His victories over Charley Massera and Lee Ramage in December 1934 placed him in the rankings. Heavyweight champion Max Baer was at ringside in Chicago when Louis knocked Massera out of the ring.[22]

Louis's performance against Ramage was even more impressive. One press account referred to him as "another Jack Johnson," adding that Louis was the "new Black Panther of the ring."[23] Ramage certainly became a respectful admirer of Louis's prowess after his fateful encounter with the undefeated prospect. "He'll stop anyone he can hit and he couldn't miss against either Baer, Lasky or Levinsky if they could be persuaded to get in the ring with him," Ramage told a reporter.[24]

In early 1935, Louis faced Patsy Perroni—another number-10 contender— in Detroit. Louis dropped Perroni several times and won a 10-round decision. In February 1935, Louis knocked out Ramage in a rematch in the second round. Press accounts called Louis "the greatest coming fighter this country has known."[25] After the bout, Scotty Monteith, a promoter from Detroit, told Roxborough: "The kid can't miss. He's going to be a champ. He's a bomber. Come to think of it, that boy is a real brown bomber."[26] In later years, sportswriters Grantland Rice, Paul Gallico, and others would create all sorts of alliterative appellations for Louis, including "the tan-skinned terror, the sepia slugger, the mahogany maimer, the dark dynamiter and the zooming Zulu."[27]

The current champion, Max Baer, took notice of the young challenger, though he spoke brashly that he would drape Louis "over those chairs in row G" when they squared off in the ring.[28] Baer added that he would be willing to fight a colored fighter if the money was right, breaking a promise he made to his mother that he wouldn't face a black fighter.[29]

Louis continued to dominate the heavyweight division, winning 18 fights in a row. The *Chicago Defender* wrote that "Joe Louis has no equal" and proclaimed him the future champion. The paper called Louis's rise through the ranks as "the biggest sensation in sports history."[30] Hyperbole aside, Louis first had to start defeating top contenders. Paul Gallico, a prominent sportswriter, predicted accurately: "He will be a pugilistic success and unquestionably a champion."[31] Gallico remarked that Louis was a natural fighter, a true destructive force: "He is a splendid, vicious, male animal, completely destructive. He was made for fighting and nothing else."[32]

Roxborough and Black made a deal with "Uncle" Mike Jacobs, a major power broker in boxing and the key to boxing in New York City. The two numbers runners knew they needed Jacob to take Louis to the title. The first step was to match Louis against former champion Primo Carnera. The fight had an interesting international flavor, as Carnera was from Italy, a country ruled by Benito Mussolini. The Italian dictator had invaded Ethiopia in an act of international aggression condemned by other nations. "The international crisis provided the backdrop for the Louis–Carnera battle."[33]

More than 60,000 fans attended the Louis–Carnera match at Madison Square Garden—the mecca of boxing—in June 1935. Many predicted a Louis victory, but others thought Louis was overrated and untested. Braven Dyer criticized Louis's lack of competition: "For the most part, however, Joe's victims have been the below-average run of stumblebums who adorn the heavyweight division."[34]

Dyer was dead wrong, as Louis handled the former champion with ease. His performance earned raves from boxing experts. Wilfrid Smith referred to it as "the most spectacular since the days when Jack Dempsey strode across the pugilistic stage."[35] Invoking biblical references, Smith wrote that "the modern David moved in to finish the Golaith."[36] Louis dominated his larger opponent, dropping him three times in the sixth round to earn the victory.

Louis followed that victory with a one-round slaughter of overmatched King Levinsky, a fighter who had won more than 60 professional bouts. Louis dropped Levinsky three times in the first round. The referee "stopped the slaughter to keep the King from having the top of his head knocked off," wrote famed sportswriter Grantland Rice.[37] Louis began to attract fans of all races with his dominant performances. However, race was always a factor at that time in the United States. Controversy ensued in Washington, D.C., when sports radio announcer Arch McDonald called Louis a nigger when describing the bout.[38] Still, Louis had clearly placed his young face on the public consciousness. President Franklin D. Roosevelt shook hands with Louis in August 1935 and congratulated him on his victories.[39]

That led to the biggest match of Louis's career to date, with former champion Max Baer. Former champion Jack Dempsey contended that Baer would be too much to handle for the inexperienced prospect. "How many great ring men were sensations in one year?" he asked.[40] But sportswriter Grantland Rice predicted doom for the former champion: "Max Baer will need the hardest training camp he has ever known to carry even an outside chance against this murderous machine that can throw a grenade from ten inches and apparently blow up anything in sight."[41]

It turned out Rice had better prognosticating skills than Dempsey, as Louis dominated Baer, turning him into a "bloody hulk" by the third round. Rice colorfully wrote: "Max Baer left the primrose path, wandered into the jungle and came near losing his life."[42] Louis stopped Baer in the fourth round. It appeared that Baer could have beaten the count, but he stayed down for the full ten count. When asked about it afterward, the former champion said: "I could have struggled up once more, but when I get executed, people are going to have to pay more than twenty-five dollars a seat to watch."[43] Meanwhile the South Side of Chicago—largely African American—exploded in exultation at the triumph of this new, great black fighter. "By the end of 1935, he had become the most famous black man in the United States."[44] The Associated Press voted Louis the best athlete of 1935—a rare feat for a boxer and, particularly, for one who did not hold a world championship.[45] Many were calling Louis the "uncrowned champion" or "uncrowned king of the heavyweights."

Louis then reeled off two more wins in 1936 over proven commodities—Paulo Uzcutun and Charley Retzlaff—to solidify his top ranking. Uzcutun lasted into the fourth round, while Retzlaff didn't even make it out of the first round. Louis ran his record to 24–0. He was, in the eyes of many, the best heavyweight boxer in the world.

Jacobs then matched Louis against his third former world heavyweight champion—Max Schmeling, a man who had begun his professional career in his native Germany in 1924. Schmeling had lost seven fights in his professional career. It was assumed that Schmeling was on the downside of his career. Louis seemingly entered the contest overconfident. "I don't think he's so hot," Louis said of his opponent. "From those pictures it looks like he can be hit with either hand and I don't think he can punch—at least not enough to hurt me much."[46]

But Schmeling was a shrewd fighter. He noticed a flaw in Louis's style—that when Louis jabbed, he sometimes would drop his left hand. Schmeling's money punch was his straight right hand. He believed that he could land that straight right hand over Louis's left jab. Schmeling wrote that "Louis's one weakness matched perfectly my great strength."[47] Still, many expected that Joe Louis would win easily and "flatten Max Schmeling."[48]

In June 1936, Schmeling's prior preparation trumped Louis's lackadaisical approach. In the fourth round, Schmeling landed a right cross over Louis's jab. Schmeling followed up with a fusillade of punches that dropped Louis for the first time in his professional career. Louis rose quickly at the count of two and survived the round. "I couldn't believe that I was on my ass, and I could've sworn my damn jaw was broken," Louis said. "This was my first knockdown as a professional. To be honest, I never fully recovered from that blow."[49]

"Round after round, Schmeling's right found its mark," writes historian Randy Roberts. "Louis' face swelled grotesquely."[50] Schmeling knocked Louis out in the 12th round in a shocking upset. Bill Henry of the *New York Times* exclaimed:

They said he was a sucker.
They said he was too old.
They said he couldn't box.

They said Louis would knock him out whenever he pleased.
They said he was whistling past a graveyard when he said he wasn't afraid.
Well, Max showed em.[51]

Louis's stepfather, Pat Brooks, had suffered a debilitating stroke the day before and did not see the fight. He died never knowing that his stepson had lost a fight. "Sadness enveloped Harlem, the South Side, and the Black Bottom," Roberts explained. "Almost twenty years later Langston Hughes could still recall the pall of grief that hovered above black Americans."[52] Louis toppled from the precipice of a world title shot that he craved. Schmeling appeared to be first in line to fight James J. Braddock for the championship. Meanwhile, Louis seemingly would have to wait in line and try to climb back to the top. "Louis must now begin again the long climb toward the championship," wrote Wilfrid Smith of the *Chicago Daily Tribune*. "It remains to be seen whether he ever will scale the height."[53]

BECOMING A CHAMPION

Max Schmeling suddenly received the support of his home country. Prime Minister Joseph Goebbels telegraphed Schmeling immediately with congratulations: "I know you won for Germany. Heil Hitler."[54] Schmeling's victory confirmed Hitler's misguided nonsense about Aryan superiority. Schmeling appeared ready to challenge Braddock for the world championship.

Two months after losing to Schmeling, Louis returned to the ring and added another former world champion to his list of knockout victims. He kayoed Jack Sharkey in the third round. He then kayoed Al Ettore, a younger heavyweight, in five rounds. Louis appeared to need a few more wins to land the coveted title shot. Fortunately for Louis, he had "Uncle" Mike Jacobs working behind the scenes to get him a title shot in front of Schmeling. Part of the problem for the German was that his scheduled fight with Braddock was called off due to a hand injury suffered by the champion. It seemed as if Braddock and Schmeling would meet in June 1937 in Madison Square Garden. Jacobs managed to work out a deal between Joe Gould, Braddock's enterprising manager, and Roxborough. In exchange for Braddock granting Louis a title shot, Gould and Braddock would receive a hefty $500,000 or half the gate and broadcast revenue. Not only that, they also would receive 10 percent of Jacob's net profits in promoting Joe Louis over the next decade. In other words, James J. Braddock ended up a wealthy man in part because of Joe Louis winning future championship bouts.

Jacobs managed to stir up anti-Nazi fever in order to quell demands for a Braddock–Schmeling match instead of Braddock–Louis. Schmeling and his team filed a lawsuit, but it was unsuccessful in preventing a Braddock–Louis bout. Schmeling knew that he was being denied a title shot in part because he was from Germany. "After the Braddock fiasco it was finally clear to me—a German world champion could be tolerated in 1931, but one coming from Hitler's Germany was acceptable to no one."[55]

Braddock contributed to social history by not making race a factor in his prefight buildup with Louis. George Nicholson, a black heavyweight who sparred with Braddock and Louis, confirmed that Braddock was simply a genuinely good human being. "Joe was always grateful to Braddock for not drawing the color line," biographer Richard Bak writes. "For the rest of his life, whenever their paths would cross, he would always warmly address Braddock as 'Champ.'"[56]

On June 22, 1937, Braddock defended his title against Joe Louis. Braddock—who had not defended his title since winning it—actually dropped Louis in the first round with a right uppercut. Louis rose and proceeded to slowly wear down the champion. Braddock took a beating in the middle rounds, finally succumbing in the eighth round. "When he knocked me down," Braddock later said, "I could have stayed down three weeks."[57] Braddock referred to feeling Louis's jab in his face as "getting a light bulb rammed into your face."[58]

Joe Louis had become the second African American to hold the world heavyweight boxing title. But Louis had another idea on his mind. He needed to defeat Max Schmeling to prove he was the real champion. "I don't want nobody to call me champ until I beat that Schmeling," he said.[59]

Louis made his first title defense against Tommy Farr, a tough, gritty Welshman who gave the champion a tough fight. Farr's bobbing and weaving style frustrated Louis, and Farr clearly won some rounds along the way. The bout went the full 15 rounds, with the referee scoring it 13–1–1 for Louis. The two judges were more realistic, scoring it 9–6 and 8–5–2 for Louis. Blackburn praised Farr after the bout: "Louis hit Farr with shots that would have dropped, yeah, flattened most other fighters in the world. Farr is a real tough man and he has an awkward style. He is a better fighter than people give him credit for."[60] Louis offered a similar assessment of Farr: "Tommy Farr fooled me. He was one tough guy, with a peculiar style. He didn't look too effective, yet he was puzzling and his punches were annoying."[61]

Louis made two other title defenses, against Nathan Mann and Harry Thomas, before facing the man he most wanted—Schmeling. The buildup for the Louis–Schmeling fight was extraordinary. It took on geopolitical implications as the United States and Nazi Germany headed toward collision in what would become World War II. President Roosevelt urged Louis to win the fight, saying: "Joe, we're depending on those muscles for America."[62] For many reasons, the second Louis–Schmeling fight has been called "the Battle of the Century."[63] As Louis said, "the whole damn country was depending on me."[64]

Experts were divided in how they viewed the second encounter. But two former champions sided with Louis. Gene Tunney commented that "Louis had the best right hand punch I have ever seen," and James J. Braddock added "Louis can punch harder than any man I ever met."[65]

The battle of the century was a one-sided slaughter, as Louis destroyed Schmeling in the first round. Louis dominated early with his jab and then crushed Schmeling with a right hand to the body. Schmeling turned his body to avoid the blow, which ended up hitting him in the back. Schmeling's camp complained that the shot was an illegal kidney shot, but the final result was never in doubt from the opening bell. Louis showed his utter dominance over his rival. Schmeling himself acknowledged that the blow was aimed at his heart and that he had turned his body to avoid the punch. "In any case, it wasn't a question of a foul," he said.[66] Schmeling spent 10 days in the hospital after the bout, suffering two fractured vertebrae in his back.

Celebrations broke out all over the country. Andrew Young, who later became the first black mayor of Atlanta, said: "When Joe Louis knocked out Max Schmeling, that was freedom day."[67] Numerous musicians released songs devoted to Louis and his ring triumphs, including Count Basie, Ike Smith, Billy Hicks and the Sizzling Six, and others.

Schmeling never again competed for the heavyweight title, but he and Louis later stayed in touch. Schmeling became a wealthy man, head of Coca-Cola in Germany. He traveled all the way from Germany to Las Vegas to help Louis celebrate his 56th birthday.[68] Schmeling also reflected years later that his most painful defeat may have been a blessing. "A victory over Joe Louis would have made me forever the 'Aryan Show Horse' of the Third Reich."[69]

Louis continued to dominate in the ring, dispatching former light heavyweight champion John Henry Lewis—a personal friend of Louis and the first black man to win the light heavyweight crown—in the first round. Lewis had fine boxing skills but simply was no match for the power of Louis. "I felt funny all of a sudden," Lewis told reporters after being felled by the champion.[70] Joe Louis continued his dominance with a first-round stoppage over an overmatched, 36-year-old Jack Roper. A game Roper tried hard but was "helpless before [Louis's] left hooks."[71] Media reports began to ask whether the dominant heavyweight champion was the greatest heavyweight or even the greatest fighter of all time. Frank Young of the *Chicago Defender* wrote that Louis would have "disposed" of former greats Jack Dempsey and Jack Johnson.[72]

Louis's next bout provided more intrigue due to the colorful nature of his opponent, "Two Ton" Tony Galento. This short, rotund, balding bar owner from Orange, New Jersey, made a career out of crazy antics. He once ate 50 hot dogs right before a fight to win a bet. He openly head-butted and even bit opponents on occasion. He also possessed the gift of gab. When asked one time about Shakespeare, Galento—not the literary type—replied: "Never hoid of him. What's he, one of those foreign heavyweights. I'll moida da bum."[73] "He boxed kangaroos, wrestled bears, and claimed to have once choked an octopus to death."[74] He sometimes even drank beer between rounds.[75]

Galento didn't look like much of a fighter, outside of a bar fighter. "He was a saloon keeper, and from the looks of him he must have had a drink with every customer."[76] But appearances aside, Galento had two character-istics that made him a tough opponent: He could absorb massive amounts of punishment, and he could punch. Galento had a powerful left hook that gave him a puncher's chance in any bout. Galento had been the number-one challenger for the crown as far back as 1939. He had consistently railed that he would knock out Joe Louis if given the chance. Louis responded with verbal volleys of his own: "Galento is only a third-rate fighter who happens to have a good punch. He's a great fighter if he can hit you, but he won't hit me if we meet."[77]

A few months later, in June 1939, at Yankee Stadium, "Two Ton" Tony Galento and Joe Louis engaged in an exciting fistic encounter that featured "savage fury and methodical brutality."[78] Galento hit Louis with a solid com-bination in the first round that rocked the champion. The crowd at Yankee Stadium roared in approval, as they knew the champion faced a real threat. Louis rebounded quickly and controlled the action and, by the middle of the third round, was dominating the bout.

Then Galento landed a left hook out of nowhere that dropped the cham-pion. Galento's punch actually lifted the "Brown Bomber" off the canvas. "When Galento knocked Louis down, said referee Arthur Donovan, "I could see that the champion was badly hurt, even though he jumped onto his feet without a count. If Tony could have landed another left hook, he would have won the title."[79] Galento never landed another left hook. Instead, Louis rose to his feet and pummeled Galento, stopping him in the fourth round.

Galento had made insults of every kind at Louis in the prefight buildup. But years later, Louis and Galento were on quite friendly terms. Louis would come to visit Galento's bar often.[80] "Funny thing, though, me and Tony are still friends," Louis wrote. "I used to go to his saloon in Jersey quite a bit, and we'd laugh about all the things we'd been so serious about."[81]

Louis kept defending his title in the early years of his reign. Jack Milloy of the *New York Post* dubbed Louis's opponents collectively as "the Bum of the Month club."[82] But these fighters had decent credentials. Johnny Paycheck had a record of 38–3–2 when he fought Louis, and the Chilean Arturo Godoy had more than 50 professional wins when he tangled twice with the "Brown Bomber." Godoy even lasted the full 15 rounds in his first bout with Louis, often making the champion backpedal during the bout. Louis earned only a split-decision victory over Godoy, as one judge favored the Chilean fighter. Jack Cuddy, covering the bout, referred to Godoy as the "roughest, toughest man that Louis ever met."[83] Trainer Blackburn defended Louis against heavy criticism for his performance: "This fellow [Godoy] came in weaving and bobbing, crouched like one of those monkeys who used to see begging for pennies while his owner held the string and played the hand organ."[84] In June 1940, Louis defeated Godoy more decisively, stopping him in the eighth round.

Louis stayed active, defending his title four times in 1940 and then seven times in 1941. In some of his title defenses, Louis faced little opposition. For example, Louis crushed Gus Dorazio in February 1941 by second-round knockout. The fight, which was held in Philadelphia, outraged Pennsylvania state senator John J. Haluska. He called for an investigation into the bout, calling it a "complete frame-up." Haluska said: "We should investigate who was responsible for such a farce of a fight. It was a disgrace to take the people's money."[85]

But not all of Louis's opponents were overmatched or bums. In 1941, the champion faced some serious opposition, first in Max Baer's larger brother Buddy and then in a brash, young light heavyweight named Billy Conn. Louis stopped Baer by disqualification in the seventh round, after Baer's corner protested what they felt was a blow after the bell by Louis. But it was the first fight with Conn in June 1941 that left a lasting impression on the boxing world.

Conn—officially weighing just more than 170 pounds—had quick hands and feet with exceptional boxing skills. He had dominated the light heavyweight division and won fighter of the year honors from the New York boxing writers' group in 1939 over Joe Louis.[86] At the end of 1940, *The Ring* magazine rated Conn the number-one fighter in its annual poll.[87]

In their June 1941 fight, Conn used his superior speed to box Louis effectively for much of the bout. In rounds 8 through 12, Conn boxed beautifully and took the lead on the judges' scorecards. During the bout, Conn told Louis: "You got a fight tonight Joe," to which the champion replied, "I knows it."[88]

In the 12th round, Conn staggered Louis with his combination punching. Conn told his corner after the round: "I'm going to knock this son of a bitch out."[89] That proved his undoing, for Louis—though behind on the scorecards—always possessed one-punch knockout power.

Tragically for him, Conn fought the 13th round more like a slugger than a boxer. He actually believed he would knock Joe Louis out cold. Instead, Louis coolly landed a series of blows culminating in a right hook that felled the challenger. Louis retained his title again with only two seconds remaining in the 13th round. The crowd at the Polo Grounds went berserk. Roberts wrote that "the fight was so damn dramatic that it killed people."[90] Sid Ferer summed it up best: "Joe Louis held onto his world heavyweight championship tonight—but he never came closer to losing it."[91]

After the bout, Conn reflected on his stupidity in going for a knockout. "What's the sense of being Irish if you can't be dumb."[92] The two men did not fight a rematch until five years later, in June 1946. World War II intervened, and both men served in the armed forces. Roberts writes that Louis–Conn I was "Joe Louis' last great fight."[93]

Instead of defending his title on a regular basis, Louis became a war hero of sorts, even though he wasn't fighting on the front lines overseas. But he was admired for his patriotism. Some of his straightforward comments became legendary. Most notably, he said to a Navy Relief Society benefit: "I have only done what any red-blooded American would do. We gonna do our part, and we will win because we are on God's side."[94]

World War II deprived Louis of a few more years of his prime. Louis often fought charity bouts and occasionally gave away his entire purse for army relief funds and other charities. That didn't stop the U.S. government from pursuing the champion for back taxes—a situation that plagued Louis for much of his adult life. His managers faced legal trouble, as Black faced income tax evasion charges and Roxborough served time for illegal gambling.[95]

Louis quietly battled against segregation on military bases. He once saved future baseball great Jackie Robinson from serious trouble after Robinson had a conflict with a superior white officer. Louis privately demanded that all of his boxing exhibitions be integrated or he would not participate. Louis knew that he needed boxing. He had tax troubles, as well as money spending problems.

Louis knew he wasn't the same fighter after the war. "When I came out of the army I wasn't the fighter I was before I went in," he said. "Nobody can lay off that long and come back as good as he was."[96]

In 1946, Louis defended his title twice—first in a rematch with Conn and then in a first-round kayo over Tami Mauriello. The bout with Conn did not live up to the expectations generated by their first epic encounter. For one thing, Conn's skills had deteriorated; he wasn't nearly the same level of fighter.

In 1947, Louis defended his title against Jersey Joe Walcott. Born as Arnold Cream, Walcott began his career as a talented welterweight. He gradually grew bigger and acquired an array of savvy ring skills. But Walcott was not considered a serious challenger to Louis's title. He was anywhere from a 10–1 to 20–1 underdog. But in December 1974, Walcott outboxed Joe Louis. He dropped Louis in the first and fourth rounds. Walcott boxed cautiously in the final two rounds, not wanting to repeat the mistake of Billy Conn. At the end of the fight, everyone thought Walcott had pulled off one of the sport's monumental upsets. Louis told Walcott that Jersey Joe had won the fight and tried to leave the ring before the decision was announced. However, Louis later claimed that he just was disgusted with his performance, but thought he did enough to win, as he was the one who was the aggressor.[97]

But boxing has always been—in the words of HBO boxing analyst Larry Merchant—"the theatre of the unexpected." Referee Ruby Goldstein scored the bout for Walcott, but the two judges somehow scored the bout for Louis, who allegedly apologized to Walcott for the decision. Many in the press thought that Louis had been beat, plain and simple. "There is a widespread opinion among most of the sports writers, sent here to cover the fight, that Joe Louis retained his world title by being a popular champion."[98] Wilfrid Smith summed it up accurately: "Joe Louis still is heavyweight champion of the world. But he is no longer the Brown Bomber."[99]

Louis granted Walcott a rematch. The two met in June 1948 at Yankee Stadium. Walcott's clever boxing surprised Louis again in the third round, as the champion was knocked down again. Walcott had a lead, but Louis stayed in the fray. In the 11th round, Louis reached Walcott with a series of heavy blows to close the show. Louis had won the rematch by knockout. The crowd gave him a standing ovation, and he received a hero's welcome around town. He announced his retirement from the ring, saying "I will definitely retire from boxing."[100]

That should have been the end of Joe Louis's boxing career. But he couldn't stay away—largely for economic reasons. He needed the money to pay Uncle Sam his tax debts. In September 1950, Louis challenged new champion Ezzard Charles, who badly outboxed Louis over 15 rounds. The judges gave Louis only two, three, and five rounds, respectively. Louis cried in his dressing room after the bout, saying "I'm through."[101] Ringside reporter Russ J. Cowans presciently wrote that Charles was "probably the most underrated champion of all time."[102]

Louis kept fighting, winning eight straight bouts. He still had designs on recapturing the heavyweight title. Those dreams came crashing out of the ring literally, when, in October 1951, he faced an undefeated contender named Rocky Marciano. Louis jabbed effectively at times but could not thwart the younger man's aggressive attack. Marciano packed wallop in his fists, and he knocked Louis out of the ring in the eighth round. An era had come to an end. The great Joe Louis was done in the ring. "There was no doubt Marciano had beaten the shit out of me," Louis said.[103]

Louis's postfight career did not equal his ring greatness. In the 1960s, he battled heavy drug problems. He often hung out with heavyweight boxer Sonny Liston in Las Vegas. He worked for Caesar's Palace as a greeter. He died in April 1981 at the age of 67.

LEGACY

Joe Louis was one of the greatest fighters in history. He set records that have never been broken. He held the heavyweight championship for nearly 12 years and defended it an astonishing 25 times. But the legacy of Joe Louis extends far beyond his fistic accomplishments. He became a national hero for his win over Max Schmeling in the rematch and for his service during the war. He quietly battled for racial equality in the armed forces. He boxed more than 90 exhibitions and entertained more than 2 million troops. Budd Schulberg expressed it well: "Never part of the civil rights movement, he might be considered its one-man forerunner."[104]

Joe Louis made history in and out of the ring. One obituary remarked that Louis never said that he was the greatest, but "everybody knew it."[105] He inspired a generation of people of all races. In the famed words of sportswriter Jimmy Cannon, "he was a credit to his race, the human race."[106]

Chapter 4

ROCKY MARCIANO: UNDEFEATED AND UNDERAPPRECIATED

Today people still talk about "the great white hope"—the white fighter who can compete in a sport dominated by African Americans and Latinos. Recall that when Jack Johnson lifted the crown from Tommy Burns in Australia in 1908, a collective groan across much of the Western Hemisphere was heard. The racist sentiments of white America clamored in vain for a white heavyweight fighter.

African American Joe Louis held the heavyweight title for 12 years, the longest championship reign in boxing history. After Louis, the title was held by Ezzard Charles and Jersey Joe Walcott—two other African American boxers. It was not until the 1950s that a white man captured the heavyweight crown. He was a most unlikely champion who never harbored any racist sentiments. He seemed much more interested in baseball than boxing for much of his youth.

This future champion's story began on September 1, 1923, in Brockton, Massachusetts, when Pierilion and Pasqualena Marchegiano had their second child, Rocco Francis. His birth was a blessing for the Italian immigrants, as their first child had died at birth. Legend has it that, upon Rocco Francis's birth, the Marchegianos received a card welcoming the birth of their son with the message "Hail to the Champ."[1]

Young Rocco developed toughness growing up as a child during the Great Depression. The family often had no hot water or heat, as Pierilion's job in a shoe factory failed to bring home sufficient funds. The family lived in tight quarters, particularly after the couple had three daughters and two other sons after Rocco. As a youngster, Marchegiano played football and his first love, baseball. He played on an American Legion team as a catcher. He wielded a powerful swing that allegedly caught the attention of a few minor league scouts.

Marchegiano dropped out of school during his sophomore year for economic reasons—to help his family pay the bills. For the next several years, he worked many manual labor jobs—on a coal truck, in a candy factory, and as a short-order cook. The U.S. Army then drafted him into service in 1943. He served in the army for three years, though he never saw combat action. He returned home in December 1946.

He worked for a gas company in Brockton and honed his baseball skills. In early 1947, he and several of his friends tried out for a minor league team under the aegis of the Chicago Cubs. Rocco failed to impress the scouts. His baseball dreams dying, the young man turned to another sport in which he had dabbled and shown some natural ability—boxing.

Marchegiano had displayed his natural power during his stint in the army, knocking out fellow GIs in several bouts. In the spring of 1947, he actually had one pro bout on St. Patrick's Day against Lee Epperson in Holyoke, Massachusetts. Both fighters were making their pro debuts. Epperson was the favored fighter in his hometown and won the first two rounds over his awkward opponent. In the third round, the outsider from Brockton landed a mighty right uppercut that kayoed Epperson, who never fought professionally again.

For the rest of 1947, Marchegiano plied his trade in amateur boxing. He had about 30 bouts, in which his lack of experience showed. He did not possess great boxing skills and relied on natural power and aggression to carry him through the opposition. His biographer, Russell Sullivan, writes: "As an amateur, Rocky Marciano [as Marchegiano was later known] was extremely raw. He would simply flounder around the ring, graceless and awkward, absorbing punishment from his opponent until he saw an opening to land a big one."[2] He lost a bout in a Golden Gloves tournament to Corey Wallace, who was being billed by some as the next Joe Louis. In a later bout, Marchegiano broke his right hand, depriving him of an opportunity to pursue a national Amateur Athletic Union title and a potential shot at making the U.S. Olympic team.

Rocco and his best friend, Allie Colombo, set their sights on finding a manager and trainer in the Massachusetts area to guide his career. But several leading managers in Massachusetts did not view Marchegiano as having legitimate pro potential. They focused on his shortcomings in technique, speed, and size rather than his positive attributes. Mostly, his awkward style turned them away from taking the chance on Marchegiano, who was already 25 years old.

Through a local connection, Marchegiano and Colombo managed to contact New York–based fight manager Al Weill, who agreed to take a look at the heavyweight. Marchegiano stepped into the ring at the gym on West 17th Street against Wade Chancey, a big heavyweight from Florida. Chancey got the better of the sparring for a little while, when all of a sudden, a powerful roundhouse right from Marchegiano dropped Chancey to the canvas. Al Weill became interested.[3]

Weill often worked in tandem with trainer Charley Goldman. They had found success in the past in lighter weight classes, including with lightweight Lou Ambers, featherweight Joey Archibald, and welterweight Marty Servo. Goldman maximized the ability of his fighters. He was a former bantamweight contender who had nearly 140 professional bouts. After his fighting days were over, he turned to training. Goldman was a great teacher of the sweet science, and in young Marchegiano, he had his ultimate protégé.

ENTERING THE PROFESSIONAL RANKS

Rocco Marchegiano began his professional career at various bouts in Providence, Rhode Island, in 1948. He won all eight of his bouts by knockout. He defeated some undefeated prospects, such as Bobby Quinn and Eddie Ross. Local promoter Sam Silverman, who handled some of Marchegiano's early fights, said he knew that Rocco had real potential after he flattened the undefeated Ross.[4] *Providence Journal* boxing writer Mike Thomas was even more prescient: "If punching power will do it, Rocky Marchegiano may one day become the world heavyweight champion."[5]

After these wins, Marchegiano changed his name to Marciano—a more announcer-friendly name that showed off his Italian heritage better. His handlers knew that Marciano had two qualities that could not be taught: (1) great punching power and (2) a great chin. He showed the ability early in his career to take his opponents' best shots and then flatten them with one of his own.

In 1949, Marciano kept winning, though he finally faced a fighter who went the distance with him: the clever, defensive Don Mogard. In July 1949, Marciano faced an even tougher foe in "Tiger" Ted Lowry, a man who had more than 100 professional bouts. Lowry's experience and ring savvy gave Marciano fits, but Marciano rallied in the last few rounds to take a close unanimous decision. Marciano rebounded at the end of 1949 by stopping fringe contender Phil Muscato, who had more than 55 pro victories.

The victory over Muscato earned Marciano some name recognition and the opportunity to fight on a bigger stage. He traveled to Weill's home base of New York to face Carmine Vingo at Madison Square Garden. The 20-year-old Vingo entered the ring with a record of 16–1 and was hailed as a prospect. He and Marciano waged war for six rounds. "Head-to-head, toe-to-toe they fought like lightweights instead of the heavyweights they are," wrote James P. Dawson.[6] The first round had more action than most complete bouts, as each pugilist rocked the other. In the sixth round, Marciano felled Vingo with a devastating left hook that rendered him unconscious. Vingo fell into a coma and nearly died. Although Vingo recovered, he never fought professionally again.

The bout and its impact on Vingo affected Marciano. That was not good news for the Weill–Goldman prospect as Marciano next faced the toughest challenge of his career to that point in Roland La Starza in March 1950. The showdown featured the 25–0 Marciano against the 37–0 La Starza, who had been called the second coming of Gene Tunney. Oddsmakers tabbed La Starza as a slight favorite in the bout.[7]

La Starza possessed not only good looks like Tunney but also some of the former champion's boxing skills. He used those to good advantage early in the bout with Marciano and managed to survive a fourth-round onslaught from Marciano. Marciano's superior power rocked La Starza several times in the final two rounds. Still, the result was in doubt at the end of 10 rounds. In those days, there were two ringside judges and the referee weighed in as the third judge. Marciano captured a split-decision victory after the two judges split and referee Jack Walton cast the deciding vote in favor of Marciano.[8]

One New York boxing writer disagreed, calling the decision a "paper thin and exceedingly odd decision."[9] Matt Ring, writer for the *Philadelphia Evening Bulletin,* also criticized Marciano's performance, writing: "Watching him pitch those haymakers, one couldn't help wondering if the twenty-four knockouts on his record weren't scored against cigar store Indians."[10]

Marciano continued to improve under Goldman's tutelage. He began to throw straighter punches, and he became more consistent in his punch output. He also utilized a vicious body attack—something that would serve him well in his championship years.

The near-setback against La Starza also caused Weill and Goldman to reassess their heavyweight's career path. They decided to move Marciano slowly and match him carefully—building both his record and his confidence. However, Marciano sometimes learned slowly and won a few of his matches against nondescript opposition in less-than-crowd-pleasing fashion. But he remained undefeated and ready for the next big challenge.

That challenge came in July 1951, against the favored Rex Layne of Lewiston, Utah—a fighter who evoked memories of Jack Dempsey. A former national Amateur Athletic Union champion, Layne possessed a gaudy record of 37–1, including victories over Jersey Joe Walcott and Bob Satterfield. Like La Starza before him, Layne also entered his bout with Marciano as a favorite with the odds at 8–5.[11] Sportswriters gushed about the power-punching Layne, calling him "spectacular."[12]

But Marciano devoured Layne with a two-fisted attack to the head and body. Marciano stopped Layne in the sixth round, effectively ending his opponent's title dreams. Marciano landed a right-hand bomb that knocked Layne cold. Layne had to be assisted back to his corner.[13] The victory propelled Marciano into the heavyweight championship scene and the public eye. One columnist wrote that Marciano "had been fed on a milk diet so to speak, in his buildup, but he showed he could devour raw meat as well."[14] Marciano even landed an appearance on Ed Sullivan's television show *Toast of the Town.*

He came even closer to the title when he faced the former champion Joe Louis—his idol. Louis, only the second African American to hold the crown, kept the title for more than a decade, defeating all comers in still the most dominant championship reign in boxing history. But Louis had retired after defending his title against Jersey Joe Walcott in 1948—though he fought an exhibition in 1949. Louis—needing money because of tax problems—returned to the ring and challenged champion Ezzard Charles, who easily outpointed Louis over 15 rounds. Louis continued to ply his trade and managed to put together eight straight wins, including victories over Lee Savold and Jimmy Bivins.

Weill put together a match between the former great champion and Marciano, who some viewed as the uncrowned champion. Louis had significant height, weight, and reach advantages—not to mention a wealth of experience. Perhaps for this reason, Louis entered the ring as a slight favorite over his undefeated opponent in October 1951.

Louis used his potent left jab to keep Marciano at bay for many of the early rounds, but Marciano kept coming. He hit Louis wherever he could—head, body, and arm. Louis began to tire as the fight progressed. In the eighth round, Marciano dropped him with a left hook—further evidence that Marciano was not—as some critics alleged—a one-armed fighter. Louis rose, but Marciano pounced with a flurry of heavy blows and knocked him through the ropes. Referee Ruby Goldstein didn't even bother to count to 10, as Louis slumped to the canvas. Marciano had stopped his idol in the eighth round. "It was a nerve-pounding moment—one signaling the end of an era," wrote Gene Ward.[15] Some historians reported that Marciano felt bad about the bout, even shedding some tears for his former idol. "I was glad I won but was sorry I had to do it to him," he told reporters after the bout.[16]

For his part, Louis was gracious in defeat, saying he had lost to the better man. "He hits harder than Max Schmeling," referring to the only man who had ever stopped Louis before this bout.[17] Louis said that "Schmeling must have hit me a hundred times . . . I went out from exhaustion more than anything else. It took Marciano only two shots to do it."[18]

Marciano won three more bouts in 1952 before facing Harry "Kid" Matthews in a heavyweight title eliminator. The winner of the bout would land a title shot against champion Jersey Joe Walcott. Matthews was no slouch, entering the ring with an impressive record of 81–3–5. But, as was so often the case in Marciano's career, his opponent could not stand up to his pressure and power. Marciano landed two crushing left hooks that stopped Matthews in the second round.[19]

BECOMING THE CHAMPION

Next up was the greatest challenge in Marciano's career. Born Arnold Raymond Cream, Jersey Joe Walcott was a pro's pro who had to labor for many years without a title shot in the light heavyweight division because of racial prejudice. He simply could not land the big fights for much of his career. He served as Joe Louis's sparring partner in the early 1940s but lost that job because he did too well against Louis in the sparring sessions. In December 1947, Louis gave Walcott a title shot—and nearly regretted it. Many ringside observers felt Walcott deserved the decision, but Louis escaped with his belt. He did stop Walcott in the 11th round in their rematch—Louis's last title defense.

Walcott then lost in consecutive bouts to the next champion, the talented Ezzard Charles. Walcott landed a third shot against Charles and made the most of it. He stopped Charles in the seventh round to become heavyweight champion. Marciano faced a tough challenge in Walcott, who possessed clever ring skills and deceptive power. One sportswriter termed Walcott the "Satchel Paige of pugilism," referring to the ageless pitching ace.[20]

Experts were divided in their assessment of who would win the bout. Marciano had youth and power on his side, but Walcott had the edge in ring savvy, boxing skills, and experience. Sportswriter Frank Finch picked Walcott, believing that Marciano was too awkward to contend with the clever footwork of Jersey Joe.[21] Joe Louis picked Walcott to retain his title, but former champion Gene Tunney picked Marciano. Tunney said that Marciano hit harder with both hands than any fighter he had ever seen.[22]

In the first round, Walcott showed Marciano his deceptive power by dropping the man from Brockton in the first round. Marciano rebounded and continued on the attack. But Walcott won the bulk of the rounds with excellent counterpunching and his obvious skill at throwing punches from different angles. A master of distance, Walcott would hit his opponents with a left hook when they least expected it. Heading into the 13th round, Marciano trailed on all three scorecards. Judge Pete Tomasco had Walcott ahead 7–5 in rounds, judge Zach Clayton had Walcott ahead 8–4, and referee Charley Daggert had Walcott ahead 7–4–1.

But the 13th round served as the defining moment of Rocky Marciano's career. He managed to trap Walcott in the corner and landed one of the greatest punches in boxing history—a short right hand that contorted Walcott's jaw and cheek. "Referee Charley Daggert tolled the fatal '10' over

Jersey Joe, but he could have counted in the hundreds," wrote Finch. "It sounded like the proverbial dull thud of a blunt instrument on a human skull."[23] Jack Kearns, Jack Dempsey's manager, said "that was the hardest blow I ever saw."[24]

Rocky Marciano had done the impossible—he had won the world heavyweight championship. He had done so in one of the epic heavyweight title bouts in history. Columnist Wilfrid Smith called it "the greatest fist fight" since Jack Dempsey–Luis Firpo in the 1920s.[25]

Eight months later, Marciano faced Walcott in a rematch at Chicago Stadium. This time Marciano entered as the dominant favorite, as Walcott was in his 40s. Marciano served notice that his championship victory was no fluke, as he stunned Jersey Joe in the first round to retain his title. Marciano dropped the former champion with a left hook followed by a sharp right. Walcott jumped up ready to defend himself, but referee Frank Sikora had counted to 10. Walcott and his corner insisted that Jersey Joe could have gotten up, but he thought the count was only at eight.[26]

Marciano made five more defenses of his title—against former champion Ezzard Charles twice; his old rival Roland La Starza; Don Cockell; and the ageless Archie Moore, the former light heavyweight champion. In his second title defense, Marciano faced his former rival, La Starza. Recall that some experts believed that Marciano received an unwarranted split-decision win during their previous encounter. La Starza boxed well early and held the lead after seven rounds. But one of Marciano's great attributes was his stamina. He continually placed the pressure on La Starza, who began to wilt. When Marciano landed his patented left hook in the seventh round, the die was cast for La Starza. Reporter Al Wolf wrote it well: "He [La Starza] didn't have the power to hold Marciano at bay. And when the champion came to that conclusion, he became a careless tornado bent on destruction."[27]

La Starza became a believer in Marciano after losing the rematch. He said that the only way to beat Marciano was for someone to have the ability to box him for 15 rounds, reasoning that there was no way to knock him out. La Starza also echoed what other opponents said—that Marciano is much harder to hit than he appears. La Starza said: "Rocky fools you. He doesn't take as much punishment as he seems. He looks easy to hit but he isn't."[28]

Marciano's toughest fight by far was his first fight against Charles. Ezzard Charles was a gifted boxer with power. He dominated the light heavyweight division to such an extent that the champions avoided him like the plague. Charles had killed an opponent in the ring—Sam Baroudi in the 10th round. Some speculated that Charles never fought the same after the Baroudi tragedy in 1948. But Charles relished the opportunity to regain the heavyweight title from Marciano.

On June 17, 1953, Marciano faced Charles at Yankee Stadium. Charles dominated the early rounds with his superior boxing skills. In the fourth round, Charles opened a nasty cut over Marciano's left eye. Fortunately, Marciano had in his corner one of the sport's best cutmen, Freddie Brown. Marciano rallied in the middle rounds, hurting Charles in the sixth. Heading into the championship rounds, the fight hung in the balance. Marciano pressed the action. In the 15th and final round, he battered the courageous Charles with dozens of shots. Still, Charles survived and sent the fight to the judges, who scored the bout for Marciano in a close, unanimous decision. Charles earned praise for going the distance and surviving Marciano's attack, but Marciano retained his title.

Arguably, Marciano's next toughest defense was his last against one of the true characters of the sport—the legendary Archie Moore. As biographer Russell Sullivan wrote: "When it came to rags-to-riches stories, Archie Moore made Rocky Marciano look like Little Lord Fauntleroy."[29] Moore had labored under the race bar for many years, unable to land a title shot against the white champions. Boxing historian Mike Fitzgerald aptly labeled Moore "the ageless warrior."—Moore had turned professional in 1938 but didn't receive a title shot until 1952, when he defeated Joey Maxim to win the light heavyweight crown. He fought until the mid-1950s, even challenging a young heavyweight named Cassius Clay in 1962.

Moore had mastered the art of what he termed "escapology"—the ability to avoid punishment. But he was much more than a defensive cutie. Moore possessed serious power, still owning the all-time record in boxing history, with more than 130 knockouts to his credit. Moore genuinely believed he had the skill to defeat Marciano, whom he viewed as a crude brawler. Moore embarked on a national campaign tour to attract enough attention to earn a shot at boxing's ultimate prize: the heavyweight championship.

On September 21, 1955, Marciano faced Moore for the belt in Yankee Stadium. In the second round, Moore showed that he came for more than a sizeable payday—he came to win the fight. Marciano missed with a wild shot, and Moore connected with a strong right-hand counter that dropped the champion—only the second time Marciano had tasted the canvas. Undeterred, Marciano rose at the count of two and proceeded on the attack.

Marciano proceeded to do what he did over his entire career: relentlessly attack and wear down his opponents. He knocked Moore down twice in the sixth round and finished him off in the ninth.

In 1956, Marciano shocked the boxing world by retiring at the age of 33. Many thought that he would at least defend his belt one more time to become 50–0. But he didn't. He retired. And unlike most boxers, he never returned to the ring to tarnish his ring legacy. He toyed with the idea of coming back to face Floyd Patterson and then Sonny Liston but wisely stayed retired. Marciano died at the age of 46 in a plane crash.

LEGACY

Some modern boxing scribes insist that Marciano would not be able to compete with the behemoth heavyweights of today. They point out that Marciano was a cruiserweight in modern-day boxing with a limited reach. But Rocky Marciano was no ordinary fighter.

Rocky Marciano remains a legend entitled to a place in the high pantheon in the sport of boxing if for no other reason than his near-mythical 49–0 record. No one ever defeated Rocky Marciano in a professional boxing match.

Over the years, some fighters have approached Marciano's record. Larry Holmes ruled the heavyweight division for more than seven years from 1978 until 1985. He came agonizingly close to Marciano's record by compiling a record of 48–0. However, he lost his next fight by decision to Michael Spinks, prompting his now infamous remark, "Rocky Marciano couldn't carry my jockstrap." In more recent years, the Russian giant Nikolai Valuev came close by compiling a record of 47–0 against relatively limited opposition before dropping a decision to Ruslan Chagaev.

The ghost of Rocky Marciano still lives and so does his 49–0 record. No one can ever take it away from him and no one may ever match it.

Chapter 5

THE INCOMPARABLE ALI

In the early 1960s, boxing needed help; it needed someone to revitalize the sport. Critics had increased their cries for abolishing the "brutal" sport, citing the tragic deaths of featherweight champion Davey Moore and welterweight champion Benny "Kid" Paret in high-profile, nationally televised bouts. Opponents of the sport emphasized that shadowy mob figures played too great a role in the sport. Boxing needed a superstar to elevate the sport out of its doldrums. The great welterweight and middle-weight champion Sugar Ray Robinson was well past his prime. Dominant heavyweight champions Joe Louis and Rocky Marciano had receded into distant memory. The championship currently resided in a foreboding—though formidable—figure named Charles "Sonny" Liston, known as much for his lengthy arrest record and mob connections as for his fistic dominance.

Fortunately, boxing received a boost from a pugilist with an uncommonly pretty face, fast feet, and an even quicker tongue. His mantra would become: "Float like a butterfly, sting like a bee. I am the greatest Muhammad Ali." But before he was Ali, he was known by his birth name, Cassius Marcellus Clay. This young man became a darling of the 1960 Rome Olympics, capturing a gold medal in the light heavyweight division. He turned pro and began winning bouts. The loquacious Clay emulated the wrestler "Gorgeous George" Wagner in braggadocio and rodomontade. He would not only predict victory in his bouts, but also would correctly pick the round in which he would end the fight. He bantered playfully with the press and recited outrageous poetry. This young black man later became a Black Muslim, a follower of Elijah Muhammad and a protégé of sorts of the charismatic Malcolm X. His religious conversion and opposition to the Vietnam War led to antipathy toward the young boxer. In some circles, he was the most hated man in the United States. Boxing authorities stripped him of his title at the peak of his pugilistic powers—when he was an undefeated heavyweight champion.

Several years later, he returned—still great—but not as great as he was in the mid-1960s. But he shocked the world again by regaining the title against all odds. A funny and strange thing happened along the way: he became a hero, a cultural icon, and the most recognizable face on the planet. Of course this was Muhammad Ali—"the Greatest." His story transcends boxing and all of sports. His social and political significance eclipses every other athletic figure.

BEGINNINGS AND A GOLD MEDAL

Born on January 17, 1942, Cassius Marcellus Clay entered this world in Louisville, Kentucky, as the son of Cassius Sr., a house painter, and Odessa, a maid. He attended church regularly with his mother, who was a devout Baptist. "I've changed my religion and some of my beliefs since then, but her God is still God; I just call him by a different name," he told his biographer, Thomas Hauser.[1]

Clay wandered into a boxing gym at age 12, looking to learn the art of fighting. Someone had stolen his bicycle and he wanted to learn how to beat that person to a pulp. A local white police officer named Joe Martin ran the gym. He told Clay that he "better learn how to fight before you start challenging people that you're gonna whup."[2] Martin said that Clay did not look like anything special when he first started boxing. "He was just ordinary," Martin recalled.[3]

But Clay progressed quickly, showing amazing agility and an obsessive desire to improve. By age 17, he became a force in amateur boxing—a threat to win Golden Gloves and other amateur titles. He won the national Amateur Athletic Union championships in 1959. But he was not unbeatable—yet. He lost a split decision to a Marine named Amos Johnson in the 1959 Pan American Games.[4] Defeat did not sit well for Clay—another trait that inspired him to become a true champion. In April 1960, he once again won a national Amateur Athletic Union championship in the 178-pound light heavyweight division. After a tough first round, Clay knocked Joe Davis of Mobile, Alabama, under the ropes and scored the only knockout of the competition.[5] Clay's amateur ledger earned him a spot in the Olympic trials and then a trip to Rome in the 1960 Olympics.

He cruised through the international competition, winning the gold medal with a three-round unanimous-decision victory over Poland's Zbigniew Pietrzykowski. The tall southpaw from Poland was no slouch, having won more than 200 amateur bouts with only 13 defeats. But he was no match for the combination punching of the fleet-footed kid from Louisville.[6] Clay exhibited patriotism and defended his country when asked a question about segregation by a reporter from the Soviet Union. "To me, the USA is still the best country in the world, counting yours."[7] He exhibited his flair for rhyme in his early days too, announcing:

> To make America the Greatest is my goal
> So I beat the Russian and I beat the Pole
> And for the USA won the Medal of Gold.[8]

Clay then set his sights on turning professional.

TURNING PRO

Clay made his professional debut in October 1960, against a police chief from Fayetteville, West Virginia, named Tunney Hunsaker—a tough fighter with 15 professional victories. Hunsaker couldn't cope with Clay's superior speed and lost a six-round decision in Louisville's Freedom Hall. Clay bloodied the police chief's nose and nearly closed one of his eyes but had to settle for a verdict from the ringside judges. Still, the promise was apparent for all to see.

Clay's boxing skills led him to a string of victories. In only his sixth pro bout, he stopped LaMar Clark of Utah—a fighter known for kayoing more than 40 straight ring opponents. Clark was no match for the gifted Clay and fell easily in two rounds. Clay began to engage the press even more, as he piled up the victories. Jim Murray, the famed sportswriter for the *Los Angeles Times,* wrote: "Cassius' love affair with himself is so classic in proportion if Shakespeare were alive he would write a play about it."[9]

When he was 10–0, Clay faced his toughest test to date in Sonny Banks, a young fighter with a good punch. "Banks could punch, no doubt about that," Clay's trainer Angelo Dundee later wrote in his autobiography. "He would be Cassius' toughest opponent to date."[10] The fight took place at the mecca of boxing—Madison Square Garden in New York City. In the first round, Banks landed a quick, powerful left hook that dropped Clay—the first time he had ever tasted the canvas as a professional. He rose quickly at the count of two, took the mandatory eight count, and survived the round. In round two, Clay boxed more smartly, listening to his expert trainer Dundee, who told him to move laterally and utilize his speed. He dropped Banks in round two and proceeded to dominate the fight until the stoppage in the fourth round. Boxing experts began to take notice of the Olympic gold medalist, considering him a real prospect.

Clay also met an athlete outside of his sport who would affect his professional career and persona greatly through the years—the colorful and outrageous wrestler George Wagner, better known as "Gorgeous George." This flamboyant character dyed his hair platinum blond, posed with women, and made his ring entrances a veritable spectacle. In other words, Gorgeous George perfected the art of self-promotion. "Cassius was completely bowled over by the theatrical and outrageous George," Dundee recalls.[11]

Clay attracted even more national attention for his boxing and his showmanship leading up to his 16th pro bout against the ageless Archie Moore—"the Ole Mongoose"—the former world light heavyweight champion who had floored Rocky Marciano in a valiant losing effort in the Rock's final fight. The war of words escalated between the two pugilists. Clay predicted that Moore would fall in four, while Moore retorted that he would give "the kid a much needed spanking."[12] Clay's verbal histrionics attracted the attention of the then-invincible world champion, Sonny Liston who said: "He is a great talking fighter. This is outside the ring I mean."[13]

Clay insisted he would knock out Moore in four. "It takes a great fighter to call the exact round, and that's why Cassius Clay is the greatest,"[14] the young fighter said, referring to himself in the third person—a trait that numerous confident athletes would follow in the future. In November 1962, Clay proved true to his word—dropping Moore three times in the fourth round to finish the lopsided bout. With champion Sonny Liston sitting in the third row, the brash challenger told Liston he was next and that he would "fall in eight."[15] Clay continued his nonstop verbal banter: "I'm the greatest and I'm here to resurrect the fight game."[16]

A few months after defeating the veteran Moore, Clay faced fellow prospect Charlie Powell, a former football star, in Pittsburgh, Pennsylvania, in January 1963. Powell entered the ring with a record of 23–6–3 and was an imposing figure with a muscular physique. Clay seemed undeterred, predicting that he would stop Powell in three rounds.

Amazingly, Clay proved prescient again, as the rugged Powell fell in three rounds. The Associated Press referred to Clay's performance as a "dazzling display of ring savvy."[17] It was the 13th time that Clay had correctly predicted the round in which he would win.

Sportswriter Mort Sharnik first saw something special in Clay in the Powell fight. In the second round, Powell landed a tough body shot that would have dropped many fighters. But Clay showed no facial expression. He simply endured the punishment and proceeded to annihilate Powell. Sharnik said that "it was at that fight that I recognized he was an extraordinary fighter."[18]

Clay's next fight would not be that easy, as he faced contender Doug Jones at Madison Square Garden in March 1963. Jones entered the contest with a record of 21–3–1. Jones was coming off victories over future light heavyweight great Bob Foster and heavyweight contender Zora Folley. His only losses were to light heavyweight champion Harold Johnson, perennial contender Eddie Machen, and Folley in their first encounter. Clay seemed unfazed by the step up in competition. He predicted: "This boy likes to mix, so he must fall in six."[19] For his part, Jones seemed unimpressed with the brash fighter known as the "Louisville Lip." Jones said that Clay had a weak chin and that he would expose it in their upcoming encounter.[20] At a press conference, Jones warned: "When he gets to New York, he might have some trouble keeping up with the Joneses."[21] Clay continually talked trash leading up to the fight, changing his prediction to a first-round knockout. United Press International reported: "Brash Clay Has Volumes to Say."[22]

Jones proved more accurate than Clay, extending the talented prospect the full 10 rounds. Some observers even felt that Jones did enough to win the bout. Judges Frank Forbes and Artie Aidala gave Clay the 10th and final round, giving him the slightest of edges at 5–4–1. Fights were scored by round in New York at that time. The referee Joe Loscalzo scored it an incredible 8–1–1 in Clay's favor. Clay won three of the first four rounds, but Jones controlled the action for many of the middle rounds. At the end of eight rounds, Clay's undefeated record hung in the balance, as Jones looked on his way to victory. But Clay displayed what would become one of his vaunted trademarks—the ability to recuperate and rebound in the later rounds. Gene Ward of the *Chicago Daily Tribune* wrote that "Clay somehow found a hidden reservoir of strength for a stretch run in the final two rounds."[23] The crowd booed the verdict, yelling "Fix . . . fix . . . fix" when Clay was announced the winner. The crowd gave Jones significant applause as he waited in the ring.[24] For his part, Clay retained his ability to rhyme: "Jones came here as fat as a hen, but he tricked me and lasted to ten."[25]

Boxing sportswriters, many fans, and the heavyweight champion Sonny Liston were not impressed by Clay's lackluster performance. Liston told reporter Frank Finch: "Clay showed me that I'll get locked up for murder if we're ever matched."[26]

Clay next traveled overseas to face Henry Cooper, England's top heavyweight, known for his courage and powerful left hook. In June 1963, Clay stepped into Wembley Stadium to face the hometown fighter. Clay had predicted that he would stop Cooper in five rounds in unflattering language: "If that bum goes over five rounds, I won't return to this country for 90 days."[27] In his more typical, playful style, he said: "I talk no jive, Cooper will fall in five." His trainer Angelo Dundee, however, realized that Cooper was a live opponent: "In my book Cooper could give Clay a tough night despite Cassius' claim that he'll win in five."[28]

Dundee and Clay were both right. "Cooper could do one thing," Dundee reflected years later to Thomas Hauser. "He could whack with that left hand."[29] Badly cut, Cooper nailed Clay with a vicious left hook near the end of the round. Clay fell flat on his back, seemingly badly hurt. "When he went down he was in trouble," Cooper said years later. "He had gone. He had gone. I said to myself, I've got him. And then the bleedin' bell went."[30]

But Clay was saved by the bell and managed to get on his feet anyway. In the middle of the round, trainer Dundee performed one his miracles. He noticed a small split in Cassius's gloves. "I stuck my finger in the split, helping it along—now it was a bigger split."[31] Dundee gained extra minutes of rest for his fighter. "I wanted more time for Cassius to get himself together more," he admitted, calling it "gamesmanship."[32]

The gamesmanship helped Clay fully recover, and he proceeded to punish Cooper, who began gushing blood like a geyser. Referee Frank Little mercifully called a halt to the bout in round five, making Clay a Nostradamus again.[33] After the bout, Clay recanted his labeling of Cooper as a bum. Perhaps he was in a generous mood, as he had just earned a date with the world champion, Sonny Liston—assuming the champion would successfully defend his title against former champion Floyd Patterson. Liston annihilated Patterson in one round in July 1963. Clay was next in line.

A CHAMPIONSHIP

Many predicted that the 35–1 Sonny Liston would annihilate the undefeated Cassius Clay. In hindsight, perhaps some of that was understandable given the fighters' recent histories. Liston had just come off two straight knockouts of Floyd Patterson in the first round. He looked invincible, with a left jab nearly as potent as the great Joe Louis's. On the other hand, Clay had looked vulnerable against his last two opponents: Doug Jones and Henry Cooper. He had struggled to win a close, controversial decision over Jones and had nearly been kayoed by Cooper in the fourth round.

Most of the press certainly believed that Liston would defeat Clay. Al Monroe wrote: "And it might take much, much longer for the Louisville Lip to become man enough to make a bout with Liston more interesting than a movie cartoon."[34] Oscar Fraley wrote that Clay "possibly has created an impression in some quarters that he really does have a ghost of a chance."[35] Steve Snyder wrote: "the guess here is Sonny in four after a bit of a chase."[36] Sid Ziff got it marvelously wrong in his column for the *Los Angeles Times:* "Cassius should go two or three rounds. He might even avoid fate for a few more but he's got to go. He's bound to get tagged. He's fast but not fast enough to stay away forever and his defense is full of holes."[37] Arthur Daley of the *New York Times* was equally off base: "He'll [Clay will] be seeing stars when Sonny hits him on Tuesday but those stars will be coated by pure gold."[38] He remarked that Sonny Liston "is a real pro meeting a comparative novice."[39] Robert Lipsyte recalls that his instructions from the *New York Times* were to find out the distance to the nearest hospital because they wanted him to obtain a story on Clay's health condition after the bout.[40]

On the eve of the fight, Leonard Koppel summed it up well: "The experts, almost unanimously, expect Sonny Liston to keep his world heavyweight boxing title Tuesday night by knocking out Cassius Clay in short order."[41] Liston entered the bout as a 9–1 favorite. Las Vegas bookies took more action on which round Liston would win by knockout than on which fighter would win.[42]

But Cassius Clay had other ideas. At the weigh-in, Clay went nearly hysterical, screaming and yelling how he would destroy "the big ugly bear"—his favorite name for Liston. Mort Sharnik said it looked like Clay "was having a seizure," while respected scribe Jerry Izenburg wrote that Clay "behaved like a complete lunatic."[43] Many believed that Clay's histrionics showed that he truly was scared to face the formidable Sonny Liston.

Liston had a glowering stare in the ring that literally could freeze his opponents. Ali admitted to Hauser that he was scared by Liston's stare in the ring. "He was one of the most scientific boxers who ever lived; he hit hard; and he was fixing to kill me," Ali said. "It frightened me, just knowing how hard he hit. But, I was there; I didn't have no choice but to go out and fight."[44]

Clay proved them all wrong with a virtuoso performance that showcased his incredible, cat-quick reflexes and beautiful boxing ability. Clay boxed cautiously the two rounds, making Liston miss most of the time. Liston landed a few good punches in the second round, but Clay survived. In the third round, Clay opened up and tagged Liston with pistonlike combinations. His hand and foot speed were overwhelming for Liston. Toward the end of the round, Clay opened up a sizeable cut over Liston's eye.

In the fourth round, Clay appeared agitated. Some irritant had entered his eye and caused him some temporary blindness. It may have been a substance used on Liston in his corner. Some speculated that Liston's corner put it on his gloves for him to put it on Clay. Whatever the case, Clay screamed at the end of the fourth round for his corner to stop the fight. Angelo Dundee refused to let that happen and pushed Clay out into the ring. Clay used his speed to avoid Liston as much as he could. Midway through the fifth round, Clay could see again and he proceeded to tag Liston with combinations. In the sixth round, Clay opened up even more, clearly winning the round. Then, the unthinkable happened. Liston refused to come out of his corner for the seventh round.

Cassius Clay had won the heavyweight championship. He exclaimed loudly in the ring for all to hear, "I am the greatest" and "I shook up the world." He yelled at the press section, telling them to apologize and that he was right all along. Sid Ziff of the *Los Angeles Times,* one of Clay's most vocal critics before the fight, acknowledged his superiority that night: "Cassius Clay whipped Sonny Liston here and won the heavyweight championship of the world, fair and square."[45]

RELIGION, NAME CHANGE, AND CONTROVERSY

Cassius Marcellus Clay "shook up the world" not only when he defeated the formidable Sonny Liston, but also when he announced that he was a Muslim who would change his name to Muhammad Ali. He referred to Cassius Clay as a "slave name" and emphasized that he didn't need to go to court to change it.[46] Mike Marqusee reflects in his marvelous book *Redemption Song:* "The ritual and regimen of the Nation [of Islam] appealed to Clay for some of the same reasons he loved the discipline of training and the gym. Both demanded care and respect for the body and rewarded deferred gratification."[47]

The announcement sent reverberations far beyond the sporting world. In January 1964, the press reported that Clay had traveled to New York to address thousands of Muslims—only one month before he was scheduled to face Sonny Liston. Clay talked about how he abhorred the racial violence perpetrated against blacks and against the civil rights demonstrators in Alabama and other places. When asked, he denied that he was a member of the Black Muslims.[48]

Just one day after Clay won the title, Nation of Islam leader Elijah Muhammad indicated that Clay was a member of his religious group. "Clay had confidence in Allah, and in me as his only messenger."[49] The Nation of Islam advocated for black separatism. Muhammad often referred to the white race as "devils."

Clay's conversion to Islam placed him at the center of a maelstrom of controversy. In many circles, it also made him public enemy number one. Today, we know that hero worship and Ali go hand-in-hand, like ham and eggs. But the opposite occurred for many years, as many considered him the divisive symbol of evil. Particularly when his conversion to Islam under the tutelage of Elijah Muhammad—the feared leader of the Black Muslims—became publicly known in early 1964, Ali was a subject of mass vilification.

When he refused induction into the military to fight in Vietnam in 1967, many hated the man who would years later become a world hero. In March 1964, the army originally indicated that Clay did not qualify for service because he performed poorly on two tests.[50] "I just said I was the greatest," he said. "I never said I was the smartest."[51]

Ali faced the scorn of a nation and prosecution by the federal government because he dared to speak his mind, seemingly not fearful of the consequences. He epitomized the essence of the unpopular speaker punished for his dissident political views. He boldly proclaimed to the world: "I don't have to be what you want me to be. I'm free to be who I want to be."[52] The audacity of this young African American confounded many in the United States and perhaps abroad as well.

Many in the popular press excoriated the young champion for his religious beliefs. Ali's former trainer Angelo Dundee wrote in his autobiography *I Only Talk Winning* that "I couldn't help feeling that if the media hadn't hyped up the 'Black Muslim' issue, the authorities might have treated the whole affair differently."[53] Muhammad Ali certainly exercised his religious beliefs to his own financial detriment, when, in April 1967, he refused induction at the Armed Forces Induction Center in Houston, Texas. One of his lawyers, Chauncey Eskridge, said that Ali could easily have gone into a state national guard and avoided the front lines, but that his sincere religious beliefs compelled him to take his stance.[54]

Ali stood up for his beliefs, refusing induction into the armed forces in Houston in 1967. That action led to subsequent prosecution and conviction under federal law for not reporting. "If necessary, I'll have to die for what I believe. I'm fighting for the freedom of my people," he proclaimed in March 1967.[55] His conviction called for a five-year imprisonment and a $10,000 fine.

Skeptics questioned how a man who made his living punching other people in the face could object to war, but Ali remained steadfast. He replied that, "in the boxing ring we have a referee to stop the fight if it gets too brutal. The intention is not to kill, as it is in war. We don't use machinery, artillery, guns."[56]

Ali sought a religious exemption from the draft requirements, saying that he should be entitled to a clergyman-type exception. Ali claimed that he was a conscientious objector, opposed to war on religious grounds. Many hated Ali for continuing to advance his claims as a conscientious objector. Others gave him support. Jackie Robinson, who broke major league baseball's color barrier in the 1940s, said he respected Ali for his stand. "In my view, the deposed champion has demonstrated that he is fighting for a principle," Robinson said. "While I cannot agree with it, I respect him sincerely."[57]

The Supreme Court in *Clay v. United States* (1971) eventually reversed his conviction, writing: "the Department [of Justice] was simply wrong as a matter of law in advising that the petitioner's beliefs were not religiously based and were not sincerely held."[58] Even though Ali prevailed 8–0 before the high court, Bob Woodward and Scott Armstrong later reported in *The Brethren* that the justices initially voted against Ali, finding that he wasn't really a conscientious objector and that he should go to jail.[59] Apparently, a law clerk of Justice John Marshall Harlan loaned the justice a copy of Alex Haley's *The*

Autobiography of Malcolm X. Harlan read the work and changed his views on Black Muslims.

Ali thanked the Court for their decision in late June 1971, for "recognizing the sincerity of my belief in myself and my convictions."[60]

A DOMINANT CHAMPION

Although he had to deal with public hatred, Ali dominated the heavyweight division for several years after his upset of Liston. He defeated Liston in a rematch that was even stranger than their first encounter. Initially Clay and Liston would meet again in November 1964. Liston trained hard for the rematch. But a few days before the bout, Clay needed emergency hernia surgery, forcing a postponement of the fight until May of the following year. Originally the fight was scheduled to take place in the Boston Garden, but the fight ended up taking place in tiny Lewiston, Maine.

In the first round, Clay hit Liston with a short right hand that some have derisively called the "phantom punch." Liston fell to the ground and rose 14 seconds later. The confused referee, former world heavyweight champion Jersey Joe Walcott, had trouble getting Clay to go to a neutral corner. Walcott lost track of the ringside officials' count. However, after Liston rose, the timekeeper signaled that Liston had been on the canvas for 12 seconds. Walcott then ruled that Liston had been kayoed. Many of the more than four thousand spectators yelled, "Fake, fake, fake!"[61]

Clay claimed that he had hit Liston with what he called the "anchor punch"—a secret weapon of the late, great Jack Johnson. He claimed it was "part karate, part corkscrew." It was the first time that Sonny Liston had ever tasted the canvas. Liston claimed that he didn't hear the count.[62]

Others were convinced that something fishy had occurred. Veteran sportswriter Dick Young wrote that "chances are you've hit your wife harder" and referred to it as a "phantom punch."[63] John Hall of the *Los Angeles Times* was much blunter: "It only takes one minute to kill boxing" and "Boxing just committed suicide."[64] Bob Summitt, legal counsel for the World Boxing Association, referred to the title fight as "a farce and a fraud."[65] Jim Murray of the *Los Angeles Times* wrote that "Sonny Liston hit the floor like a guy slipping on a cake of soap getting out of the bathtub."[66]

Despite mounting public criticism and pressure regarding his religious and political positions, Cassius Clay—now known as Muhammad Ali—dominated the heavyweight division before being stripped of his title for refusing induction into the armed services. He defended his title nine times, defeating former champions Sonny Liston and Floyd Patterson, George Chuvalo—a tough-as-nails Canadian—his former rival Henry Cooper, Brian

London, Karl Mildenberger, Cleveland Williams, Ernie Terrell, and Zora Folley. It could be argued that the Ali of this period was the greatest fighter in the history of the sport. His reflexes were so fast for a man of his size that it was almost criminal. None of these fights were close.

The second Liston fight ended in a controversial first-round kayo. In his next defense, Ali dominated Patterson, a man he wanted to beat badly. Patterson said that he wanted to bring the title back to the United States and away from the Black Muslims: "Boxing has given me everything. If I can win the title back I'll take it from the organization it belongs to now and give it back to America."[67]

Ali beat Patterson badly in their November 1965 bout, carrying him until the 12th round. From the beginning of the bout, "Patterson had no chance against his bigger, younger, faster, stronger opponent."[68] At the end of the second round, Ali contemptuously yelled: "It's no contest. Get me a contender."[69]

During the bout, Ali repeatedly "taunted and tortured" Patterson in a display of "sadistic cunning," read one press account.[70] The crowd often cheered during the bout for Patterson, who showed great courage in taking a beating. A surly Ali unloaded on the press after the bout. "Write something so they'll boo me more," he said defiantly.[71]

Many in the press excoriated Ali—whom they still called Clay—for his behavior. Arthur Daley of the *New York Times* called the bout an "outrageous burlesque" and criticized the champion for his "sadistic intent."[72] Sid Ziff of the *Los Angeles Times* said there was "nothing admirable about the beating."[73]

What was admirable was the utter ring dominance, the ability to pick apart highly ranked heavyweights—former world champions no less—with remarkable ease. In March 1966, Ali outpointed the tough Chuvalo over 15 rounds in Ontario. Some in the press criticized Ali for not finishing his Canadian foe, but those individuals did not know boxing. Chuvalo had never been knocked off his feet when he faced the champion. In fact, Chuvalo was never knocked down his entire professional career. Joe Frazier and George Foreman stopped him, but they didn't knock him down.

Ali crossed the Atlantic Ocean for his next three title defenses against his former foe Henry Cooper, Brian London, and Karl Mildenberger. Overseas seemed a better option for Ali, as he faced mounting public protests targeted at him in the United States for his antiwar and antidraft stances. The second Cooper fight—held in May 1966—was a one-sided affair that Ali ended with combination punching that opened up a gusher over Cooper's eye. Shirley Povich of the *Washington Post* wrote that "Clay gores Cooper."[74]

The Brian London fight was even easier, as the Brit was unable to deal with Clay's speed. The bout ended in the third round. Arthur Daley of the *New*

York Times had a memorable lead: "It was as easy as breaking a stale crumpet."[75] London came away from the encounter convinced that the champion was the greatest: "He's as fast as greased lighting. . . . the fastest I've ever seen. He punches faster than a flyweight, moves faster than a lightweight. But you sure know you've been hit by a heavyweight."[76]

In his next bout, Ali faced a German southpaw named Karl Mildenberger, who was rated as the number-one contender. Unlike Brian London, who had at least 13 losses on his record, Mildenberger entered the contest with a record of 49–2–3 with a win over perennial contender Eddie Machen. Promoter George Parnassus believed that Mildenberger had a shot at winning the bout.[77] Former heavyweight kingpin Joe Louis thought that Mildenberger might give Ali trouble with his southpaw stance and good jab. "I just hope he doesn't get overconfident against Mildenberger like I was against Schmeling."[78] Mildenberger landed a hard liver shot in the eighth round, but Ali absorbed it well and began to build a big lead. He eventually stopped Mildenberger in the 12th round.

Ali next defended his title in November 1966 against a dangerous opponent—Cleveland "Big Cat" Williams, who had more than 65 professional victories. Williams was a bit past his prime when he faced Ali, and it showed in the ring. Ali put on a clinic, stopping Williams in the third round in their encounter at the Houston Astrodome. "The greatest Ali was as a fighter was in Houston against Cleveland Williams," said Howard Cosell. "That night he was the most devastating fighter who ever lived."[79]

Ali made the next defense of his title against Ernie Terrell, a 6' 6" fighter with an incredibly long reach. The World Boxing Association actually had declared that Terrell was world champion—something that rankled Ali, who rightfully considered himself the true champion. Terrell entered the ring with some serious credentials, including wins over Eddie Machen, George Chuvalo, and Doug Jones—the man who had given Ali so much trouble earlier in his career. Terrell inspired Ali's wrath in much the same way as Floyd Patterson, because he kept calling Ali by his former name, Cassius Clay. At a prefight press conference, Ali slapped Terrell and called him an "Uncle Tom."[80] In response, Terrell called Ali an "idiot."[81]

Ali vowed to punish Terrell for the insults regarding his name. During the bout, Ali would hit Terrell and then scream, "What's my name?" "It was a vicious ugly horrible fight," recalls Jerry Izenburg.[82] Ali won a lopsided 15-round decision. Terrell was never the same fighter after the beating he took from Ali. Terrell dropped two more fights to Thad Spencer and Manuel Ramos, removing him from heavyweight contender status. He finally retired in 1973 after suffering a first-round knockout at the hands of Jeff Merritt.

Ali made one more defense of his crown against Zora Folley in Madison Square Garden in February 1967. Folley was a longtime contender who had won 74 bouts in his professional career. He had not lost in more than three years. But he faced a different breed when he faced Muhammad Ali, who easily stopped him in the seventh round. Ali, whom the crowd booed for much of the contest, coasted the first couple of rounds, causing announcer Don Dumphy to refer to him as "part clown, part bicycle rider." But gradually Ali began dominating the action with his quick left jab. He dropped Folley to the count of nine in the fourth round and then finished him off a few rounds later. Folley said that Sonny Liston was the hardest puncher he ever faced but that Ali was the "best all-around fighter he met."[83] Unfortunately, the public did not get to see Ali in the ring for nearly three and half years. He fought a foe that he couldn't defeat—the United States Army and the U.S. judicial system. In April 1967, he refused induction to the armed services at an army base in Houston, Texas. When his name was called, he refused to step forward, even after being personally told that his conduct could constitute a crime punishable by up to five years in prison for violation of the Universal Military Training and Service Act.

Ali stated: "In the end, I am confident that justice will come my way, for the truth must eventually prevail." Justice and truth took a while to prevail, because first a jury convicted him in June 1967 after only 20 minutes of deliberation. Judge Joe Ingraham imposed the maximum sentence under the law: five years. Ali stood his ground but paid the price. Sanctioning bodies and athletic commissions stripped him of his title and his boxing licenses. He essentially became a man in exile, while he appealed his case through the courts. He couldn't make a living at his chosen profession in the boxing ring. Instead, he made speeches on college campuses and lectured around the country. He also spent a week in jail in December 1968 for driving without a valid drivers' license in Dade County, Florida.[84] During this period, he also fell out of favor with Elijah Muhammad for publicly stating that he would consider getting back into boxing if the money was right. The comment upset Muhammad, who believed that Ali was favoring the white man's money over religion.[85]

But, as Hauser writes, "during his exile Muhammad Ali grew larger than sports. He became a political and social force."[86] Ali warned that boxing would suffer in his absence, saying: "Boxing be nothing when I'm gone."[87]

A COMEBACK

Early in his exile, a 25-year-old Ali exclaimed that he would come back and win his title—even if he had to sit out 10 years. "Even at 35, my slowing down would only bring me down to the level the others are at now," he said. "I don't care if I have to sit out another four years, I'm going to come back."[88]

While his legal appeal was still pending, boxing authorities finally relented and Ali had the opportunity to fight again—first in Georgia, despite the strenuous objections of segregationist governor Lester Maddux, who called for a "day of mourning" when Ali fought in his state. Ali's first opponent in a promotion known as "the Return of the Champion" was a tough customer— Jerry Quarry, a tough Californian who gave Joe Frazier a hell of a fight in 1969 before losing in the eighth round on cuts. Unfortunately for Quarry, history repeated itself, as he suffered a nasty cut over his eye in the third round from Ali's sharp punches. The cut was so bad that the referee had no choice but to stop the contest. Ali had returned to "Wonderland . . . with ultimate ease."[89]

Ali set his sights on the current world champion, "Smokin'" Joe Frazier, a former Olympic gold medalist who was undefeated in the professional ranks. In Ali's absence, there was a monstrous void. Heavyweight elimination tournaments were held with one sanctioning body crowning Jimmy Ellis, a personal friend and longtime sparring partner of Ali, and the other crowning Joe Frazier. Frazier defeated Ellis to become the undisputed champion. Frazier was not the real champion in many people's eyes—at least not until he defeated Ali. The former champion began a verbal barrage directed at the current belt holding, referring to himself as the true champion.

Frazier ignored Ali for a time, but then responded in kind. "He talks loud because he's scared," Frazier said. "He needs me. I don't need him. He has to come to me."[90]

First Ali had to get past a tough customer in the Argentinean Oscar Bonavena, a man who actually got under Ali's skin at a press conference. Bonavena mocked Ali, comparing him to a chirping bird and a chicken. Later Bonavena pinched Ali on the check and patted his rear. All of this brought out the Cassius Clay of old with the poetry:

> It's been a long time since I put my predictions rhythm and rhyme,
> But, it was Bonavena who started it all getting out of line.
> He couldn't have been talking to some angel in Heaven,
> Now he has the nerve to predict I will fall in eleven,
> If this is a joke, it's at the wrong time,
> For being so rash, he must fall in Round Nine.[91]

Bonavena had managed to get under Ali's skin more than any previous opponent. Ali handled Bonavena over 15 rounds and even managed to drop the tough Argentinean in the final stanza to win by technical knockout. "They say I'm not a knockout puncher, well what was that," Ali asked reporters after the bout.[92]

Ali and Bonavena showed the world an interesting aspect of the culture of boxing after the bout. Two men who traded verbal barbs and insults in a tense prefight buildup had nothing but effusive praise for their opponent after the bout. Bonavena said, "Ali is no chicken" and is a true champion. He even predicted that Ali would defeat Frazier if the two met in the ring. For his part, Ali called Bonavena "the toughest man I ever fought."[93]

After wins over Quarry and Bonavena, Ali attempted to reclaim his throne against Frazier, the undefeated champion. The mega-fight became known as "the Fight of the Century." It featured two undefeated fighters, with the champion Frazier at 26–0 with 23 stoppages and the ex-champion Ali at 31–0 with 25 stoppages. Jack Kent Cooke, owner of the Los Angeles Lakers, bankrolled the fight, which was held at Madison Square Garden. Cooke desired to host the fight at the Forum, where his Lakers played basketball, but both pugilists wanted the bout in New York. Cooke reasoned that his business was "cable television," so he could live with holding the fight in the Big Apple.[94]

Ali promoted the fight with his characteristic charisma, poetry, and verbal swordplay. He acknowledged that many people would watch the fight just to hope he got beat: "People want to see me whipped—because I'm arrogant, because of the draft, because of my religion and because I'm black. And for other reasons I might not even know about."[95]

He told reporters: "Then right after a certain round, and Frazier don't answer the bell, I'm going to jump over the rope and take on Cosell."[96] Frazier retorted that Ali was nothing to him, just a "silly little kid."[97] The champion guaranteed that Clay—he never referred to Ali by his name—would not take his title. Frazier said that he would finish Clay by the 10th round.[98] The fight took on ugly racial overtones, as Ali called Frazier an "Uncle Tom." Frazier retorted that Clay was a "phony" who "don't really stand for all those things he talks about."[99]

On March 8, 1971, the two undefeated heavyweights met in perhaps the biggest fight in boxing history since Jack Johnson defeated James Jeffries more than 60 years earlier. After his exile, Ali never had the same foot speed that he had during the height of his powers. "If I was young, I'd have danced for fifteen rounds, and Joe wouldn't have ever caught me," he told Hauser.[100] Neil Milbert of the *Chicago Tribune* had predicted that Ali would win a decision because of his "superior speed and boxing skill."[101] Famed gambler Jimmy "the Greek" Snyder rated the fight as dead even. However, oddsmaker Bob Martin of Churchill Downs Sports Book rated Frazier as a slight 7-to-5 favorite.[102] Former champion Joe Louis was quite prescient, predicting a Frazier victory because "the layoff has to hurt Clay, particularly his speed."[103] Before the bout, a confident Ali declared: "If Joe Frazier whips me, I'm going to get on my knees and crawl across the ring, look up at him and say, 'You are the greatest. You are the champion of the whole world.' "[104]

Ali fought more flat-footed and often went to the ropes and took punishment. He won the first two rounds with his quick jab but lost rounds three through eight on two of the three official scorecards. He gave away several of these rounds by laying on the ropes and taking punishment. At times, Ali would pepper Frazier's face with his quick jab, but Ali received numerous thundering body shots from the fists of a determined Frazier. Ali rallied in the 9th and 10th rounds to close the gap on at least two of the scores, but then came the fateful 11th round.

In the 11th round, Frazier hit Ali with a shot that nearly knocked him out on his feet. Ali's knees buckled, but his amazing recuperative powers enabled him to survive. In the 15th round, Frazier settled all doubts with a monstrous left hook that dropped Ali. Most boxers never would have risen, but somehow Ali rose to his feet at the count of four and finished the fight. But he lost a unanimous decision. Referee Arthur Mercante had it close, 8–6–1 in rounds. But the two judges had it more lopsided with scores of 9–6 and 11–4. The scorecard of 11–4 of judge Bill Recht was far too lopsided, but Frazier won the bout. Dave Anderson of the *New York Times* wrote that "Joe Frazier broke the wings of the butterfly and smashed the stinger of the bee."[105]

Frazier gave Ali credit for staying on his feet and lasting until the final bell, saying: "he really takes a good punch."[106] Ali's handler, Drew "Bundini" Brown, who often acted as Ali's foil and motivator, said that the former champion recognized after the bout that Frazier had won. "No, he never acted like he won . . . Joe Frazier is the champion of the world, without a doubt."[107] Ali had suffered his first defeat. Even worse, "he was silenced."[108] Dave Brady of the *Washington Post* wrote: "When Ali failed to make it to the post-fight interview scene, his critics finally savored the observation that someone was able to shut him up."[109]

Ali was not silenced for long. Only six days after the bout, he appeared on ABC's *Wide World of Sports,* telling Howard Cosell that he had won nine rounds in the fight and "was outpunching him with flurries."[110] Soon, chasing a rematch, Ali resumed his verbal assault of Frazier. He claimed that Frazier was afraid of him and wouldn't fight him again. "He's scared to death," he said. "If a man whupped me 15 rounds and took a beating like he did against me, I wouldn't wanna fight him again either."[111] Ali continued month after month with the vitriol: "It's a known fact that he took all the whupping. He was so ugly after that fight, his face should have been declared a disaster area."[112] Frazier did suffer damage in the bout and stayed in the hospital a long time, much longer than Ali. But Frazier was the undisputed champion, and Ali had to go back to the drawing board.

Boxing didn't have to go the drawing board, as the "fight of the century" sparked unprecedented interest in the sport. Ali–Frazier revitalized boxing in many cities across the United States. But some criticized the bout. A British doctor, Joseph Blonstein, chairman of the World Amateur Boxing Association, claimed that the fight was fixed. "I thought the fight was a complete phony," he said. "They fixed it, this way so that they could be sure of a return and a re-return."[113] Blonstein wondered in an article why Ali fought so flat-footed: "I thought Ali looked doped."[114]

Although he suffered an ignominious defeat in the ring, a few months later, Ali received a resounding legal victory from the U.S. Supreme Court—what his best friend Howard Bingham called his "greatest fight."[115] The victory relieved Ali, who could resume his boxing career with a clearer mind. He won 10 fights in a row over many big-name opponents, including rematch wins over Quarry, Patterson, and Chuvalo. He didn't get a shot at Frazier, though, who called Ali a "fat, old, fool."[116]

In March 1973, Ali suffered a shocking upset loss to Ken Norton—an ex-Marine and former sparring partner of Joe Frazier. Norton was a physically strong fighter with an awkward defense. Stylistically, he always posed problems for Ali, who was a 5–1 favorite to beat the unheralded Norton. But Ken Norton had other ideas, breaking Ali's jaw and capturing a 12-round split decision in San Diego, California. His personal physician, Ferdie Pachecho, claims that Ali suffered the broken jaw in the second round. It was a crushing defeat. It represented a "long slide downhill for one of the most famous athletes of our time."[117] Many assumed that Ali would never regain the title. "Losing to Norton was the end of the road, at least as far as I could see," Howard Cosell recalled.[118] Many said that the 31-year-old Ali was done, that he had slipped from a former great fighter to something much less. Trainer Angelo Dundee defended his fighter, saying that Ali exhibited incredible courage in going nearly the entire fight with a broken jaw. "Eleven more rounds with a broken jaw . . . what a man!"[119]

But the resilient Ali put together perhaps the greatest two years of work in boxing history. A mere six months later, he defeated Norton in another close bout by split decision. Billed as "Ali's Revenge," the former champion had another tough tussle with Norton. He boxed for seven rounds and then slugged with Norton for the last five. Judge George Latka scored it 6–5–1 for Norton but was overruled by judge John Thomas and referee Dick Young, who had it 6–5–1 and 7–5 for Ali, respectively. The difference was the final round, as Ali somehow summoned enough energy to move faster and land more punches than Norton in the final stanza. "Quickly, reacting to the drama as he had throughout his magnetic career, Ali somehow regained his speed."[120]

Ali later avenged his loss to Joe Frazier with a unanimous-decision victory in Madison Square Garden. The two had engaged in a vicious war of words that even came to blows on a taping for an ABC sports program. With Cosell moderating, the two began exchanging barbs. Frazier mentioned something about Ali going to the hospital after their first encounter, which caused Ali to launch a verbal tirade, including labeling Frazier "ignorant." The two wrestled to the floor and had to be pried apart.

The New York State Athletic Commission fined both fighters $5,000 for their brawl in the television studio. The controversy spiked public interest in the matchup, which may have needed a little extra, as the fight was not for the heavyweight championship. Frazier had lost his title to the monstrous puncher George Foreman, who floored Frazier six times in under two rounds. Ali had hoped that Frazier would win so he could receive a world title shot. He claimed that Frazier's loss proved how badly he had beat him up years earlier: "I just didn't realize I beat Joe Frazier that bad."[121] Ali even fell to the floor six times in a sparring session with Chuck Olivera to mock Frazier's performance against Foreman.[122]

In their second bout, Ali fought much more intelligently, avoiding the ropes and tying Frazier up when necessary. He also threw more jabs and won more rounds. He captured a close, but unanimous, decision. Referee Tony Perez scored the bout 6–5–1, judge Tony Castellano scored it 7–4–1, and judge Jack Gordon scored it 8–4 for Ali. Like the first fight, Ali started strong. In the second round, he hurt Frazier badly and may have finished him off, but referee Perez held him back, incorrectly thinking that the bell had rung ending the round. Instead, 20 seconds remained in the round, and the break enabled Frazier to gather himself. But Ali boxed well enough to win the bout unanimously. As sports scribe Bill Lyon wrote: "The butterfly is older, but it still floats."[123]

Ali even praised Frazier after the bout: "Joe Frazier is great. I knew I was good, but I didn't know he was that good."[124] He conceded that Frazier had hurt him badly twice in the bout.

Ali's victory over Frazier landed him what became the most famous fight of his illustrious career—the fight that author Norman Mailer later called "The Fight." Ali would face the undefeated champion, George Foreman— a supposedly indestructible force of nature who had devoured Frazier and Norton. Foreman had dropped Frazier six times and stopped Smokin' Joe in the second round in January 1973 to win the title. In his second defense, Foreman dropped Norton three times and stopped him in the second round. By matter of comparison, Ali had lost to both Norton and Frazier. While he had won the rematches with those two fighters, he only managed to win close decisions. Wouldn't Foreman annihilate Ali just as he did Frazier and Norton? Many experts thought so, pegging Ali as a huge underdog.

Many feared for Ali's life in this bout. Foreman's trainer, Archie Moore, told Norman Mailer: "I was praying and in great sincerity, that George wouldn't kill Ali. I really felt that was a possibility."[125] A few thought Ali could do it. One was his mother, who expressed confidence in her son: "George looks very big and mean and he has been knocking out everybody he's met but Sonny Liston was big and mean looking too . . . and he didn't scare my boy none."[126] Tony Blackwell of the *Chicago Defender* was one of the few who picked Ali to win, saying that Ali would win in 10 rounds. He explained: "You see, almost everyone picks Foreman because of the enormous size of his fist. Well behind the fist is the boxing glove. Foreman will have to hit Ali first, before being able to depend on his fist."[127]

The mega-fight was held in Kinshasa, Zaire—the country formerly known as the Congo—due to the promotional efforts of an enterprising ex-convict, numbers runner, and hustler named Don King. Zaire's ruler, Sese Seko Mobutu, backed the fight, believing that the heavyweight title bout would bring worldwide legitimacy and respect to his country and regime. Billed as the "Rumble in the Jungle," the fight was supposed to be a horrific mismatch. Instead, it created a super-legend, taking Ali to near mythic proportions. The bout was originally scheduled for September, but a cut over Foreman's eye postponed the bout until late October. It would be an omen for the champion.

Ali employed his famous rope-a-dope strategy, where he would lay on the ropes and do his best to avoid punches. He effectively tired Foreman out, employing a dangerous strategy that his trainer Angelo Dundee warned him against: "Don't do that Muhammad, please, please don't do that," he yelled at his fighter.[128] But Ali gradually wore out Foreman, as Big George punched himself out. In the eighth round, Ali seized the moment, landing two hard lefts followed by an even harder right cross. Foreman stumbled around the ring like a drunk and collapsed perhaps partly from exhaustion. Muhammad Ali had regained the world heavyweight championship at age 32. "Boxing's most controversial champion created the most bizarre chapter in this bizarre career."[129]

Ali stayed active in his second reign as champion. In 1975, he made four successful title defenses against Chuck Wepner, Ron Lyle, Joe Bugner, and then Frazier in a rubber match called the "Thrilla in Manila." Ali's fight with Wepner turned into a one-sided affair later in the bout, though Wepner showed great courage in refusing to go down. He even knocked Ali down in the ninth round, though many believed that Wepner stepped on Ali's shoe.

Wepner's courage so inspired Sylvester Stallone that he created a screenplay involving a pretender, would-be contender named Rocky Balboa taking on the colorful champion Apollo Creed. Balboa was loosely based on Wepner, while Creed was a caricature of Ali. The film *Rocky* (1976) won an Academy Award for Best Picture and made a mega-star out of Stallone, who played the lead role. It also spawned a series of six *Rocky* movies, all of which earned Stallone eventual enshrinement in the Boxing Hall of Fame in Canastota, New York, in 2011.

The three wins over Wepner, Lyle, and Bugner were preliminaries for the big one—the third bout with Frazier. Originally, the third bout was to be fought in either New York, Washington, D.C., or even Iran.[130] Ali boasted that he would "whup the gorilla in the Thrilla in Manila" while he pounded a plastic gorilla. William Barry Furlong presciently said before the bout: "And you know this next fight will not be a friendly fight. Or a gentle one."[131]

The Thrilla in Manila was a violent contest, a physical torture chamber for its two contestants. Neither fighter was ever the same after that brutal battle. Ali battered Frazier for much of the bout. Frazier's trainer, Eddie Futch, mercifully ended the bout, refusing to let his fighter come out for the 15th round. "I stopped it, because Joe was starting to get hit with too many clean shots. He couldn't see out of his right eye. He couldn't see the left hands coming."[132] Ali was ahead on all three scorecards. Under the five-point must system (the winner of a round receives five points), Ali was ahead 66–60, 67–62, and 66–62 on all three cards.

Ali praised Frazier effusively after their epic third battle. "He is great. He is greater than I thought he was. He is the best there is except me."[133] Ali then contemplated retirement after the bout. "You may have seen the last of Ali. I want to get out of it. I'm tired and on top. What you saw tonight was next to death. He's the toughest man in the world."[134]

With the benefit of hindsight, Ali should have retired after the Thrilla in Manila. He would have retired on top with his health still intact. Instead, he stayed in the fight game too long, took many more punches, and suffered enormous physical consequences.

A CHAMPION IN DECLINE

After defeating Norton, Ali successfully defended his title six more times against the lightly regarded Jean Pierre Coopman, defensive boxer Jimmy Young, an overmatched Richard Dunn, rival Ken Norton, Alfredo Evangelista, and hard-punching Earnie Shavers.

The toughest of the fights may have been the one with Jimmy Young, a quick boxer with fine defensive skills. Young later retired George Foreman in

1977 with a victory in San Juan, Puerto Rico. But in May 1976, when he faced the great Ali, not many gave him a chance—including Ali. That was a mistake, as Young landed some clean shots and avoided most of Ali's punches. Ali earned a unanimous-decision victory, but he seemingly earned points more with his reputation than his fists. "We almost had a new champion," Ali admitted after the bout. "I underrated Jimmy Young. I didn't know he would be as good as he was. I didn't know he would be so hard to hit."[135] The crowed lustily booed the verdict, and many in press row thought Young had won the bout.

Historically, the most significant of these bouts was his third match with Norton in Yankee Stadium. Norton controlled the action early, but Ali seemed to gain some momentum and showed glimpses of the old, dancing Ali. He won a close but unanimous decision. Ali won the fight, because he won the final round on all three scorecards. Referee Arthur Mercante had it 8–6–1, while judges Barney Smith and Harold Lederman both scored it 8–7 for Ali. "I knew I was ahead," Ali said after the bout.[136] "The judges made asses of themselves," a bitter Norton said after the bout. "I know I won 9 or 10 rounds. I was obviously the winner."[137]

Ali also narrowly avoided a loss when he faced fearsome puncher Earnie Shavers—a man who kayoed former champion Jimmy Ellis in one round and would later do the same thing to Ken Norton. The bald-headed Shavers—dubbed "the Acorn" by Ali—possessed dynamite in his right hand. But Ali managed to do just enough to win a close, unanimous-decision victory. He even shook Shavers a bit in the final round. "A younger Ali wouldn't have gotten hit by so many right hands," the champion acknowledged in the press conference after the bout.[138]

In his second reign as champion—particularly after the epic bout in Manila—Ali kept winning, but sometimes just barely. He rarely showed the explosive speed that characterized his early years. He certainly took much more punishment than in his prime. The Young, Norton, and Shavers bouts exposed Ali as a beatable, fading champion. Leon Spinks—in only his eighth pro bout—capitalized.

Spinks had won a gold medal at the 1976 Montreal Olympics in the light heavyweight division in the country's most celebrated class, which included his brother Michael, Leo Randolph, the talented Howard Davis Jr., and the charismatic Sugar Ray Leonard. But Spinks was deemed far too green to pose a serious threat to Ali, who entered as a 10–1 favorite. Instead, the aggressive Spinks pressed the action, threw more punches, and landed more as well. He captured a 15-round split-decision victory as judges Lou Tabat and Harold Buck overruled their colleague Art Lurie. Ali praised the new champion but said he was ready for a rematch. "I'd like to become the first man to ever win the title three times."[139]

Ali trained hard for the rematch, calling his upcoming matchup the "Third Coming." He claimed that he would win the title and retire after the bout. In September 1978, Ali turned back the clock just enough to win the heavyweight championship again. He moved around the ring and used his superior reach to his advantage. "He was no butterfly . . . but he can still sting," wrote one ringside reporter.[140] The judges scored it 10–4–1, 10–4–1, and 11–4 in rounds. But Ali didn't look great in making history. Jim Murray of the *Los Angeles Times* summed it up accurately: "Ali is just a shell of his former self, but against Spinks that was more than enough."[141]

Ali retired from the ring as the only three-time heavyweight champion. He was long past his prime. When Spinks decided to fight Ali in a rematch rather than the number-one contender, Ken Norton, the World Boxing Council stripped Spinks of that belt and named Norton champion. Norton became the first man in boxing history to win a world title without actually winning a world title bout. In his first defense, Norton defended his title against an undefeated fighter named Larry Holmes, a former sparring partner of Ali and Frazier. Holmes had lost to Duane Bobick during the 1972 Olympic trials, causing many to write him off as a serious pro prospect.

But Holmes worked hard at his craft and continued to improve. Holmes and Norton waged an epic 15-round battle. While Holmes seemingly had the edge in the bout, it turned out that he needed to win the final round on the judges' scorecard to capture a split-decision victory. Later, the World Boxing Association had its own champion in undefeated prospect "Big" John Tate. However, Tate lost the belt on a miraculous, come-from-behind knockout by the unheralded Mike "Hercules" Weaver.

The lure of the ring was too much for Ali, who should have picked Weaver as his opponent. Instead, Ali challenged Holmes for the title.[142]

A 38-year-old Ali looked quite lethargic when he challenged Holmes for his world championship in October 1980. Holmes won every round, and, as the fight progressed, he took a beating from his former sparring partner. One major newspaper headline captured the essence of the bout: "Holmes batters Ali from start to finish."[143] Angelo Dundee stopped the bout in the 11th round. It was a sad ending to Ali's championship career. Holmes somewhat reluctantly battered his former idol. "I don't take any great happiness in what I did," he said after the bout.[144]

Ali later claimed that it was taking a double dosage of a thyroid drug to lose weight that caused his lethargy in the Holmes fight. In the six months before the Holmes bout, Ali had dropped nearly 50 pounds. But he paid a price for it. He thought he should give it one more go in professional boxing. Ali fought one more bout against contender Trevor Berbick in Nassau, Bahamas, in December 1981. Ali lasted the full 10 rounds but lost by a wide margin.

Ali's physical condition worsened over the years. Doctors diagnosed him with Parkinson's disease in 1984. Over time, he barely spoke and his hands trembled horrifically. But despite his declining physical condition, he acquired a new level of dignity. On July 19, 1996, Ali surprised the world by lighting the Olympic Torch in the opening ceremonies in Atlanta. After taking the torch from swimmer Janet Evans, his left hand shook violently, but he managed to light the torch. "For those who saw it, remembering it will never be a choice."[145]

LEGACY

Ali's legacy is enduring and everlasting. His ring greatness alone ensures his place in the pantheon of the greatest fighters of all time. He was the first man to win the world heavyweight title three times. He defeated two of the most feared punchers in boxing history—Sonny Liston and George Foreman—to win the title. The Ali of the 1960s might be the greatest fighter in ring history. He absolutely overwhelmed the opposition with breathtaking speed. He spent three and a half years away from the ring when he was in his athletic prime. He managed to come back and reach the pinnacle of the sport. He defeated at least 10 world champions back when there was not a proliferation of sanctioning bodies and champions: Floyd Patterson, Archie Moore, Bob Foster, Joe Frazier, Sonny Liston, George Foreman, Ken Norton, Leon Spinks, Jimmy Ellis, and Ernie Terrell.

But Ali's legacy far transcends sports. He gave up millions of dollars because of religious and political convictions. He faced great punishment for his freedom of speech—"I'm free to be what I want to be" and "I ain't got no quarrel with them Viet Cong." Robert Lipsyte once described him as "America's first truly international sports hero . . . a celebrity on the streets of the world."[146] In short, Ali became a world hero idolized by millions across the globe. The man once vilified became sanctified.

Award-winning author David Maraniss wrote that "his popularity transcends politics, race, country and religion. He is universally accepted as a man who stood up for what he believed in and paid the price and prevailed."[147] Former Atlanta mayor and U.S. Ambassador to the United Nations Andrew Young said that Ali "forced us to think internationally."[148] President George W. Bush said of Ali when awarding him a Presidential Medal of Freedom in 2005: "Across the world, billions of people know Muhammad Ali as a brave, compassionate and charming man, and the American people are proud to call Muhammad Ali one of our own."[149] Maya Angelou wrote that Ali "belonged to everyone. . . . his impact recognizes no continent, no language, no colour, no ocean. He belongs to us all."[150]

Chapter 6

THE INCREDIBLE STORY AND COMEBACK OF "BIG" GEORGE FOREMAN

Imagine a prison inmate who enters a penal institution in 1973, when George Foreman ruled as the undefeated heavyweight champion, fresh off destructions of former champion Joe Frazier and top contender Ken Norton. The inmate has no contact with the outside world; he had been placed in solitary confinement, where he had lapsed into a coma. The inmate regains consciousness years later, in the fall of 1994. He first asks what year it is. The nurse says 1994. The inmate, a boxing fan, then asks, "Who is heavyweight champion of the world?" The nurse says, "George Foreman." The inmate replies, "Lord, I knew he was great, but I didn't think he'd be champion for 20 years."

George Foreman did not hold the heavyweight championship for 20 years. He lost his title in 1974, retired from boxing for 10 years, and then engaged in the most improbable of all comebacks, culminating with a come-from-behind knockout over champion Michael Moorer to capture the heavyweight championship at age 45. George Foreman defied Father Time, became a modern-day Lazarus, and shocked the world.

But more impressive than the stunning success of his comeback, George Foreman transformed his persona to become arguably one of the most beloved figures in modern U.S. history and a corporate success. He turned his excess weight into a clever marketing pitch for George Foreman Grills, which garnered him untold millions, a television show, and adoration from millions.

ROUGH BEGINNINGS

George Foreman today is rich enough to eat with platinum silverware and dishes, but he was not born with a silver spoon in his mouth. He grew up in the Fifth Ward of Houston, Texas, known as the "Bloody Ward." He lived in area marked by despair and disappointment—and also violence. As he wrote in his autobiography, "There was more than enough fury in my house and never enough food."[1] The neighborhood featured a regular dose of knifings and police beatings.

He learned to fight at an early age in the streets, and he normally prevailed, given his natural size and strength. In his own words, George Foreman was a bully. He turned to mugging, street fighting, petty thievery, and other misdeeds.

He dropped out of E. O. Smith Junior High School in the ninth grade, barely able to read and write. He only made it through middle school because he loved to play football. "I was a delinquent," he told the *New York Times.* "I was always interested in boxing, but all of my fights were outside the ring."[2]. George told others that "the cops knew me . . . You name it, I'd done it."[3]

After quitting school, George washed dishes and moved furniture, seemingly prepared for a future life of manual labor. However, his sister saw an ad at a local employment office advertising the Job Corps program created by President Lyndon Johnson as part of his Great Society vision. The program was designed to give kids a second chance at becoming productive members of society.

Foreman latched on to a Job Corps program out West that probably saved his life. He traveled first to a conservation center in Medford, Oregon, in August 1965. He did not turn into an angel overnight; instead, he returned to his bullying ways and beat up several other kids. However, the counselors showed him leniency and refused to give up on the big man-child.

After six months, the Job Corps transferred him to the Park Job Corps Center in Pleasanton, California. There, a young George Foreman met a man who would change his life: Charles "Doc" Broadus, head of security at the operation. Broadus also operated the center's boxing gym. He convinced George to test his skills in the ring against a smaller kid who had more boxing experience. The result was a large dose of humble pie; Foreman couldn't even touch the younger kid in the ring.

Foreman backed away from boxing, not wishing to embarrass himself further. But, Broadus saw something in the young man and forced him to return to the boxing ring. After a near-arrest by the police, the Job Corps considered kicking young George out of the program. Broadus intervened, saying that he could reach the young man through boxing. The authorities let Foreman stay in the program, provided that he commit himself to discipline under Broadus and boxing.

When Foreman returned home to visit his mother, he informed her that he had taken up boxing. Her initial reaction was negative, as she thought "he had done enough fighting at home."[4] But she came around after seeing noticeable changes in her former problem child.

"Overnight I became a poster boy for the Job Corps," Foreman recalled. "I'd gone from being a junior high dropout to a young man who now devoured books."[5] He also began devouring his ring opponents and absorbing skills in the ring. Still, George was not a polished boxer, which caused him to lose a decision at a national Golden Gloves tournament in Milwaukee, Wisconsin.

Foreman graduated from the Job Corps, obtained his general equivalency diploma, and moved back to Houston. He briefly returned to his thuggish ways before his mother called Doc Broadus, pleading for him to come help her son. Broadus bought George a one-way ticket to Oakland, California, and put George to work at the Job Corp center. Foreman began training in earnest to make the 1968 U.S. Olympic boxing team.

FROM DELINQUENT TO OLYMPIC CHAMPION

Foreman progressed rapidly enough to win a place on the U.S. Olympic boxing team to compete for a medal at the 1968 Summer Olympics in Mexico City. The 19-year-old Foreman crushed the opposition, but not before a scare against a squat Romanian named Ion Alexe. The Romanian hit Foreman with a straight left that knocked Foreman for a loop. "He was a short, stocky southpaw," Foreman recalled. "He didn't look like much but he hit me so hard with a straight left that a siren went off in my head. Scared me to death."[6] Foreman rebounded quickly to stop Alexe and everyone else. He knocked out Italian Giorgi Bambini in the second round to reach the finals. He then battered the Soviet Union's Ionas Chepulis before the referee halted the contest in the second round. Foreman expressed pride in himself and his country before receiving the gold medal. He waved a small American flag and smiled for the world to see. John Hall, sports columnist for the *Los Angeles Times,* reported that "the young Texan's display was a rare moment of dignity and love in the face of the adversity and suffering which we know so well."[7]

Foreman's patriotism sharply contrasted with the symbolic messages of other U.S. Olympians. Sprinters Tommie Smith and John Carlos—who won gold and bronze medals in the 100-meter dash—famously or infamously raised their fists with black gloves on the medal stand, as the "Star-Spangled Banner" was played. Smith and Carlos raised their black gloves to protest segregation and the deprivation of civil rights for African Americans in the United States.

Foreman refused to criticize Smith and Carlos for their different stance. Instead, Foreman said that all the American athletes were like a family who supported each other's quest for athletic superiority. "We were like a family," he told Dave Zirin. "And we were all focused on trying to win our own gold medals so we didn't feel the outrage, the controversy after they raised their fists."[8] Foreman focused on the fact that the United States was freer than many other places in the world. "There were a lot of people there who wanted to really protest against their countries," Foreman said, "but they couldn't do it. They don't feel free, but we can do what we want."[9] Foreman explained that his flag waving was a spontaneous reaction that many people supported. But he also felt the wrath from some who believed that he had betrayed the cause that Smith and Carlos advocated.[10]

RISING THROUGH THE PRO RANKS

Boxing trainers drooled over Foreman's vast potential. Cus D'Amato, former manager and trainer of Floyd Patterson, said that Foreman had the potential to be heavyweight champion.[11] Foreman made his professional debut on June 23, 1969, in Madison Square Garden in New York City. He flattened 187-pound Donald Waldhelm in the third round. Foreman looked less than stellar in his pro debut against a mediocre opponent who entered the ring with a record of 5–4–2. His handlers moved Foreman slowly against little opposition. In his third bout, he half punched and half pushed 185-pound Sylvester Dullaire out of the ring.

Foreman finally faced tougher opposition in his eighth pro bout when he squared off against the rugged Roberto Davila of Lima, Peru. Foreman showed a good jab and controlled the fight. But he could not put away his determined opponent.

In January 1970, Foreman faced more serious opposition in the form of 18–5–2 Jack "the Giant" O'Halloran, a 6' 6" fighter who had faced contender Joe Bugner in his pro career. O'Halloran also outweighed Foreman by more than 20 pounds. Foreman took his time and stopped his large opponent in the fifth round to earn his 15th victory.

In his next bout, Foreman faced an even tougher test—a tougher one than he anticipated. He faced Gregorio Peralta, a 35-year-old Argentine with 90 professional bouts and 77 victories. For the first time in his career, Foreman suffered a cut in the ring, a deep cut over his right eyebrow. Peralta managed to duck low and nail Foreman with several hooks and looping right hands. Still, Foreman earned a unanimous decision victory, as referee Mark Conn scored the fight nine rounds to one, and judge Jack Gordon scored seven rounds to three for Foreman. However, judge Tony Castellano only gave the fight to Foreman by a 5–4–1 vote. Many in the crowd booed upon hearing the verdict for Foreman, who emphasized the positive after the decision. "Anyhow, this was a big one, going 10 rounds. I proved myself to be a fighter."[12]

In May 1970, Foreman earned another important victory—over the tough journeyman George "Scrap Iron" Johnson, a durable and underrated opponent. Foreman stopped Johnson in the seventh round at the Forum in Inglewood, California.

Foreman intimidated some of his opponents, adopting the menacing glare of his former friend and mentor of sorts, Sonny Liston. In July 1970, Foreman's opponent, Roger Russell, looked at the floor, ceiling, and everywhere else but refused to look at Foreman. Reporters noted that Russell looked defeated before he even tasted Foreman's punching power. Sure enough, Foreman stopped his overmatched opponent in the first round.[13]

In August 1970, Foreman showed championship potential in stopping former world heavyweight title challenger George Chuvalo in the third round. Chuvalo had taken Muhammad Ali 12 rounds in 1966 and had only been stopped one time previously in more than 80 bouts by Joe Frazier. Foreman dispatched the durable Canadian as no other fighter had ever done.

Foreman's career ascent was not without some intrigue, particularly in his February 1971 bout with a fighter supposedly named Phil Smith in St. Paul, Minnesota. Foreman won the bout easily, stopping his opponent in the first round. However, Smith's handlers contacted authorities and noted that their fighter was not in Minnesota. It turned out that the fighter was Charlie Boston from Winston Salem, North Carolina.[14]

In May 1971, Foreman again tangled with Peralta, who had given him his sternest test to date in his young career. This time Foreman managed to stop the game Peralta in the 10th round to win the North American Boxing Federation title. Foreman dominated the action, and it was only due to the incredible chin of Peralta that the fight lasted as long as it did.

CHAMPION

Foreman continued his march through the heavyweight division, winning five fights in 1972 against marginal opposition. He entered 1973 with a record of 37–0 with 35 stoppages. The boxing powers ranked him as the number-two contender in the world, behind only Muhammad Ali. Foreman considered himself the number-one contender.[15]

Critics charged that Foreman had feasted upon a roster of journeymen, older fighters, and tomato cans to compile his glossy record. Foreman's manager, Dick Sadler, responded testily: "They weren't all considered stiffs until George KO'd them all. He overpowered them so easily, everyone decided they had to be stiffs."[16]

Foreman landed the shot at undefeated heavyweight champion Joe Frazier in Kingston, Jamaica. Oddsmakers listed Frazier as the favorite to defend his title, as he had defeated the great Ali in the so-called battle of the century in 1971 and had successfully defended his title two more times after that historic clash. Foreman enlisted the help of the crafty Archie Moore—the former light heavyweight champion and heavyweight contender—to help in his preparations.

Foreman overwhelmed the smaller Frazier with his devastating power. One of Foreman's uppercuts literally lifted Smokin' Joe off the canvas. Foreman dropped Frazier three times in the first round and then stopped him in the second. The *Chicago Tribune* described Foreman's performance "like a lumberjack with a hangover attacking a tree."[17]

"God intended that I be champion," Foreman said. "My victory should be a lesson to all the deprived and underprivileged kids who think they don't have a chance to accomplish anything."[18]

Foreman became a popular champion early in his tenure. Will Grimsley wrote of him: "There is no air of arrogance or pomposity about him—even now that he is champion. He is modest and mild-mannered."[19] Foreman said after winning the championship that he wanted to go home with his wife Adrienne and baby girl Michi.

But celebrity and fame took their toll on the champion and his formerly pleasant personality. He had problems with management, as he fired and then rehired Sadler. He divorced his wife and engaged in excessive spending on automobiles, buying a Mercedes, a Rolls Royce, and an Excalibur.

However, he kept winning, defending his title against Jose Roman in Tokyo, Japan, and then against Ken Norton in Venezuela. He stopped Roman in the first round and Norton—the man who had defeated and broken the jaw of the great Ali—in the second round. Some speculated that Norton might present some problems for Foreman. Norton himself referred to Foreman as "slow."[20] Foreman put to rest any doubts as to his dominance, dropping Norton three times in the second round. The *Chicago Tribune* wrote: "It was awesome. It was short. It was devastatingly decisive."[21]

Foreman's trainer Sadler—with whom he had reunited—called him the "greatest." Others began to join the Foreman bandwagon, saying he was the best of Louis, Marciano, Liston, and other great champions. Next up, Foreman signed to defend his title against another great former champion, Muhammad Ali.

ZAIRE

Foreman faced the irrepressible Ali in Zaire, Africa, due to the promotional efforts of Don King. Oddsmakers installed Foreman as the prohibitive favorite. They believed as did Foreman's Sadler: "It's just a matter of how Ali is going to get knocked out."[22] In what turned out to be an omen, the fight was postponed in September after Foreman suffered a cut during a sparring session. Officials moved the bout from September 25 to October 30, 1974. A few weeks later, in early October, a car carrying Foreman crashed.[23]

Still, most experts picked the younger Foreman to stop Ali. Foreman entered the ring at 40–0 with 37 knockouts. The standard thinking was that if Frazier and Norton beat Ali and Foreman destroyed Frazier and Norton, then Foreman will also soundly defeat Ali. A notable exception was Tony Blackwell, who predicted in the *Chicago Daily Defender* that Ali's movement would frustrate Foreman and guide him to victory.[24]

But Ali conjured up his old magic, employing psychological warfare and his surprising rope-a-dope strategy, laying on the ropes to cause Foreman to tire himself out. Foreman wobbled Ali in the second round, but for much of the early rounds, Ali avoided most of Foreman's damaging blows. He surprised Foreman by his ability to absorb many damaging blows. Ali completed his surprise by kayoing an exhausted Foreman in the eighth round in what Norman Mailer simply referred to as "The Fight."

Foreman demanded an inquiry into the fight, making all sorts of excuses. He claimed there were irregularities with referee Zach Clayton's count, the ropes, and the canvas. Foreman claimed that he got up before the count of 10. He added that there was "tampering with the ropes to Ali's benefit" and that the canvas was too "soggy."[25]

Years later Foreman realized that he had lost the mental game with Ali. He also realized that the people in Zaire connected with Ali and loved him as their hero. "Ali made them love him," he told Zirin. "That's why I couldn't beat him. He heard them chanting his name and said, 'I'm not going to lose.' That's where the stamina and taking my punches came from: they loved him, and I love him too. He's the greatest man I've ever known."[26]

EXHIBITION, A WAR AND ANOTHER UPSET

Foreman returned to the ring in April 1975 in a most unusual format. He defeated five straight foes in three-round exhibitions. He defeated Alonzo Johnson, Jerry Judge, Terry Daniels, Charley Polite, and Boone Kirkman. He stopped the first three opponents and decisioned the other two. Ali served as a ringside commentator and still appeared to get inside Foreman's head. Foreman appeared to imitate Ali in the ring, which displeased the crowd. They responded with chants of "Ali, Ali" during the exhibitions.[27]

Foreman said after the exhibitions that he had embraced the "bad guy" role to Ali's "good guy" persona. "No more of that Good Guy stuff for me," he said. "I've been abused and put down too much for it."[28] Famed African

American sportswriter A. S. "Doc" Young blasted Foreman's "exhibitions," writing that they debased the sport of boxing. He blasted that Foreman had "let the stink of 10,000 sewers over the boxing world" by defeating the "Farcical Five."[29]

George Foreman did not return to the ring for real until January 1976, when he faced rugged puncher Ron Lyle, an ex-convict who had served nine years in prison for second-degree murder. The two engaged in one of the great slugfests in boxing history, what was called a "wild swinging brawl that resembled an old Hollywood movie."[30]

Lyle stunned Foreman in the first round, only to have Foreman nearly knock him out in the second. In the fourth round, Lyle dropped Foreman, then Foreman knocked down Lyle, and then Lyle floored Foreman again. Many rate it as one of the best rounds in the annals of boxing. "It was the toughest fight I ever had," Foreman said after the war.[31]

In June 1976, Foreman once again faced Joe Frazier. The result was the same, as Foreman was simply too big and powerful for his foe. Foreman dropped him twice en route to a fifth-round victory. He continued his winning ways, defeating future world heavyweight title challenger Scott LeDoux, undefeated Dino Denis, and Pedro Agosto. Foreman continued to call for a rematch with Ali and accused his former conqueror of ducking him.

In March 1977, Foreman faced slick boxer Jimmy Young, a man who had dropped a close, controversial decision to Ali in 1976. Young used his crafty defensive skills to full effect but also displayed more offensive firepower than normal. Foreman appeared more sluggish than normal in the San Juan, Puerto Rican heat. Foreman nearly decapitated Young in the seventh round with a strong left hook. "He really hurt me," Young said after the bout. "I didn't think I was going to make it."[32] But Young survived and began putting rounds in the bank. The light-punching Young even dropped Foreman in the 12th and final round to secure a unanimous-decision victory.

In his dressing room, George Foreman suffered from dehydration and nearly died. He also had a life-changing religious experience. "Then I felt myself transported to a far-off place, to an enormous void, to the bottom of the bottom of the bottom," he wrote in his autobiography *By George.* "At that, a giant hand lifted and carried me out of that nothing-ness."[33] In a later book, *God in My Corner,* Foreman explained that, while he lay prone on the table, he suddenly raised his body up and yelled out loud: "JESUS CHRIST IS COMING ALIVE IN ME."[34] His handlers may have chalked it up to heat exhaustion and dehydration, but the religious experience was real and long lasting.

Foreman's religious experience changed him at age 28. His brother Roy— one of his chief advisors—told the *Washington Post:* "He's found God and he is fighting another type of fight. He's fighting for God and that's bigger than boxing."[35] It gave him a second lease on life. It also led to his 10-year retirement from boxing. In his time away from boxing, Foreman became a preacher, eventually forming his own church. He became an ordained minister at the Church of the Lord Jesus Christ in 1978. He had some marital disharmony during his years away from the boxing ring, fathered several children, and eventually found stability in his personal life.

For several years after his retirement, Foreman expressed little, if any, desire to return to the ring. "At first, I thought I could be a fighting evangelist, giving glory to God in the ring," he said. "I could not fight anymore. I'm not putting down boxing. But I could not do it."[36] He loved performing as an evangelist for no money. His only source of income during that time was the sale of his own considerable personal property.[37] His told the press: "Just don't put me in a ring."[38] He traveled around the country speaking to churches, schools, and prisons for First Church of the Lord Jesus Christ in Houston. He won the Distinguished American award from the Horatio Alger Association in Los Angeles in 1984. That year, he boxed in an exhibition at Fort Benning, Georgia. He did better in the ring than he thought he would. It rekindled flames that he thought were gone forever.

However, Foreman knew that he needed to do something about his weight. He tipped the scales at more than 340 pounds.

After a period of time, he needed to infuse his church with additional capital. He initially considered returning to boxing to raise money for his church. Such began the most unlikely of comebacks at the age of 37. He said half-jokingly that he was looking to become boxing's oldest champion.

THE COMEBACK

Many in the boxing community viewed George Foreman's comeback with outright derision, viewing it as another in a long line of bad jokes. Many ex-fighters attempted comebacks when they were over the hill and in desperate need of money. Foreman's excess weight made him an easy and large target for the detractors. They called it the "Battle of the Bulge" and the "Great Fat Hope."[39] The *Chicago Tribune* ran a headline: "Hey, Foreman! Fat Chance."[40] Reporter Shirley Povich referred to it as a "paunchy comeback" and the comeback attempt as "nonsensical."[41] Povich disparagingly concluded "that before abandoning the Lord's work he should have sought a second opinion."[42]

Instead of reacting with anger, the new George Foreman made his weight a joke, eventually laughing his way to the bank with food endorsements and later the mega-popular George Foreman Grill that made him a millionaire many times over.

But Foreman said he had other reasons for making a successful comeback. He wanted to "show a lot of young kids I work with in Houston what you can achieve with some hard work."[43] He began doing some serious roadwork for the first time in his career. He never ran more than four miles in his career—even when he was heavyweight champion. When he ran six miles in February 1987, he joked that "for the first time in my life, I got a second wind."[44] He also claimed that he was more mentally prepared for his comeback than during his first career. "I could be wrong, but I think I'm better now than I was when I was champ," he told the *New York Times*. "I'm thinking a lot better. I had 10 years of thinking what I should've done that I didn't do, especially in those losses."[45]

He first obtained his boxing license from the California State Athletic Commission. The commission ran a battery of tests, skeptical that the aging Foreman was a candidate to fight professionally again. To the commission's surprise, Foreman passed all the tests. Doctors said that neurologically he was in better shape than other boxers of similar ring experience.[46] However, Foreman weighed in at nearly 270 pounds.

In March 1987, Foreman entered the ring for the first time against journeyman Steve Zouski. Foreman finished his foe in the fourth round, though he looked fleshy according to ringside reports. Phil Berger noted, "there was a touch of Frankenstein in the mechanical way he fought."[47] Zouski acknowledged that Foreman had "thudding punches" but said "there's no snap in his punches."[48]

In September 1987, Foreman knocked out Bobby Crabtree—a journeyman, but one who packed a mean punch—in six rounds. In December 1987, Foreman stopped Rocky Sekorski in the third round. In January 1988, he knocked out Tom Trimm in less than 40 seconds. Foreman showed a strong left jab in many of his bouts. Mort Sharnik said Foreman's jab was still "vicious."[49] Foreman also didn't waste as much energy in his comeback. The older Foreman was slower but also more relaxed in the ring. He didn't tense up nearly as much as he did as the hulking menace in the early 1970s.

In March 1988, Foreman stopped former world cruiserweight champion Dwight Muhammad Qawi with his weight down at 235 pounds.

People began to take Foreman's comeback seriously for the first time in January 1990, when he defeated former world heavyweight challenger Gerry Cooney in a bout billed as the "Puncher Versus the Preacher." Cooney possessed a monstrous left hook that he had used to decapitate aging veterans Ken Norton and Ron Lyle in the first round. Cooney earned a title shot against Larry Holmes in 1982 and fought courageously for 13 rounds before succumbing to the champion. Cooney looked to revitalize his own comeback by dispatching of Foreman. Cooney, a fast starter, shook Foreman in the first round but couldn't drop the "Preacher." In the second round, Foreman displayed that he still possessed formidable power in his fists. He dropped

Cooney twice, the second time with a left uppercut followed by a right cross. Cooney lay on the canvas for more than 90 seconds.

Foreman praised Cooney as the most devastating puncher he had ever faced. For his part, Cooney acknowledged: "I just got caught with a great, great shot. He caught me with the bombs. He is such a strong fighter."[50]

Foreman hoped for a shot at former heavyweight champion Mike Tyson. In June 1990, Foreman fought on the undercard of Tyson's successful first-round knockout of Henry Tillman. Foreman followed Tyson with a second-round kayo of Adilson Rodriguez. "Youth and enthusiasm are great," Foreman said after the victory. "But age and craftiness are better for me."[51]

The win over Rodriguez landed Foreman what he had coveted: another shot at the world heavyweight championship against Evander "the Real Deal" Holyfield in April 1991. Foreman found a home for his left jab and occasional short right cross, but he couldn't put enough punches together. Instead, he absorbed a fusillade of punches from the much younger and quicker Holyfield. Foreman once took 19 straight punches from Holyfield without hitting the canvas. In the end, Holyfield won a unanimous, 12-round decision over the 42-year-old Foreman.

Holyfield won the fight, but Foreman emerged from the bout as a victor, too. He became a hero for his courage at an advanced age. "It was a good night for me," Foreman said. "He had the points, but I made a point. I proved you shouldn't be ashamed of being a senior citizen."[52] He also became America's great endorsement star. He did commercials with Nike, McDonald's, and other leading companies.

Foreman plodded forward with his boxing comeback. In April 1992, he survived a 10-round war with Alex Stewart. Foreman dropped Stewart twice in the first round, but Stewart survived and then pounded Foreman in some of the later rounds. Foreman earned a 10-round majority-decision victory.

In June 1993, Foreman suffered a serious setback to his boxing career when he lost a unanimous decision to Tommy "the Duke" Morrison for the World Boxing Organization world championship. Morrison, naturally a slugger, fought the smartest fight of his career by boxing Foreman from the outside. The judges scored it 118–109, 117–110, and 117–110 for Morrison. Many expected the 44-year-old Foreman would retire after this defeat. Foreman even spurred on those rumors by stating, "I had some great times in boxing and I'm proud of what I've done. God bless boxing."[53]

CHAMPION AGAIN

But Foreman received another shot at the big time in November 1994, when he faced undefeated heavyweight champion Michael Moorer—a former light heavyweight and cruiserweight star with punching power who had defeated Holyfield to win the title. A southpaw with power and boxing skills, Moorer entered the ring with a record of 35–0 with 30 stoppages. He seemed to possess too much quickness for the plodding Foreman. For more than nine rounds, Moorer outboxed Foreman, even better than Holyfield and Morrison had done. The announcers at ringside—Foreman's Home Box Office (HBO) colleagues—intimated that Foreman simply didn't have the speed to land the necessary power punch. But George Foreman was resolute.

He entered the ring in the same red boxing shorts that he had worn against Muhammad Ali in the legendary "Rumble in the Jungle" in Zaire. Foreman wore them in part to exorcise the demons that still haunted him from Kinshasa. In the 10th round, Foreman landed a short, quick right cross that flattened Moorer. "I exorcised the ghost, once and forever," he said. "Heavyweight champion of the world."[54]

Foreman retained his title with a controversial decision win over Axel Schultz. Foreman then defeated Crawford Grimsley over 12 rounds in Japan. The 35-year-old Grimsley, who was 20–0, backpedaled from the 47-year-old Foreman all night, causing Foreman to say after the bout: "It seems that the younger fellas, they love to run from me."[55] In April 1997, Foreman outpointed Lou Savarese over 12 rounds in a tough split decision.

In November 1997, the 48-year-old Foreman fought his last fight against contender Shannon "the Cannon" Briggs, who started well in the early rounds. Foreman seemingly controlled most of the rounds with his dominant left jab, nearly knocking Briggs to the canvas on a couple of occasions. The judges scored the bout 116–112, 117–113, and 114–114 in a majority decision for Briggs. The crowd at Atlantic City lustily booed the decision.

BOXING COMMENTATOR AND MONEYMAKER

After his final retirement, Foreman returned to his role as a boxing analyst for HBO. He worked alongside blow-by-blow announcer Jim Lampley and the analyst (and former boxing scribe from Philadelphia) Larry Merchant. Foreman thrilled audiences with his no-nonsense, straightforward analysis. Foreman actually began as an analyst with the network in 1992 and left in 2004.

Foreman was often known for disagreeing with Merchant, who sometimes came off as a little pompous. During one bout, Merchant pontificated on some point, prompting Foreman to inquire: "Is that from your years of experience in the ring?" Merchant obviously was less than pleased with the slap at his lack of boxing experience. On another occasion, Foreman told Merchant: "You don't know boxing, Larry. You just speak boxing."[56]

But Foreman got along well with his HBO colleagues. "George was here for 12 years," Merchant said on the eve of the first telecast without Foreman. "A lot of people seemed interested in our differences, which I understand. It's like two guys sitting side by side watching a movie and getting a different idea of what's going on."[57]

Foreman also made hundreds of millions of dollars in endorsement deals. *Business Week* estimated in December 2004 that Foreman had made in excess of $200 million on the famous George Foreman Grill.[58] He also had a book entitled *George Foreman's Indoor Grilling Made Easy.*

Foreman remains in the boxing game, serving as a trainer for his son George III—known as "Monk." George III boasts a record of 15–0 at the time of this writing, though he has not faced any stiff opposition.

The elder Foreman still makes occasional comments that he might return to the ring in his sixties. Some dismiss the idea as Foreman simply spouting off with his jocular personality. Others are not so sure—after all, George Foreman has made a career—and a life—out of defying the odds and doing things his own way.

Chapter 7

MIKE TYSON: "THE BADDEST MAN ON THE PLANET"

Cus D'Amato had trained several world champions in his illustrious career. He had guided the career of Floyd Patterson, the first man to win the world heavyweight title twice in the late 1950s and early 1960s. He also worked with Jose Torres, a former Olympic medalist and light heavyweight champion in the professional ranks. But those fighters' hey-days were in the 1960s, when D'Amato was at his peak in the fight game. D'Amato almost didn't have a peak because he refused to play ball with the mob, whose octopuslike tentacles controlled much of boxing. If he kowtowed to mob influences, he probably would have trained more world champions. A bit of a recluse, D'Amato had largely slipped from the boxing scene until he became acquainted with a young, squat, powerful-looking man-child who would one day cause seismic eruptions in the world of boxing.

In the early 1980s, D'Amato found a prodigy who he felt had the natural power and abilities to achieve the highest glories in the sport. D'Amato had a profound belief that there was something special in a troubled boy named Michael Gerard Tyson.

D'Amato first learned of Tyson when Tyson was 14 years old. Bobby Stewart, a former boxer of D'Amato's, saw promise in Tyson as the overseer of the boxing program at a juvenile reform school called Tryon School for Boys in Johnstown, New York. Tyson's juvenile delinquency can be traced to his lack of a stable home life.

Tyson was born on June 30, 1966, in the Bedford-Stuyvesant section of Brooklyn. His father left his mother Lorna when young Mike was two years old. Tyson started off well in grade school until age eight, when his family moved to the more depressed area of Brooklyn known as Brownsville, an area that "had become a classic urban slum."[1] Tyson remembers the area and time as "awful living conditions, poverty and peer pressure."[2] One of the only joys in his life was flying pigeons—a hobby that he still enjoys to this day. The life of the streets became Tyson's mantra, his life code. He became a mugger when he was just in grade school. Tyson had to live at Tryon after numerous scrapes with the law. He had been arrested more than 30 times. Violence was a part of his life. "It was part of life," he told Jose Torres. "It was acceptable."[3]

As a former professional heavyweight boxer, Stewart saw in Tyson a physical specimen unlike any he had ever seen. Stewart knew boxing, as he had enjoyed a fine amateur career before turning professional. In the amateur ranks, he had won a national Golden Gloves title and won a decision over future world heavyweight champion Michael "Dynamite" Dokes. Stewart taught the young Tyson how to box but figured the young man needed a real professional, someone who could really work with this diamond in the rough.

Tyson asked Stewart if he would teach him how to box, but Stewart had another lesson in mind. "I had a reputation for beating up other students," Tyson told the *New York Times,* "and when we boxed he tried to humiliate me so the other kids would see I was nothing. He hit me in the body and I went down. My air stopped; I thought I was dead."[4] Tyson even intentionally hit some other students at the school so he could be moved under Stewart's tutelage, because Stewart handled some of the most recalcitrant youth offenders at his residence hall at the school.[5]

If Stewart intended for Tyson to quit boxing, the teacher was sorely mistaken, as the young bully with the lisp and soft voice wanted to learn how he could drop people with one punch to the body. "Bobby Stewart was surprised," Tyson told the *New York Times.* "He thought because he humiliated me, I'd stop. I didn't. As time went by, we boxed so much, he began to like me."[6]

Stewart contacted his former professional manager, Matt Baranski, who operated a boxing gym in Albany, New York. Baranski referred Stewart to one of his friends—the legendary Cus D'Amato. Stewart took Tyson up to D'Amato's place in the Catskills. D'Amato saw immediately what Stewart had glimpsed: raw, unvarnished power and potential. Shortly after seeing the young Tyson spar a few sessions at the local police station, D'Amato told his friend Jimmy Jacobs that "Mike Tyson is going to be the heavyweight champion of the world."[7]

D'Amato became a father figure to the troubled teen and even his legal guardian when Tyson's mother passed away when he was 16. D'Amato counseled Tyson on life matters in addition to boxing. He warned Tyson about trusting people and about comporting himself in a lawful manner.

During his time at the Catskills, D'Amato overlooked certain transgressions and bent certain rules to accommodate his protégé. He even dismissed assistant trainer Teddy Atlas after Atlas confronted a young Tyson with a gun after learning that Tyson had tried to initiate sexual contact with

Atlas's 13-year-old niece. But Tyson also showed a softer side around D'Amato and Camille Ewald, D'Amato's significant other who became Tyson's adoptive mother. Tyson also showed an amazing ability to absorb information about boxing and boxing history. He watched hours and hours of tape with D'Amato, studying different fighters and techniques. He learned the art of defense, the peak-a-boo style that D'Amato had incorporated into Floyd Patterson's arsenal.

Tyson showed promise as an amateur, knocking out many foes—a relatively unusual feat in amateur boxing, where the young boxers wear protective headgear. Tyson won a silver medal at the 1982 Junior Olympics after an eight-second demolition of an opponent in the semifinal round. He lost a decision to an Eastern European fighter in the gold medal match. Tyson lost in the Olympic trials to Henry Tillman, a taller, skilled boxer who had more of an amateur style. Amateur boxing does not reward knockdowns or harder punching. Judges in amateur boxing simply count (using clickers) the number of punches each fighter lands. Tyson performed well in the amateurs but clearly had a professional style.

D'Amato turned Tyson pro at the age of 18 in March 1985 and rapidly moved him through the ranks. Jimmy Jacobs, a fight film collector extraordinaire, and Bill Cayton, a shrewd businessman, helped D'Amato manage Tyson's affairs. The pair of Jacobs and Clayton had funded D'Amato's boxing gym in recent years. The triumvirate worked wonders for Tyson in and out of the ring. Tyson fought 15 times in 1985 alone, winning all by knockout. Only three fighters even made it past the first bell. Tyson won his first 19 fights by knockout—12 of them in the first round. He showed an amazing blend of power and speed. His opponents—many of them limited in skill—simply could not deal with the speed. Early in his career, Tyson also was hard to hit, as he employed D'Amato's peak-a-boo style diligently.

D'Amato died at age 77 in November 1985 before he could witness the coronation of his young fighter. His young protégé had compiled a record of 11–0 but had not yet stepped up to face quality opposition.

Tyson showed some of his edge in his early career. In his national television debut, Tyson faced fellow contender Jesse Ferguson, who entered the ring with a 14–1 record. In the fifth round, Tyson broke Ferguson's nose. In the next round, the referee disqualified Ferguson for excessive holding, though the result was later changed to a technical knockout for Tyson. In the postfight interview, an exultant Tyson chilled some observers by saying: "I try to catch him right on the tip of the nose, because I try to push the bone into the brain."[8]

Tyson established an aura of invincibility by dispatching his opponents so quickly. He also showed excellent defensive skills and a good chin when he, on rare occasions, was hit flush. "My attributes are my elusiveness and my ability to take a punch," he proudly proclaimed after one fight.[9] He cultivated the image of a gladiator by entering the ring with no robe, just plain black trunks with a white towel around his broad shoulders.

FULFILLING HIS DESTINY

Tyson steadily moved up the ranks and overcame adversity. In May 1986, he went the full 10-round distance twice against former world challenger James "Quick" Tillis and against the rough-and-tough Mitch "Blood" Green, a former gang leader. Tyson showed frustration at times but still won both fights easily on the scorecards. After the difficulties with Tillis and Green, Tyson disposed of Reggie Gross, William Hosea, Lorenzo Boyd, and Marvis Frazier—the son of Joe Frazier—in the first or second rounds. In August 1986, Tyson faced a stiffer challenge from the tough Jose Ribalta, who somehow managed to last until the 10th round. In September, Tyson dispatched former world cruiserweight champion Alonzo Ratliff in the second round.

That led to the moment of truth for Mike Tyson, as he was scheduled to face World Boxing Council (WBC) heavyweight champion Trevor Berbick. If Tyson won, he would become the youngest heavyweight champion in history, passing D'Amato's former protégé Floyd Patterson. In November 1986, Tyson fulfilled D'Amato's vision and his life goal by dispatching Trevor Berbick for the WBC world heavyweight championship in the second round. It was a mismatch, as Berbick had no answer for the quicker, younger Tyson. "I was throwing, what can you say, hydrogen bombs," Tyson said after the fight. "Every punch with murderous intentions."[10]

On that day—November 22, 1986—Tyson made history. He overwhelmed Berbick in the second round to win the title. Experts gushed at the potential of the young champion. Angelo Dundee said: "At his stage, I've never seen anyone like him. How do you fight him? With a gun."[11]

Tyson not only won one heavyweight title but he also added belts from the other two major sanctioning bodies—the World Boxing Association (WBA) and the International Boxing Federation (IBF). In March 1987, he easily outpointed WBA champion James "Bonecrusher" Smith—a man with a college degree and a devastating right hand. But Smith held Tyson for most of the night, losing virtually every round. Only in the last round did Smith ever appear to hurt Tyson. For most ringside observers, Bonecrusher simply wanted to survive and turned into Boneclutcher.

After defeating Smith, Tyson faced a talented, if somewhat troubled, ex-champion by the name of Pinklon Thomas in May 1987. Some boxing observers dismiss this Tyson victory as nothing more than "Iron" Mike beating an over-the-hill ex-champion, but Pinklon Thomas possessed one of the finest jabs in recent memory and a 29–1–1 record. Tyson overwhelmed Thomas, stopping him in six rounds.

In his next bout, in August 1987, Tyson unified the heavyweight championship with another easy unanimous decision over IBF champion Tony Tucker. For a man nicknamed "TNT," Tucker showed very little firepower and employed the Bonecrusher Smith strategy of jab, move, and hold. That enabled Tucker to last the 12 rounds but led to a lopsided decision victory for Tyson.

Tyson cemented his hold over the heavyweight division by defeating former longtime champion Larry Holmes in January 1988. The former champion, who had lorded over the division as kingpin from 1978 to 1985, had vowed he would school the young Tyson on the art of boxing. Holmes returned to the ring after 21 months, convinced that he could use his superior height and reach to frustrate the younger champion. But Holmes couldn't beat the younger, quicker, stronger man—and Father Time. Tyson stopped Holmes in the fourth round. No one had ever stopped Holmes in his career of more than 50 pro bouts. "He's better than I thought he was," Holmes said after the fight. "He's very hard to hit, and punches very good."[12]

While Tyson held all the belts, many clamored for a showdown with Michael Spinks, the undefeated former light heavyweight champion who had dethroned Larry Holmes three years earlier. Spinks's charismatic promoter Butch Lewis referred to Spinks as the "uncrowned champion" and the "true heavyweight champion."[13] This infuriated Tyson, who held all three belts and began to believe the hype that he really was the "baddest man on the planet."[14]

On the night of the fight, June 27, 1988, Lewis enraged Tyson further by objecting to Tyson's hand wrappings in his dressing room. Tyson vowed to punish Spinks for this affront. Tyson overwhelmed Spinks with a 91-second demolition that cemented his domination over the heavyweight division.

The demolition of Michael Spinks elevated a young Tyson into the pantheon of dominant heavyweight kingpins. Pundits began to compare Tyson to the division greats of yesteryear. Tyson also pervaded popular culture and public consciousness. He graced the cover of *Time* magazine and countless other publications. Celebrities flocked to his fights, and millions watched him on HBO and on pay-per-view.

TROUBLES CONTINUE

Unfortunately, Tyson pervaded public consciousness because of his penchant for headline-generating behavior. Tyson's personal life became front-page

news in tabloids and mainstream newspapers. He wrecked cars, allegedly as-
saulted women, and punched people. He also attracted more attention when
he married actress Robin Givens of *Head of the Class* fame in February 1988.
As Phil Berger wrote in the *New York Times,* since his marriage to Givens,
"Tyson has been hip-deep in conflicts and crises."[15] Tyson seemed to unravel,
as his boxing inner circle changed dramatically. Tyson's career had been handled expertly by Jimmy Jacobs and Bill Cayton, who had funded D'Amato's
gym for years. They had guided him to the position of heavyweight champion and enabled him to earn millions of dollars.

Four days after wedding Givens, Tyson renewed his managerial contract
with Jacobs and Cayton. However, Jacobs—the more personable of the two
and the one with a better personal relationship with Tyson—died. Promoter
Don King, Robin Givens, and Givens's mother, Ruth Roper, all counseled
Tyson against Cayton. By all accounts, they played the race card to perfection
against Cayton, an older white man. Later, Roper and Givens realized that
Cayton was a good businessman and encouraged Tyson to resign with Cayton
under more favorable terms to Tyson. But Don King played the race card
continually, eventually leading to litigation and the breakup of the last member of the original D'Amato team. Tyson severed ties with Bill Cayton and
then sued him, alleging that Cayton and Jacobs failed to advise the fighter
that Jacobs was terminally ill when the contract was signed.

In August 1988, he got into a street fight with former opponent Mitch
"Blood" Green in Harlem. The next month, in September, Tyson took bigger
blows than he faced in the ring when he appeared with Givens on a *20/20*
interview with Barbara Walters. Givens described Tyson's violent behavior to
a national audience: "It's been torture. It's been pure hell. It's been worse than
anything I could possibly imagine. . . . Michael is intimidating."[16]

Even stranger than the Givens's accusations was Tyson's placid, passive
demeanor. Some speculated that his antidepressant medication kept him in
check. Whatever the case, a few days later, the real Tyson emerged, as the
police responded to an enraged champion who allegedly threatened Givens
in a violent rage.

In 1988, Tyson also made another move that many boxing analysts considered one of his bigger mistakes: he let go of his trainer Kevin Rooney, who
had been a D'Amato protégé. Rooney had been a decent welterweight who
fought professionally out of the Catskills for D'Amato from 1978 until 1985.
He compiled a decent record of 21–4–1 but lost badly when he stepped up
in competition and fought the great Nicaraguan warrior Alexis Arguello in
1982. However, Rooney had made his mark as a young, up-and-coming
trainer under D'Amato's tutelage. When D'Amato died, Rooney took over
as Tyson's lead trainer. However, Rooney had the temerity to speak his mind

about the negative influences of Tyson's wife and her mother. This led to Rooney's dismissal.[17]

King replaced Rooney with Aaron Snowell, Richie Giachetti (who had been Larry Holmes's trainer for much of his career), and Jay Bright. Other key members of the entourage—known as "Team Tyson"—were John Horne and Rory Holloway. With the exception of Giachetti, none of the men had the experience of Rooney. However, Giachetti angered King over another matter and was replaced. Boxing analysts feared that the corner changes for Tyson were not ideal for Tyson.[18]

But for all his troubles that were brewing, Tyson cut a swath through the heavyweight division, dominating the division in way that perhaps had never been done. As author Joe Layden writes, "He resurrected boxing, brought it to a place in the public consciousness that it hadn't held for two decades, and he accomplished this not through style but swagger."[19]

STUNNING UPSET

After he had dispatched Michael Spinks in June 1988, legal and other troubles kept Tyson out of the ring for the rest of the year. He successfully defended his title twice in 1989 with convincing wins over Carl "the Truth" Williams in 90 seconds and a fifth-round stoppage of the courageous Brit Frank Bruno. Tyson's promoter Don King then avoided Evander Holyfield and instead looked for an opponent that looked good on paper but that would not provide a true threat to the champion's title. After all, King had the king of all possessions in boxing—the undisputed heavyweight champion.

Eventually, King selected a talented but inconsistent performer named James "Buster" Douglas, who sported a record of 28–4–1. Douglas had quit in his only shot at a world title, losing in the 10th round to Tony Tucker. Douglas also had quit earlier in his career, when he fought a less talented David Bey. However, Douglas was a tall man (6' 4") and a good athlete who had been a star basketball player in high school. He had the ability to defeat future champion Oliver McCall, Randall "Tex" Cobb, and other quality fighters on his resume. But the book on Buster Douglas was that he lacked the fire in his belly that his father—former middleweight contender Billy "Dynamite" Douglas—possessed.

Oddsmakers did not believe that Buster Douglas presented much opposition. The few casinos that even took bets on the February 1990 title defense in Tokyo, Japan, provided staggering 42–1 odds. But Buster Douglas focused like never before, partly energized by the recent deaths of his mother and the mother of his young son.

Buster Douglas shocked the world in February 1990 by doing the impossible—knocking out Mike Tyson. He dominated the fight with his left jab, movement, and combination punching. Tyson had one shining moment near the end of the 8th round, when he caught Douglas with a right upper-cut. However, Douglas rose at the count of nine, further benefiting from a slow count by referee Octavio Meyran. Douglas returned with zeal in the 9th round and pounded the champion. He finished him off in the 10th with a frightening fusillade of blows. The mighty had fallen, though promoter Don King filed a protest based on the referee's long count in the 8th round. The media responded with vitriol, leading King to back off from his challenge. James Douglas was world heavyweight champion.

Shockingly, if Tyson had been able to survive the 10th-round attack and fight reasonably well in the last two rounds, he may have retained his title by split decision. While U.S. judge Larry Rodzadilla accurately scored the bout 88–82 in favor of Douglas, the two Japanese judges were way off base. Ken Morita actually had Tyson ahead by one point—a shockingly egregious scorecard.

PRISON TIME

Tyson returned to the ring four months after the Douglas debacle against a familiar foe—Henry Tillman, the same fighter who had thwarted Tyson's Olympic ambitions. Tillman had a quick jab and decent boxing skills but was no match for Tyson's power. Tyson blasted Tillman out in the first round in their June 1990 bout. Later that year, Tyson began to rebuild his ring mystique with another first-round kayo over Alex Stewart, a contender with a 26–1 record. In 1991, Tyson had two battles with the rugged Donovan "Razor" Ruddock. In their first bout in March, Tyson stopped Ruddock in the seventh round. In their rematch, Tyson won a 12-round unanimous decision.

Tyson did not win another fight for five years because he lost in the court-room. In July 1991, Tyson attended a Miss Black America pageant in India-napolis, Indiana. On July 19, he allegedly raped an 18-year-old contestant, Desiree Washington, though the young woman willingly entered Tyson's hotel room late at night. King hired Washington, D.C., attorney Vincent Fuller to defend Tyson. Fuller had successfully defended King on tax evasion charges but was more well known for obtaining a not-guilty-by-reason-of-insanity defense for John Hinckley Jr., who shot President Ronald Reagan in 1980. Fuller's performance in Tyson's defense was less than stellar, as he played up Tyson's sexual desires and appetite to show that Washington must have known what was expected when she came to his hotel room. Prosecutor

Greg Garrison performed much better before the Indiana jury, which convicted Tyson of rape and sexual assault after nine hours of deliberation. The Marion County, Indiana, system enabled the prosecutor to select the judge. Garrison wisely chose Judge Patricia Gifford, who was a rape prosecutor before ascending to the bench as a judge. Even an Indiana appeals court later affirmed Tyson's conviction and urged that this system be changed to appear fairer to defendants: "The existing system of filing cases is totally inappropriate and must be abandoned in favor of a system in which the prosecutor cannot control the assignment of a case to a particular judge."[20]

Judge Gifford sentenced Tyson to two 10-year sentences that would run concurrently but suspended four years. "Something needs to be done about the attitude you displayed here," Gifford said in sentencing the former champion.[21] This meant Tyson had a six-year sentence that he could shave in half with good behavior in prison. The "Baddest Man on the Planet" became inmate number 922335, and that is where he remained for several years. Much like the boxing world was deprived of Muhammad Ali for more than three years in his prime, the same thing happened with Tyson—albeit for dramatically different reasons.

Tyson consistently maintained that he did not rape Desiree Washington, that it was consensual sex. In a 2009 documentary appropriately entitled *Tyson,* the former champion referred to her as a "wretched swine of a woman." Some commentators publicly questioned whether the sentence and the trial were fair to Tyson. Wallace Matthews said that there was reasonable doubt.[22] Tyson's appellate attorney, Alan Dershowitz, tried mightily to convince the Indiana appeals court to reverse the conviction and gain Tyson a new trial, but he lost by a single vote of 2–1.[23] The dissenting judge wrote: "My review of the entire record in the cause [*sic*] leads me to the inescapable conclusion that he did not receive the requisite fairness which is essential to our system of criminal justice."[24]

Subsequent appeals in state and federal court were not successful. In the Indiana Court of Appeals, Dershowitz lost by a vote of 2–1. In an op-ed, Dershowitz maintained that Tyson was innocent of the rape charges: "Mike Tyson has done his time, even though in his view and mine he never did the crime. Asking him to apologize for a crime he honestly believes he did not commit is wrong. Mike is entitled to maintain his innocence. I'm proud of him for sticking to his principles."[25]

Tyson read voraciously in prison, considered converting to Islam, and avoided major trouble behind bars. Upon his release in 1995, he returned to the ring against Peter McNeeley, the son of former world heavyweight title challenger Tom McNeeley, who had fought Floyd Patterson in the 1950s. McNeeley charged Tyson at the opening bell but simply didn't have the firepower to compete with even this lesser version of Tyson. In his next bout, Tyson faced Buster Mathis Jr., who, like McNeeley, was not as good a boxer as his father, former Joe Frazier opponent Buster Mathis Sr.

Don King managed to land Tyson a title shot against Frank Bruno. In March 1996, Tyson dispatched Bruno in the third round—much like their previous encounter seven years earlier. Later that year, in July, Tyson added the WBA belt by overwhelming Bruce Seldon, who seemingly didn't have the heart to compete in the fight. By some accounts, Mike Tyson was back, capturing two world heavyweight belts.

In November 1996, Tyson finally faced Holyfield in a fight billed as "Finally." Many expected Tyson to dominate the 34-year-old Holyfield, who had looked less than spectacular in recent bouts. In his previous four bouts, Holyfield had lost his title to Michael Moorer (there were reports Holyfield had a heart problem), he won a tough decision over Ray Mercer, lost via stoppage to Riddick Bowe, and looked bad in defeating blown-up cruiserweight Bobby Czyz. But Holyfield had the belief that he could beat Tyson; the Tyson mystique meant nothing to him. Holyfield effectively used his elbows, head, and hands to beat down Tyson over 11 rounds.

THE BITE

The first Tyson–Holyfield encounter led to the infamous rematch and the most widely reported and remembered actions in Mike Tyson's career and life. Tyson actually landed some good body punches in the bout but came undone after a Holyfield head butt opened a cut above his eye. Tyson's detractors believe he simply looked for a way out of the fight. Whatever the motivation, Tyson took a bite—literally—out of Holyfield's ear twice. A piece of Holyfield's ear flew across the ring, while an enraged Holyfield looked to punish Tyson. Mills Lane disqualified Tyson, who went mad in the ring. Tyson later justified his actions because of Holyfield's head butts, which opened cuts on Tyson's forehead. "I got to feed my family," he yelled to the world. Years later, in October 2009, Tyson sincerely apologized to Holyfield in person on the *Oprah Winfrey Show*.[26]

The Nevada Athletic Commission fined Tyson $3 million and revoked his boxing license. It took him a while to regain the right to fight, and he didn't step into the ring until January 1999 against former champion Francois Botha. The "White Buffalo" frustrated Tyson for much of the fight, as evidenced by Tyson trying to break Botha's arm during a clinch. However, Tyson still retained his power, and he felled Botha with a single punch in the fifth round. In his next bout, Tyson pummeled former cruiserweight champion Orlin Norris but then kept punching when Norris was down, turning a sure victory into a no contest. In October 2000, he blasted Andrew Golota, called the "Foul Pole" for his Polish ancestry and penchant for throwing low blows against Riddick Bowe. Tyson stopped Golota in the second round, but the result was later changed to a no contest after Tyson tested positive for marijuana.

Even though his ring decline was obvious even to ardent Tyson supporters, he still had drawing power. Part of the drawing power came from his outrageous public statements. He told a woman interviewer for CNN/SI television: "I normally don't do interviews with women unless I fornicate with them, so you shouldn't be talking any more unless you want to."[27] He later told Rita Crosby of Fox News: "I think I'm capable of evil. . . . I'm a depressant kind of dude."[28]

Despite his radioactivity in certain circles, a seeming bidding war took place for who would host the next Mike Tyson bout. District of Columbia mayor Anthony Williams publicly pressed for the fight to be held in the nation's capital. Instead, the bout took place in Memphis, Tennessee—a place known more for entertaining club shows than worldwide, incredible events. But a regional boxing promotion company named Prize Fight Promotions and the mayor of Memphis, Willie Herenton, helped bring the fight to Memphis at the Pyramid.[29]

In June 2002, Tyson squared off against Lennox Lewis, a 6' 5" former Olympic gold medalist who dominated the heavyweight division in the first decade of the 21st century. The two squared off in Memphis, in a surreal atmosphere. Because officials feared Tyson's bizarre behavior, a line of guards separated the fighters in the ring. The guards had been put in place largely because of Tyson's unruly behavior at an earlier press conference.

The first round showed glimpses of the old, attacking Tyson. He moved forward with a couple of crisp jabs and threw a few devastating hooks. Lewis seemed content to avoid major damage, circling the ring cautiously and countering with an occasional jab. Tyson won the first round on three judges' scorecards. After the first round, the bout proved anticlimactic and disappointing to the largely pro-Tyson crowd of more than 15,000 people at the Pyramid. Lewis utilized his 6' 5" frame and long reach to keep Tyson at bay. He began punishing Tyson heavily in the middle rounds. Lewis, a former Olympic gold medalist, long had been the best heavyweight in the division. He had emerged during Tyson's hiatus from the sport along with his former amateur rival, Riddick Bowe.

Although Lewis and Bowe never met, Lewis did put his stamp on the heavyweight division. He also put the clamps on Mike Tyson, stopping him in the eighth round. It was an absolute beatdown. Tyson showed none of the elusiveness that defined his early career. He showed a solid chin, as he took a litany of hard right hands and countless jabs. But it was an unmistakable mismatch. Dave Anderson wrote for the *New York Times* that Tyson had entered the "Tomb of Doom."[30] "This is my most defining fight," said Lewis after the bout. "I'm the best fighter in the world. I wanted to prove it to the whole planet."[31]

A different Tyson emerged after the bout. He seemed almost timid and childlike, kissing Lewis on the forehead and wiping his sweat. Many in the sporting world reacted with surprise at this behavior. Some speculated that Tyson was being nice for a rematch. Others didn't know what to make of it and just called it "nuts."[32]

For all practical purposes, Tyson's career ended when he lost to Lewis. Boxing observers knew that Tyson at age 35 was a shell of the man who had decimated the division, unified the titles, and became the most talked-about man on the planet. He fought three more times in his professional career. He returned to Memphis in February 2003 against a brawling fighter named Clifford "the Black Rhino" Etienne, a once-promising football star who spent time in prison for armed robbery. Etienne had a crowd-pleasing style and owned victories over Lawrence Clay-Bey, Terrance Lewis, and a few other fringe contenders. But Etienne had fought a draw with previous Tyson victim Francois Botha and had been stopped by Fres Oquendo, who dropped the Black Rhino seven times. In other words, Etienne had a suspect chin and moved forward. That recipe was perfect for Tyson, who could still punch hard—particularly in the early rounds. He kayoed Etienne in the first round in only 49 seconds with a powerful right hand. Tyson admitted he really wasn't prepared to fight and wasn't ready for a rematch with Lennox Lewis.[33] "If I have to fight Lennox Lewis in my next fight there's no way I can continue fighting," a frank Tyson admitted. "I don't want to fight Lewis at this moment."[34]

Many thought that Tyson would land a lucrative rematch with Lewis, but it was not to be. Instead, Tyson still attracted headlines for the wrong reason. In an interview with Greta Van Susteren, Tyson spoke of his alleged victim, Desiree Washington: "I just hate her guts. She put me in that state, where I don't know. I really wish I did now. But now I really do want to rape her."[35] In a documentary for the Fox Sports Net "Beyond the Glory" series, Tyson realized that many perceived him as an animal. "White society thinks I'm an animal. Wild beast out of control. Ready to rape their daughters or hurt them or do something drastic to them," he said.[36] Writer Richard Sandomir nailed the essence of the dichotomy of Tyson and his appeal to the public: "He can prompt sympathy and horror simultaneously."[37]

More bad news followed Tyson, as he filed for bankruptcy in August 2003, even though he reportedly made more than $350 million in his prizefighting career.[38] He allegedly owed more than $13 million to the Internal Revenue Service, $4 million to the Inland Revenue Service (in the United Kingdom), and $2 million to a mortgage company in Las Vegas.[39]

In February 2004, Tyson pleaded guilty to disorderly conduct with regard to a June 2003 scuffle with two men outside the Marriott Hotel in Brooklyn. Under the deal, Tyson would perform community service and undergo counseling but receive no jail time. He read in court: "I was involved in a situation in the lobby of the Marriott Hotel in which I, Mike Tyson, was very disorderly."[40]

Tyson finally returned to the ring in July 2004, against Great Britain's relatively unheralded Danny Williams, who sported a record of 31–3, but most of his victories were over British fighters of little renown. Williams possessed some power, though, as he had dispatched future WBO world title challenger Kali Meehan in the first round. Most pundits expected Tyson to walk through Williams, as he had done to Etienne in his last bout. But the 265-pound Williams had other ideas and told the press before their clash in Louisville, Kentucky, that he would win the bout.

Tyson and Williams staged a thrilling slugfest for nearly four rounds, trading vicious shots. In the first round, Tyson landed a savage uppercut that wobbled Williams. In glimpses, Tyson looked like the old "Iron" Mike Tyson. But he appeared to twist his knee, which affected his power shots greatly. Williams took advantage and waylaid Tyson to the great surprise of the more than 17,000 fans at Freedom Hall in the hometown of Muhammad Ali. Williams called the victory "the greatest feeling in the world and by far my biggest moment in boxing."[41]

Tyson's nadir came in his last fight against journeyman Kevin McBride, a tall (6' 6") fighter from Ireland known as the "Clones Colossus." Even at age 39, Tyson was supposed to destroy the relatively immobile McBride. Instead, McBride used his considerable height and weight (he weighed more than 275 pounds for the bout) to lay on Tyson and tire him out. Tyson quit on his stool after the sixth round. "I don't have the guts to stay in the sport anymore," Tyson said after the abysmal performance. "I most likely won't fight anymore. I won't disrespect the sport by losing to a fighter of this caliber."[42]

Author Bob Mee said it well: "It was a terrible way to go."[43]

CULTURAL REDEMPTION

Tyson never fought again after the embarrassing loss to Kevin McBride. He ended his career on a serious down note, losing three of his four final bouts. But he has never faded completely from the public consciousness. In fact, in recent years, he has made a surprising comeback.

In 2009, a DVD entitled *Tyson* was released to critical acclaim. Critics called it "riveting," "absorbing," and an engaging look at the two sides of Mike Tyson.[44] Famed movie critic Roger Ebert raved about the piece, calling Tyson "surprisingly persuasive."[45] That same year, Tyson graced the cover of the highly anticipated video game Fight Night Round 4 with none other than Muhammad Ali. "I'm honored to be on the cover of Fight Night Round 4 with Ali," Tyson said. "He was a special champ, and I have the highest respect for him as a person and a fighter."[46] Tyson graced the cover by the vote of the public, as fan voting determined which two pugilists would have the honor. It was a fitting testament to Tyson's continuing popularity. He also appeared in the hit movie *Hangover*—an uproarious comedy set in Las Vegas. Tyson would later appear in the sequel as well.

In 2009 Tyson also experienced a tragedy of epic proportions. In May, his four-year-old daughter fell on a treadmill and died. Tyson told Larry King that the event changed his life and forced him to make major changes. "I had to grow up," he said. "I had an incident where I lost my daughter in some family accident at home and it was just time to grow up and wake up."[47]

In May 2011, he appeared on a segment of *Animal Planet*, discussing his famous love of pigeons. The softer side seemingly had conquered the dark side, at least in certain aspects of media coverage.

BOXING ASSESSMENT

For much of his career, "Iron" Mike Tyson captivated the boxing public. He engendered a searing degree of media scrutiny. He transcended the sport that he dominated to become a cultural icon. But he became famous because of his ferocious performances in the ring. He ended that career with a mark of 50–6 with 44 knockouts. Revisionists now insist that Tyson was overrated and could never have competed with Lennox Lewis, Evander Holyfield, and other top heavyweights. Legendary boxing authority and publisher Bert Sugar barely lists Tyson in his list of 100 greatest fighters, pegging him last at number 100.[48] But Tyson fought those fighters when he was already well past his prime. Prison robbed Mike Tyson of his physical prime, though he had already reached and passed his peak condition by that point.

The reality is that, from 1986 to 1990, Mike Tyson was one of the most dominant heavyweight champions in boxing history. He fully earned his moniker the "Baddest Man on the Planet." He became the youngest man in history to win the world title (at age 20), and he unified the division. In one stretch, he won nine straight bouts—eight of them coming against men who held world heavyweight championship belts: Trevor Berbick, James "Bonecrusher" Smith, Tony "TNT" Tucker, Pinklon Thomas, Larry Holmes, Tony Tubbs, Michael Spinks, and Frank Bruno.

Tyson remains the only man in boxing history to stop Larry Holmes—one of boxing's all-time greats.[49] He placed the only loss on Hall of Famer Michael Spinks's career. He was the first man to stop Pinklon Thomas—a gifted fighter in his own right. For all these lofty ring achievements, Tyson earned the ultimate accolade for boxers with his 2011 induction in the Boxing Hall of Fame in Canastota, New York. He earned enshrinement alongside boxing great Julio Cesar Chavez and *Rocky* film superstar Sylvester Stallone.

When Tyson spoke, he mentioned some of the sport's greats, such as Carmen Basilio and Gene Fullmer. But when he began to talk about his old mentor and father figure, Cus D'Amato, he couldn't hold it together. He wiped his eyes and couldn't finish his speech. "Hey guys, I can't even finish this stuff," he said. "Thank you! Thanks!"[50]

Perhaps at that moment, D'Amato would have been just as proud of his former protégé in his vulnerability as he was years ago with his ring invincibility.

Chapter 8

JOURNEYMEN: FORGOTTEN WARRIORS OF THE SWEET SCIENCE

Boxing movies, books, and other media focus their attention on famous champions and forlorn contenders—hungry pugilists at the top of the food chain in the supermarket of boxing. Recent movies in boxing have depicted the lives and careers of champions and top contenders. Consider that *Ali* depicted the life and times of the great Muhammad Ali, including his triumph in the "Rumble in the Jungle" over George Foreman; *Cinderella Man* told the harrowing, heartwarming tale of former heavyweight champion James J. Braddock, who overcame injuries and poverty to revive his career and claim the heavyweight title; and *The Fighter* told about the heartaches and triumphs of welterweight contender and popular slugger "Irish" Micky Ward.

This is not surprising, as cinema and boxing have always had a close, even symbiotic, relationship. Society rewards the talented and often ignores the average and mediocre. Boxing reflects society, as the sport heaps fabulous riches and rewards on the top champions, while the vast majority of fighters struggle for sustenance. The boxers who ply their trade at club shows sometimes get paid as little as $50 or $100 per round. They are fodder for the hungry up-and-comers, the ones groomed by promoters for bigger and better paydays down the line. These opponents are supposed to lose to the prospects. That is how the sport works.

You don't often (with a few rare exceptions) see the lives and times of average, run-of-the-mill fighters depicted on the silver screen. You don't often see them reach up and grab the brass ring. But these fighters are crucial to the lifeblood of boxing. The business of boxing relies on the average fighter of limited or little ability who serves as fodder for rising prospects.

Examine the records of the fighters the next time you watch a bout on television; most of the time, these shows feature fighters with gaudy records. Such records are built at the expense of a veritable number of so-called opponents—also known as journeymen or more pejoratively as tomato cans. "Journeymen earn their monikers because, largely, they are fighters without hometowns," writes boxing author Ted Kluck. "They are the boxers who travel, often without cornermen, to take, and most likely lose, fights on short notice."[1]

Michael Murray, an English heavyweight who compiled a losing record of 16–26 from 1988 to 2001, later wrote an autobiography appropriately entitled *The Journeyman.*[2] He describes journeymen:

> The matchmaker's job is to find a broken and defeated fighter and ensure almost certain victory for the prospect. The men already beaten and broken are called "bodies." The men not yet beaten, but who are believed to be close, are called "journeymen." We are men willing to fight anyone, anywhere, and all we require is money and enough time to put on our shorts and glove-up.[3]

Journeymen regularly travel to opponents' hometowns, where the deck is stacked against them. While they may have poor ledgers, they are essential. Without these sacrificial lambs, boxing could not exist. Prospects need to build their records to gain experience and to land bigger opportunities. Managers often seek out lesser fighters who pose little risk for their valuable commodities. But don't be deceived. Records are often quite deceiving. Many fighters have poor records because they take fights on short notice in other fighters' hometowns. It is not unusual for a boxer to take a fight on ridiculously short notice.

But some journeymen have a good degree of boxing skill and savvy. Take the example of Emanuel Augustus—formerly Emanuel Burton. He sports a less-than-flattering record of 38–34–6. He regularly took fights on short notice and received a litany of bad decisions. But Emanuel Augustus can fight with the best fighters in the world. He has been described as a "fighter of world-class skill with a journeyman's record."[4] "I think I am the only fighter who has had to fight the referee, the judges, the trainers before I fought the opponent," he told another reporter. "But I was blessed, blessed because I at least realized this a long time ago."[5]

Augustus bloodied Floyd Mayweather's nose before finally succumbing in the ninth round in their October 2000 bout. "I gave him hell," Augustus recalled. "And I took that fight on very short notice."[6] He gave Micky Ward absolute hell in a 2001 fight-of-the-year candidate, and he has defeated a laundry list of prospects. For example, he took a fight on two days' notice against Carlos Vilches—a fighter with a 37–1–2 record—and defeated him in the eighth round. In 2004, Augustus outpointed 23–1 prospect Alex Trujillo, even though he was a late-hour substitute. He mocked and taunted Trujillo during the 12-round bout, even placing his hands behind his back. "If people could guess what you are going to do, it's going to make for a boring fight," said Augustus. "I'm an entertainer first, fighter second."[7]

These fighters often provide trainers and managers with a good barometer to see if their young prospect has what it takes to make something of himself in the fight business. If a prospect can beat a fighter like Augustus, he has world-championship potential.

But managers have to be wary of some journeymen, like Augustus, who are much better than their deceiving records. These journeymen are a most interesting breed. They learned through the years that they could earn nice, steady paychecks if they could provide a little—but not too much—competition. In other words, go the distance and lose to the prospect. Some journeymen make names for themselves simply by going the distance and never being knocked out. If a matchmaker selects a durable journeyman, he at least knows that the prospect will get some rounds under his belt.

A classic example is heavyweight Marion Wilson. Though he sports a pathetic record of 12–41–4, he has never been knocked out in his professional career, which spanned from 1989 through 2007. Francois Botha, Jeremy Williams, Tyrell Biggs, and Andrew Golota tried to knock him out—they couldn't. Neither could former world heavyweight champions Ray Mercer, Shannon Briggs, and Oliver McCall. Wilson possesses an iron chin. He was stopped only once in his career, in 1991, on cuts. He has never been knocked down. "Mo Wilson is as reliable as running water—he'll lose an eight or 10-round decision every time out," said Showtime boxing analyst Steve Farhood. "But, if you check out his record closely, he's surprised two or three heavily favored heavyweights."[8]

Wilson the journeyman defeated undefeated, would-be prospect Thomas Williams in 1994 and undefeated prospect Paea Wolfgramm in 1998. He fought a draw with Ray Mercer in 1994. But Wilson is known—above all else—for his incredible ability to take punches without going down. "I believe it has something to do with my background as a basketball player," he told me in 2002. "I played basketball in high school and a little in college. I acquired ability, balance and agility in playing basketball. I learned the importance of footwork and legwork."[9] He also gave the classic journeyman's credo when asked about how long he would fight: "I know that many now look at me as a stepping-stone. But, you better be ready for an all-out war when you step into the ring with Mo Wilson."[10]

Matchmaker Eric Bottjer explains that journeymen have real economic value in the fight game. "Often times, a journeyman will make more money than the prospect facing them, as that's how valuable they are in a 'one-off' situation. And if you can't fight, a journeyman will kick your ass."[11]

Keys to the journeymen playbook are landing many fights, making some money, and staying competitive enough to land more opportunities. Journeymen often employ creative ways to land more fights—including fighting under different names. "Fighting under different names is what we needed to do, to get paid," said Verdell Smith, a clever journeyman boxer from Oklahoma. "A journeyman, that's all you can really be coming up from here [in the Midwest]."[12]

"Opponents and journeymen are very important in boxing and unfortunately, they are going by the wayside," says Tim Lueckenhoff, chairman of the Association of Boxing Commissions and the chief boxing official in the state of Missouri. "Championship-level boxers need to stay busy and the journey boxer has allowed for such. Back in the mid 1990s, there were several boxers from Oklahoma, Indiana, and Nebraska that could compete with championship-level boxers and we used to see them at many fight cards."[13]

"Most of these guys found out that they could make more money losing than winning," Lueckenhoff explained. "They could hold their own in the ring and today when you speak with most of them, it is as if they never had a fight in their life. There is no outward indication that they are suffering from any medical conditions due to their time in the ring. They were good enough to slip punches and do just enough to lose."[14]

No one epitomized slipping punches and doing just enough to lose than the incomparable Reggie Strickland out of Indiana.

REGGIE STRICKLAND

No journeyman—or any fighter in boxing history, for that matter—has ever lost more fights on paper than Reggie Strickland—or Reggie Buse or Reggie Raglin. One reporter aptly referred to him as a "professional loser."[15] Another dubbed him "the king of the journeyman."[16] Strickland earned his dubious distinction because he was known for losing decisions to fighters with prettier records. Plain and simple, Reggie Strickland boxed just enough to lose—though he rarely lost by knockout.

According to BoxRec (boxrec.com; the best source on boxing records around), Reggie Strickland had 363 bouts in a professional career that spanned from 1987 to 2005. His career ledger reads a remarkable 67–263–17. That is 263 career losses. His ultimate opponent status garnered him attention from the late 1990s, as he graced the front page of the *New York Times*,[17] an interview on Bryant Gumbel's *Real Sports* show on HBO, and stories in various nonboxing magazines such as *Gear* and *Men's Fitness*. Matchmaker Eric Bottjer calls Strickland "the most famous" of all journeymen.

Before the adoption of federal legislation that provided greater regulation of boxing, Reggie would fight under different aliases, presumably so he could obtain more paydays. "I never knew whether his real name was Strickland or Raglin for many years," says Jake Hall, former Indiana boxing commissioner.[18] Sure enough, Reggie Strickland sometimes fought as Reggie Strickland, Reggie Raglin, or Reggie Buse. Reggie disagreed with the increased regulation of the sport. "You have all these commissions and politicians that want to put stipulations on boxing," he said. "My thing is, if they've never been in the ring themselves, how can they put a stipulation on it?"[19]

Most commissions require fighters to sit out for 30 days after suffering a technical knockout loss. But active journeymen want more paydays, so they find creative ways to avoid the detection of state officials. Or—like Reggie Strickland—they showed enough skill to avoid major punishment and went the distance.

"I thought Reggie Strickland was a very good fighter who could have done much better," Hall says. "But he made more money taking fights as an opponent, competing hard enough to make the fight somewhat competitive but not trying hard enough to win. I wouldn't say the fights were fixed, but I don't think he tried his best."[20]

"Reggie was one of those guys who could fight with anyone and not get hurt," Lueckenhoff recalls. "He knew his role and that was to put on a show and do just enough to lose. I remember one time in Missouri when Reggie was hit by a low blow and it upset him. He showed that night he could fight and beat anyone that he wanted."[21]

Hall recalls one fight in November 1998, when Reggie faced local product Tim Bryan in Indianapolis for the Indiana State super middleweight championship. Most in attendance expected Bryan, who had a winning record, to outwork Strickland and capture a decision victory. But Bryan apparently had disrespected a close associate of promoter Fred Berns. Strickland entered the ring with a different mindset that night—to punish Bryan, which he did to win the Indiana championship.

Another night that Strickland came to fight was February 17, 1998, at the Music City Mix Factory in Nashville, Tennessee. The Mix Factory—a nightclub—featured a live professional boxing card nearly every Thursday evening for fight fans. Promoted by Jimmy Adams, the cards generally consisted of prospects and former champions squaring off against nondescript opposition. For example, Adams lined up bouts for former world heavyweight boxing champions Greg Page, Tony Tucker, and Oliver McCall—all of whom fought at the Mix Factory.

Adams and matchmaker Jim Westmoreland also brought in younger fighter prospects whom they would build up and establish better records in hopes of bigger paydays down the line. One such prospect was Brent Cooper, a muscular middleweight who entered the ring on February 17 with a record of 16–1. Cooper later parlayed the padded record into a spot on *The Contender*—a television show for would-be contenders, though he lost his first bout on the show. Cooper possessed some decent pop in his punches, but his record was built against a litany of nondescript also-rans. Most of his victories came against fighters who never won a single bout.

For whatever reason, Strickland came to fight that night against Cooper, using his superior boxing skills to outbox the prospect over four rounds. Cooper was aggressive and pressed forward for much of the bout; Strickland showed his typically evasive abilities but also atypically threw many more punches than usual. At the conclusion of the bout, two of the three judges awarded Strickland the split-decision victory.[22] The bout caused a near-riot in the ring, as former world heavyweight champion Greg Page—who was in Cooper's corner—squared off with Terry Hogan, a local fight judge who was working Strickland's corner.

I remember the fight well, as I was one of the two judges who scored the bout for Strickland. The ring became a circus as punches started flying. Fortunately for me—one of the judges—I managed to leave the arena with the local timekeeper—Charles "Give 'Em Hell" Welfel, a colorful character who doubled as a constable in a neighboring county. With his gun in his pocket, the former police officer Welfel led me out of the riotous and dangerous situation, as we ran through a back door and out a fire exit to escape. Welcome to the crazy world of undercard boxing.

But the Bryan and Cooper fights were aberrations. Usually, Strickland would not expend full effort—at least on the offensive end. Often he would slip punches but not aggressively throw countershots. Strickland often would not fight to the best of his ability, seemingly doing enough to go the distance but not win the rounds. "Reggie knew there was more money in losing than winning," Lueckenhoff explains. Strickland even admitted as much to sportswriter George Diaz: "As long as I come out of the fight OK and I'm able to count my money when it's over, I'm fine. I'm ahead of where I was before I got there."[23] A journeyman who loses gets more fight opportunities, as managers for prospects eagerly seek to add another win to their fighter's ledger. Strickland fit the bill perfectly.

Fred Berns, a longtime boxing promoter in Indiana, knows Strickland well. "He couldn't have been a world champion but he could have competed at a very high level had he paid his dues," Berns says of Strickland. "He was a natural with a high skill level, but being a champion had little or no interest to him. It was an income that allowed him to avoid a job."[24]

Strickland ended his career in a fitting note—by losing nine straight decisions. He lost his last bout in October 2005 to Dante Craig by an eight-round decision. Sadly, Strickland suffered an auto accident that effectively ended his boxing career. In May 2005, he fought a 5–0 prospect named Tavoris Cloud. Strickland lost all four rounds but took Cloud the distance for the first time in the young prospect's career. Cloud later became the IBF world light heavyweight champion.

Cloud was not the only former or future world champion that Strickland faced in his professional career. Strickland also squared off against Randall Bailey, a former junior welterweight world champion; Keith Holmes, a former junior middleweight world champion; Lonnie Smith, a former junior welterweight champion; Raul Marquez, a former junior middleweight champion; Cory Spinks, a former welterweight world champion; and Charles Brewer, a former super middleweight world champion.

Often Strickland would face the same fighter multiple times on the Midwestern circuit. He fought Rob Bleakley seven times. Bleakley, who retired in 2001 with a record of 77–37–1, has fond memories of his days on the Midwestern circuit. "Those club shows were great back in the day," he recalls. "All this federal legislation basically killed boxing, it certainly killed the club shows." He explains that, just as major league baseball needs the minor leagues, so does boxing. "It was those club shows that provided training ground for fighters to get better. Plus, we provided a lot of entertainment for the fans."[25] He recalls Strickland as a fun-loving character who understood his role in the sport. "Reggie basically embraced the role of a loser, realizing that he could make some decent paydays and avoid having to have a real job," Bleakley says. "I fought him many, many times." Strickland actually won a six-round decision in their sixth matchup in Kentucky, near Strickland's hometown of Cincinnati. "I won the fight, but it was a hometown decision in his favor," Bleakley says.[26]

Toward the end of his career, Strickland took a few more punches. "Unfortunately, late in his career, he began to cover up and absorb more punches and did not try to win, Lueckenhoff said. "That is why ultimately his boxing career ended."

When his boxing career ended, Strickland stayed in the fight game, serving as a matchmaker for Fred Berns. "Reggie was my matchmaker for the past 12 or so years. He was a little on the laid back side and didn't always stay on top of things until the very last minute, but he was good and knowledgeable. I mean who knew more about boxing or different styles than he?"[27]

Reggie Strickland really could fight. He didn't care about his poor record that garnered him worldwide attention as the legendary journeyman. "You've got to understand that a record doesn't make a fighter," he lectured me in 2001. "Hell, I could make you 30–0 by matching you with the right opponents."[28] Reggie Strickland knew more about boxing than virtually anyone. "If I told you all the things I've seen in this game, you wouldn't believe me," he told me.[29]

BRUCE STRAUSS

Another colorful journeyman was Bruce "the Mouse" Strauss. A middleweight from Omaha, Nebraska, Strauss opened his career on June 1, 1976, with a four-round decision win over Gary Maize in Oklahoma City, Oklahoma. The very next day—on June 2—he stopped a fighter named Tony McMinn in Topeka, Kansas. His promising 2–0 start ended with a loss in his third bout.

In all, Strauss compiled a record of 78–53–6—or something in that ballpark—according to BoxRec. Honestly, there is no way to know for sure his real record, as fighters in the Midwest in those days used various aliases. Strauss says he lost hundreds of fights, but he fought under numerous names. "I won 70 or 80 fights and lost about 260," he told a reporter with *Newsday.* "But under my real name, I only lost about 100 or so. Back then, I got away with a few things that are not allowed now. I actually helped the commissions."[30]

Called the "Prince of Palookas,"[31] Strauss relished his role as a loveable loser. He even bragged about losing fights on different continents around the globe. "If you haven't seen me knocked out," Strauss said. "You're nobody."[32]

Strauss also made a career out of fighting at various weight classes from welterweight to light heavyweight. He allegedly would have hidden weights in his trunks when he needed to fight in the middleweight, super middle-weight, or even light heavyweight divisions. He also made a habit of doing whatever it took to survive at times, including the occasional, well-timed blow below the belt. Once a referee came into his corner and told Strauss that it was not fair that he was landing low blows on his opponent. Strauss retorted: "Well, it ain't fair that he's better than me, neither."[33]

These were the days before the Muhammad Ali Act and the standardization of boxing records. Strauss became something of a legend because of his journeyman status. A movie title *The Mouse* starring John Savage was made in the 1990s.[34]

SIMMIE BLACK

Another legendary journeyman was a fighter named Simmie Black—though he fought as Spider Black, Tommy Tucker, Sammy Jackson, Fred Johnson, and probably a few other names, too. He often appeared on small fight cards in Memphis, Tennessee, on Beale Street. Black was known for losing fights and entertaining crowds. He performed cartwheels in the ring—often after he was knocked down or out. He mocked his opponents, talked to the crowd, and virtually anything else. He took the act of clowning in the ring to an art form. "I got a lot of fans," Black told sportswriter Wallace Matthews. "Because even when I lose, I lose good."[35]

According to BoxRec, Black's career ledger was 35–164–4. He often put on impressive losing streaks. From September 1993 to May 1995, he lost 15 consecutive bouts. But that was not his most dubious losing streak. From September 1987 to October 1989, he lost 21 consecutive bouts.

"He was like a James Brown in the ring," said Memphis boxing promoter Mike Glenn, who regularly held club shows at the New Daisy Theatre on the famous Beale Street in Memphis, Tennessee. "He even looked a little bit like a young James Brown."[36]

But Glenn said that Black was a much better fighter than his record, which is often the case for well-traveled journeymen. "He was a pretty damn good fighter really," Glenn said. "His record was very deceiving. He often coasted because he was more of a showman."[37]

Glenn recalls that Black's favorite move was to fake like he was really hurt and fall down, then spring back up and get in his opponent's face. "He got disqualified in New York when he did that," Glenn recalled. "They didn't appreciate his particular brand of showmanship."[38]

But the fans in Memphis loved Simmie Black, even if he lost, because he entertained them. "Everybody loved Simmie," Glenn says. "He was a true original. I've been around musicians for about 35 years. Simmie had that special type of charisma that made people like him."[39]

GEORGE "SCRAP IRON" JOHNSON

Strickland, Strauss, and, particularly, Black campaigned in lighter weight classes. But all divisions have journeymen or gatekeepers—fighters that prospects must defeat in order to be considered contenders. A classic gatekeeper-style journeyman was George "Scrap Iron" Johnson. Though he stood only 5' 9", the rotund Johnson was not afraid to stand toe-to-toe with the toughest heavyweights of his day. He tangled with Sonny Liston, George Foreman, Joe Frazier, Jerry Quarry, Eddie Machen, Ron Lyle, and Joe Bugner.

Johnson was, in the words of journalist John Allen, "one of the best punch absorbers in the business."[40] He didn't possess the greatest athletic physique in the world. Columnist Jim Murray once quipped that Johnson "regularly visited the Pizza Hut for the family size with everything."[41]

In September 1966, Scrap Iron gave longtime contender Machen a tough-as-nails fight that had the fans at the Olympic Auditorium in Los Angeles roaring with approval.[42] In May 1967, Johnson extended a young Smokin' Joe Frazier the full 10 rounds. In 1969, Scrap Iron tangled with former heavyweight champion Sonny Liston. Johnson moved forward and pressed Liston the entire fight. Liston finally stopped Johnson in the seventh round, hitting him with pulverizing jabs and right-hand bombs. Amazingly, Johnson never went down. Watch the YouTube video of the bout. The ring announcer expresses amazement that Johnson won't go down. But that was the essence of Scrap Iron Johnson. He wouldn't go down.

Sometimes Johnson put a real scare into a legitimate contender. He certainly did that to Jerry Quarry the second time they fought, in May 1970. Johnson lost a close—and unpopular—unanimous decision to Quarry at the Olympic Auditorium. After the bout, "Johnson was virtually unmarked and Quarry had cuts over both eyes which his handlers claimed were from butts."[43] Later that month, Johnson stepped into the ring against undefeated heavyweight George Foreman, a monstrous puncher. Foreman pounded on Johnson but didn't knock him out. The referee stopped the bout in the seventh round because of damage to Johnson's swollen left eye. Dan Hafner of the *Los Angeles Times* reported that "the durable Scrap Iron never seemed in danger of going down."[44]

For his many entertaining ring battles, later in life—long after his fighting days were over—Johnson was inducted into the California Boxing Hall of Fame and received a special recognition award by the World Boxing Hall of Fame.

JOE GRIM

The original journeyman may have been a fellow named Joe Grim, otherwise known as the "Human Punching Bag" for his ability to absorb massive amounts of punishment. One newspaper writer contended that this unique pugilist had nearly 500 bouts in his infamous career. Even world heavyweight champions Bob Fitzsimmons and Jack Johnson could not knock out Joe Grim, who also was billed as the "Iron Man of Philadelphia." They could knock him down, but the resilient Italian American would not stay down. Nat Fleischer, the longtime editor of *The Ring* magazine, recalls that, in his early days as a reporter, he witnessed the courageous Grim taking brutal punches from Fitzsimmons, a former champion in the middleweight, light heavyweight, and heavyweight divisions in their October 1903 encounter. Before the bout began, Grim shouted to the crowd, "I'm Joe Grim. I fear no man on earth."[45] Fleischer noted that Fitzsimmons was one of the "most murderous punchers" in the sport, but he couldn't knock down Joe Grim, who lasted the full six rounds. Grim then stumbled to the ropes and yelled again: "I'm Joe Grim and I fear no man on earth."[46] Fitzsimmons dropped Grim numerous times in the bout, but each time the resilient Italian American rose to his feet.[47] The *Washington Post* reported that Grim hit the canvas 20 times during the bout with Fitzsimmons, but he just wouldn't stay down.[48]

"Grim was the hardest proposition to knock out I ever met," Fitzsimmons reportedly said. "He was the most amazing man, in his own way, I knew. . . . Every time I hit him with what I thought was a knockout blow he either burst into laughter or launched a speech. . . . He was insensitive to physical pain."[49]

Even Jack Johnson—the greatest heavyweight in that era—could not knock out Joe Grim. "I just don't believe that man is made of flesh and blood," Johnson allegedly told his cornermen during his bout with Grim. Instead, Grim took Johnson's best shots, stuck out his tongue at Johnson, and called his opponent a bum.[50]

Other Hall of Fame fighters tried their hand at knocking out Grim. Joe Gans, the great black lightweight champion, utilized his superior boxing and speed to hit Grim numerous times. Gans knocked Grim down repeatedly but couldn't keep him on the canvas.[51]

Grim would fight anybody. He never drew the color line, as he often tangled with black fighters. All-time great Joe "the Barbados Demon" Walcott, Jack Blackburn, and the Dixie Kid—talented African American fighters—fought Grim. They all beat him—Blackburn several times—but they couldn't knock him out. Philadelphian Jack O'Brien, future world light heavyweight champion, and big heavyweight Al Kaufman, who later challenged Jack Johnson for the heavyweight title, also couldn't knock out Joe Grim.

Unfortunately, Grim did not possess much boxing skill. Boxing writer George Siler referred to Grim as "the rankest failure in the business" after Grim took a six-round beating from Hugo Kelly in Chicago in December 1903.[52] Siler became so disgusted at the mismatch at ringside that he declared in his column: "It is hoped, for the good of the sport, that Grim will never again be given the opportunity to illustrate to the Chicago public his ability to take punishment."[53]

Grim became a sideshow attraction of sorts, as promoters would put him on the card simply to see whether a superior fighter could knock him out. Occasionally, Grim would go on the offensive. He put on a good show against Joe Thomas in a July 1906 bout in Philadelphia. A fight report indicated that Grim "put up a rattling good fight . . . and celebrated the end by turning a handspring."[54]

Toward the end of his career, he suffered a couple of knockout losses, but Joe Grim remained defiant to the end. He died at the age of 58 in a mental hospital in Philadelphia. The Associated Press wrote an obituary for the man who rarely won a fight but often put on a show.[55] John J. Daly wrote it best for the *Washington Post:* "There probably has never been another like him. . . . There is no doubt that Joe Grim was the toughest man who ever entered the squared circle."[56]

CONCLUSION

Their names may not end up in the record books. They might not make the boxing Hall of Fame (though Scrap Iron Johnson made one of them). They may not win as many fights as they lose. But journeymen represent the life-blood of the sport. "Boxing could not survive without them," says Bottjer. "The common denominator is that they are real professionals. They know how to protect themselves, know that they are there for the education of younger, more talented fighters."[57]

Chapter 9

DEATH IN THE RING

It is the most awful reality for boxing and its aficionados. It terrifies many pugilists who acknowledge its omnipotent possibility. It worries some medical professionals sitting at ringside who know their skills could be tested in the ultimate way. The awful reality is that some boxers die from injuries suffer in the ring.

"Most of the boxers who died from ring engagements were poorly trained and really had no business in the ring, many of them suffering from physical defects."[1] So wrote the *Washington Post* more than 100 years ago in an article entitled "Fourteen Boxers Die." That list included Jack McKenzie, who died after a taking a fusillade of punches from his opponent Terry Martin in a bout held in Portland, Maine, in September 1906. A right hand from Martin landed on McKenzie's throat and apparently hastened the demise. Six doctors rushed to the ring to save the pugilist's life, to no avail.[2] McKenzie served as a last-minute substitute for Herman Miller in the bout. A day earlier, a fighter from Buffalo named Richard Munson suffered the same fate at the hands of Walter Robinson. The *Chicago Tribune* characterized Robinson as a "colored fighter" who was arrested after the bout.[3]

Fast-forward more than 100 years, and fortunately African American boxers aren't called "colored" by the press and fighters are not arrested if their opponent dies. But the reality is that boxers die every year. Similarly, many boxers enter the ring at less than optimal condition, and some take bouts on very short notice. Through the years, the sport of boxing has passed a series of regulations designed to improve the safety and security of the sport. But deaths still occur. After all, the goal of the sport is to pound your opponent in the head, to knock your opponent unconscious.

Sometimes a fighter takes a severe beating in the ring. Other times the boxer seems to be holding his own and then suffers at the hand of a powerful flurry from his opponent. Consider the plight of Chicago bantamweight Thomas Perry, who battled veteran Sammy Marino of New York for 9 rounds without any significant perceptible damage. In the 10th and final round,

Marino landed numerous blows, dropping Perry to a sitting position on the canvas. The referee stopped the bout, and Perry walked to his dressing room under his own power. However, he lost consciousness in his dressing room and died three days later in a Milwaukee hospital.[4]

LEGAL PROBLEMS FOR THE SURVIVING BOXER

In the early part of the 20th century, opponents of boxers who died in the ring faced significant legal problems. Often they were charged with murder or manslaughter because their opponents died from ring injuries. Sammy Ciminielli of Youngstown, Ohio, was taken to jail in McKeesport, Pennsylvania, after his opponent, Billy Light, died from injuries in their bout.[5] Sometimes nearly everyone associated with the bout was arrested after a boxer died. When Charley "Kid" Hill died from ring injuries suffered after his bout with Jack Gross in Philadelphia, local officials arrested "all of the officials connected with the bout," including the fighters' seconds, the referee, and the owners of the arena where the bout was held.[6] Herman Follins, a featherweight from Newark, New Jersey, faced manslaughter charges after his opponent, Johnny "Kid" Sullivan, died following their encounter in Jersey City in August 1929. What made the tragic event puzzling was that Sullivan actually was winning the bout handily before fatiguing badly in the later rounds.[7]

Even more puzzling was a 1954 bout between Ralph Weiser and Teddy Hall in Klamath Falls, Oregon. Weiser had knocked Hall down in the first round. The referee counted to 10, and Hall should have been counted out, but Weiser protested on behalf of his fallen opponent, because it was obvious that Hall was not hurt and simply didn't know the proper count. Weiser's sportsmanship didn't seem to hurt him for much of the bout, as he built a commanding lead heading into the ninth round. However, Hall rallied with a series of blows that dropped Weiser. "He got to one knee, then pitched forward on his face," wrote the Associated Press.[8] A doctor reported that Weiser had died from a brain hemorrhage.

At the very least, the surviving boxer should have expected to be taken to the local district attorney's office for further questioning. A particularly unlikely event took place in a fight card in Omaha, Nebraska, where two boxers died in different bouts. Sammy Dissalvo died from a body blow delivered by Chuck Patterson, and another fighter, Joe Parizek, suffered a brain concussion after being kayoed by Nebraska football star Louis Dunkak. The local district attorney summoned both winning pugilists for further questioning.[9]

If a black boxer killed a white opponent in the ring, it seemingly always led to criminal charges. A newspaper account reveals that, after German boxer Carl Baldus died after collapsing in the ring against "Larry Hogan, a Negro,"[10] Hogan faced "a technical charge of homicide" and was held for questioning by the local district attorney.[11]

Many times charges would be dropped after it was shown that the surviving boxer had not violated any rules. World lightweight champion Sammy Mandell had to undergo the booking process at a police station in Kansas City, Missouri, in June 1927, after his opponent, Steve Adams, died following their nontitle bout. Mandell stopped Adams in the second round. The champion landed a solid body blow, and, moments later, Adams collapsed to the ring following a clinch. "Spectators were amazed at Adams' collapse," according to a newspaper report.[12] Mandell faced what the *Chicago Daily Tribune* called "technical charges," pending further inquiry. The referee said that Mandell had fought cleanly, and the charges were dropped.[13] Often local district attorneys would question the prevailing boxer and the officials connected with the bout. Usually the district attorney would then determine the death accidental, and no formal legal charges would be filed. Other times, local judges would hold inquests on the death of boxers to determine what would happen next.[14]

Sometimes cases would go to juries, though those juries usually exonerated fighters of the charges. A jury in Wilkesboro, Pennsylvania, of 10 men and 2 women exonerated amateur boxer Joe Ritchie in January 1922, after his opponent, George Bliss, died from their ring encounter.[15] Likewise, a judge in Boston ordered the release of Joseph St. Hilaire after his opponent, Ambrose J. Melanson, died from their ring encounter in the fourth round of their eight-round bout. Hilaire dropped Melanson twice in the fourth round, with Melanson hitting his head on the canvas on the second knockdown. Melanson had taken the fight on short notice but apparently had passed the prefight physical.[16]

Gradually, as the 20th century progressed, the prevailing fighter was not taken into custody. The trend toward not holding boxers whose opponents died picked up in the 1930s. In July 1934, in Alhambra, California, Vic Vidales stopped Jimmy Costello—whose birth name was John Thomas Patrick—in the fourth round. Costello was dropped several times, causing his manager, Al McCoy, the former middleweight champion of the world, to throw in the towel. Unfortunately, McCoy didn't throw in the towel soon enough, as Costello died the next morning. The newspaper reported that "no action is planned against Vidales pending an inquest."[17]

Similarly, criminal charges were not leveled against Young Aduette, who stopped opponent James R. "Cyclone" Sawyer in a lightweight bout in Bath,

Maine, in June 1935. Sawyer apparently entered the ring with indigestion and later died due to heart failure.[18]

Future world lightweight champion Lou Ambers did not face arrest after stopping his opponent, Tony Scarpati, in a New York City bout in March 1936. Ambers dropped Scarpati in the seventh round, causing Scarpati to fracture his head on the canvas. Scarpati had won 19 straight bouts heading into the match with top contender Ambers. The event impacted Ambers, who sent to the Scarpati home several times and visited his opponent in the hospital.[19]

PREFIGHT INJURIES AND CONDITIONS

Many fighters entered the ring with injuries from previous bouts or serious health conditions. Either the fighter failed to disclose these injuries at the prefight physical or the examination was too cursory an exam, a rubber-stamping matter that amounted to little more than a fighter signing a piece of paper. Donald "Tiger" Huff, a featherweight, died in November 1928 after taking "a severe beating" at the hands of Chuck Mangin. The *New York Times* reported: "It is understood that Huff had been suffering from heart trouble."[20]

Nat Hines, a light heavyweight boxer, died from brain injuries after a March 1946 bout against Billy Eck in Philadelphia. The Pennsylvania Athletic Commission stated that a brain operation revealed that Hines had suffered brain damage from a bout two weeks earlier. Hines was stopped in that previous bout. The state athletic commissioner, Leon Rains, told the Associated Press: "There was no evidence that Hines was not in good condition before he entered the ring Friday night. He signed a waiver to the effect that he was in good condition and we had no reason to believe otherwise."[21]

Ed Sanders had won the gold medal for the United States in the heavyweight division at the 1952 Olympic Games in Helsinki, Finland. He turned pro but never fought for a world title. Instead, he died from ring injuries in December 1954 in a bout against Willie James. An autopsy showed that he had suffered previous brain trauma, most likely in his two bouts earlier that month against Bert Whitehurst.

CALLS TO BAN BOXING

Detractors of boxing throughout history have pointed to ring deaths as a primary reason to ban the sport. Sometimes a ring death would cause state officials to consider banning the sport in their respective state. This happened in Ohio in March 1929, after Tony Azzera died after losing a six-round decision to Young Sweeney. Azzera showed no ill effects during the bout but collapsed an hour later in his dressing room.[22]

Many of these calls occurred after boxers died on television bouts. In February 1950, Raymond "Lavern" Roach, an ex-Marine from Texas, faced George Small in a nationally televised middleweight bout. The stakes were high for both contenders, as the winner might receive a date against the great Sugar Ray Robinson. Roach boxed well and built a lead heading into the 8th round. Boxing historian Ted Sares recalls that Small landed a desperation left hook that floored Roach. The tide turned dramatically, as Small battered Roach in the 9th and 10th rounds until the referee stopped the contest. "As Lavern lay glassy eyed on the blood-spattered canvas, he motioned that he was ok, but he was anything but," writes Sares. "All of a sudden, he went slack eyed and unconscious."[23] The Roach–Small bout took place at St. Nicholas Arena in New York City.

St. Nicholas Arena was the site of another boxing tragedy in December 1950. Percy Bassett and Sonny Boy West, both contenders in the lightweight division, also fought live on television. Bassett stopped West in the seventh round. West fell unconscious in the ring, and a two-and-a-half-hour operation could not save his life.[24]

Boxing took another public blow when amateur boxing champion Charlie Mohr died from injuries suffered in a college boxing bout against Stu Bartell. In 1959, Mohr went undefeated during the collegiate boxing season and won the National Collegiate Athletic Association (NCAA) championship. A lanky southpaw, Mohr possessed serious boxing skills. Mohr wanted to be a priest for most of his life and regularly prayed for his opponents before he entered the ring.[25] In April 1960, he faced Bartell, a navy veteran, for the NCAA championship. Mohr took a hard punch in the second round, and the referee stopped the bout. Mohr left the ring on his own power but collapsed about 10 minutes later. The tragedy not only felled Mohr but also the sport of college boxing. The talented writer Michael Weinrub notes: "There are still boxing clubs at schools across the country, but there are no scholarships, and the NCAA hasn't held an officially sanctioned championship since the day Charlie Mohr went down."[26]

BENNY PARET

In March 1962, boxing took a serious blow when Cuban welterweight champion Benny "Kid" Paret defended his title against archrival Emile Griffith. In April 1961, Griffith had defeated Paret in the 13th round to take the welterweight title. Six months later, Paret regained his championship when he won a close 15-round decision over Griffith. That led to the fateful third bout between the two rivals. At the weigh-in, Paret had hurled insults at Griffith, calling him a *maricon*—Spanish for faggot.

The third bout was a back-and-forth affair for the excited Madison Square Garden crowd and the NBC televised audience. Paret nearly knocked out Griffith in the 6th round, but Griffith rebounded. In the 12th round, he unleashed a barrage of more than 20 straight punches. The ropes held a defenseless Paret up from the canvas, leading to a fusillade of blows. Paret lay motionless for eight minutes in the ring, while physicians worked on him, to no avail. He was taken to Roosevelt Hospital, where surgeons performed brain surgery, finding two subdural hematomas. The neurosurgeons drilled four burr holes to relieve the pressure and try to save his life.[27]

The fight led to a state investigation and repeated calls to ban boxing. Howard A. Rusk, a medical doctor, explained in the *New York Times:* "Since Paret's injury many persons have called for the elimination of professional boxing. Others have recommended that professional boxers be required to use protective headgear and larger, softer gloves. The later proposal would certainly do much to reduce the cumulative disability among boxers."[28]

Much blame was directed at referee Ruby Goldstein, a former top-flight boxer in the 1920s, who had refereed nearly 40 world championship bouts. Critics said he did not intervene quickly enough—though the New York Commission later absolved him in a letter to Governor Nelson Rockefeller.[29]

Paret clung to life for nine days after the bout, but died at 1:55 A.M. on April 3, 1962. His death had reverberations far beyond New York. California governor Edmund G. "Pat" Brown called for a review of boxing in his state, referring to the sport as "brutalizing" and urging the commission to do everything in its power to limit crippling injuries in the ring.[30] The state legislature later considered various reform measures designed to improve safety for boxers. A bill introduced by Assemblyman Lester A. McMillan would create a medical advisory committee to advise the commission on all medical health issues in the sport and require two physicians at ringside.[31]

In May 1962, a joint New York legislative session convened to hear testimony about the Paret–Griffith bout. The committee convened to determine what happened during the bout that led to Paret's death and whether professional boxing should continue in the state of New York. During the first day of the hearing, referee Goldstein testified for more than an hour.[32] He testified that Paret seemed to be in excellent condition for much of the fight. Goldstein rarely refereed again. He retired shortly after the bout, though he did come back to referee a bout in 1964 between Holly Mims and Luis Rodriguez in Madison Square Garden. "For months I had to take pills to get to sleep," he said in 1967. "Sometimes they don't even work. It is one of those things where you can't come out on top. If I had stopped it sooner, Paret's manager and his followers would have said it should continue."[33]

Griffith had nightmares following the bout. He said there were many nights "with a lot of crying, a lot of screaming."[34]

Paret's handlers also faced tough questions, as they put their fighter in the ring only a few months after he had taken a beating from middleweight champion Gene Fullmer. In fairness, Paret was known as a fighter who had the ability to come back after absorbing punishment. But Fullmer was a full-fledged middleweight, while Paret was a welterweight. The weight difference between the two fighters contributed to the beating.

In November 1962, Nat Fleischer, editor of *The Ring* magazine, testified before the committee. He urged the committee to not outlaw boxing in the state. He testified that more individuals died playing football (32) in 1962 than professional boxing (12).[35]

Fleischer offered several recommendations to state legislators to improve the sport, including using a smaller, more elite group of referees, refusing a license to any boxer who has been retired for more than two years and seeks to return to the ring, supervising fighters' seconds more strictly to ensure they can provide first aid to their fighters, banning a boxer in all states if he is banned in any individual state, and holding regular clinics for referees and judges.[36]

Many in the media jumped on the bandwagon, lambasting the sport. Sportswriter Jim Murray wrote in his column: "Boxing will abolish itself if you separate it and identify it for what it is because even a weed will die without water and the weed of boxing thrives on the water of ignorance."[37]

The Paret tragedy impacted boxing more than many other pugilists' deaths. For one, Benny Paret was a world champion fighting on television in one of the meccas of boxing—Madison Square Garden. He was not a relatively unknown fighter in a remote club show. The last time a fighter had died from a world title bout had been the overmatched Jimmy Doyle, who faced the great Sugar Ray Robinson in 1947 in Cleveland.

Years later, in 2005, a powerful documentary entitled *Ring of Fire* was shown to the world. It featured prominent sportswriters discussing the fateful third bout between Paret and Griffith. Most movingly, it featured Emile Griffith hugging Paret's son.

DAVEY MOORE

Paret's death sent shock waves through the nation. And just one year later, in 1963, another tragedy shook the sport to its core and caused even more scrutiny of the sport by lawmakers and society. "Davey Moore's death sent the boxing world into mourning," wrote *Los Angeles Times* sportswriter John Hall.[38]

Davey Moore, a popular world featherweight champion from Kentucky, died defending his title against Ultimio "Sugar" Ramos in March 1963 at Dodger Stadium in Los Angeles. Dodger Stadium was only a year old at the time. But promoters believed that Moore, known as the "Springfield Rifle," was popular enough to draw a crowd, along with two other championship fights. Ironically, one of those other two championship bouts featured Luis Rodriguez challenging Emile Griffith for the welterweight title.

For his part, Moore had won the title in March 1959, over Hogan "Kid" Bassey. He had defended his title five times successively before facing Ramos. Moore did well in the early rounds, staggering the younger challenger in the second round. It was an even battle through eight rounds, but gradually the younger, stronger challenger took control. In the 10th round, Ramos dropped Moore, who fell down on the ropes, his neck snapping from impact on the lower ring rope. Cyril B. Courville, a neurologist who treated Moore after the bout, said, after watching a tape of the bout: "It was highly unusual. I've never seen anything like it. The films answered what we suspected—that Moore suffered his injury not from punches but from a fall against the ropes."[39]

Moore died, leaving behind a wife and five children. Sugar Ramos repeatedly went to the hospital, saying "*Lo sientro much*" (I'm very sorry). He wasn't the only one sorry, as thousands mourned the death of Davey Moore. Ten thousand people attended the popular champion's funeral at Angelus Funeral Home.

Reaction was swift in condemning professional boxing. Pope John XXIII called professional boxing "barbarous" and "contrary to natural principles."[40] California governor Brown ratcheted up his attack on pro boxing, calling for its abolition. "I have been opposed to professional boxing for this reason since I was a boy selling soda at the prize fights in San Francisco," Brown said. "And it is for this reason that I will strongly support legislation asking the people of California to outlaw professional boxing in the 1964 election."[41] Promoter Aileen Eaton shot back at what she termed Brown's political grandstanding when he was already bashing boxing while Moore still lay in a coma. "This is no time for politics or for politicians to make hay out of something like this. Pat Brown should go to a church and say a prayer for Davey Moore."[42]

The Maryland House of Delegates considered a bill to ban the sport in Maryland.[43] Legislators in Connecticut, Illinois, Oregon, Ohio, and New Jersey considered similar measures.[44] However, the New York legislature voted to continue professional boxing, though it did offer a series of recommendations. These included federal control of the sport and the use of larger boxing gloves. "The weight of evidence accumulated is heavily in favor of the continuance of professional boxing at this time, but with additional safeguards to be applied to the supervision of the sport," said legislative leader Hayward H. Plumadore.[45] New York governor Nelson Rockefeller agreed that boxing should continue, stating: "I always considered boxing a manly art. Look at the death record on the highway and I haven't heard anyone suggest we abandon automobiles."[46] Al Weill, the former manager of Rocky Marciano, challenged suggestions of banning boxing. The feisty manager declared that the blame should fall with incompetent boxing officials who allow fighters in the ring when they have no business being in there.[47]

Popular opinion remained divided on the subject of boxing. A Gallup poll in April 1963, conducted shortly after Moore's death, showed that 41 percent favored the abolition of boxing, while 42 percent favored its continuation.[48] The year before—after Paret's death—the numbers had been 37 percent against boxing and 47 percent in favor of the sport. Columnist Jim Murray referred to boxing as a "Dracula of Sport," where he placed professional boxing on trial as a criminal defendant.[49] Harry Golden wrote that boxing was not a sport, but "our rationalization of the instinct to see blood spilled."[50] He added: "I would joyously join any movement which has for its purpose the abolition of this monstrous 'sport' of blood, death, and corruption."[51] Illinois state senator Paul Simon said: "Boxing is a seamy sport linked with hoodlums. It should be banned."[52] The great songwriter-singer Bob Dylan, at the height of his popularity, wrote the song "Who Killed Davey Moore"—a legendary lyric that still brings chills to listeners and fans.

Perhaps the words of Davey Moore himself should be considered. The night before his fateful bout with Sugar Ramos, he said: "There are a lot of sports that you get crippled and die in. A race driver—he can get killed . . . why don't they stop the 500 auto races."[53]

New York passed a rule requiring all fighters to wear gloves at least eight ounces in weight. Previously, many fights had been waged with only six-ounce gloves. The state also instituted the mandatory eight-count, which allows a referee to give an eight-count to a clearly hurt fighter who has not been knocked down.[54]

However, others pointed out that boxing's television ratings remained high.[55] The early 1960s featured a rising young heavyweight named Cassius Marcellus Clay, who took boxing to another level. But boxing remained under heavy scrutiny. U.S. senator Estes Kefauver (D-Tenn.) conducted extensive hearings into boxing and proposed legislation that would place boxing under federal control. Kefauver felt a duty to investigate after the deaths of Paret and Moore. Much of his impetus also came from the presence of criminal underworld figures in boxing, who served as the real managers of many championship-level fighters, including heavyweight champion Charles "Sonny" Liston.[56]

DEATHS IN THE 1970s AND 1980s

The specter of death always remained on the sweet science. Willie Classen was a journeyman middleweight who plied his trade earnestly enough. In November 1979, Classen entered the ring with a mediocre record of 16–6–2. He had lost his only two bouts in 1979 by knockout to power-punching John LiCicero and future middleweight title contender Tony Sibson. Both LiCicero and Sibson kayoed Classen. After LiCicero stopped him in three rounds, New York officials suspended Classen's license temporarily.

However, Classen traveled to England and took a fight against British middleweight champion Tony Sibson on only two days' notice. The Sibson–Classen fight of October 1979 was particularly brutal. Sibson floored Classen several times, and Classen complained of double vision.[57]

Only one month later, Classen was allowed to step into the ring to face undefeated puncher Wilford Scypion, who was 12–0. Classen lied to New York boxing officials, telling them he had been stopped in his bout against Sibson on cuts. Classen showed great courage, but Scypion was too good, stopping Classen in the 10th and final round at the Felt Forum of Madison Square Garden. Unfortunately, Willie Classen never recovered, dying five days later, on November 28, 1979.

A subsequent investigation revealed that Classen's prefight physical before the Scypion fight was conducted by his personal physician, a clear conflict of interest.[58]

During the bout, Scypion clearly began to impose his greater power and skill over the game Classen. "During the ninth round, fans in the crowd had started yelling for the fight to be stopped," wrote Robert Boyle for *Sports Illustrated*. "Harold Valan, a referee at ringside, called out, 'Lew! Lew! Stop it!' [referee Lew Eskin] Eskin was one of several persons who could have stopped the fight. Either of the doctors could have stopped it, and so could Minuto [Classen's manager and one of his cornermen, Marco Minuto], although he later testified he didn't know that he could. In any event, no one did."[59]

No ambulance was at the boxing event. An Amateur Athletic Union official managed to flag down an ambulance, which transported Classen to the hospital for brain surgery. It did not save his life.

A horrifying irony was that Scypion's trainer for the bout was none other than Emile Griffith, who was forced to relive the Benny Paret tragedy. "It flashed at me too," Griffith said. "But I tried not to think of it."[60]

In June 1980, Sugar Ray Leonard defended his world welterweight title against former lightweight great Roberto "Hands of Stone" Duran in a battle appropriately billed the "Brawl for It All in Montreal." The fight actually featured Bob Arum and Don King, boxing's biggest rival promoters, joining forces to co-promote the mega-bout. History recalls the card as Duran handing Leonard his first professional loss in a close, but unanimous, decision.

On the undercard, Gaetan Hart faced his nemesis, Cleveland Denny, in a lightweight bout. Denny had won the first bout by decision over 10 rounds, while Hart had won the last bout in a 12-round split decision. This time, Hart stopped Denny in the 10th round. Denny died nearly three weeks later.

TITLE FIGHT TRAGEDIES IN THE 1980S

Another tragic death involved popular British boxer Johnny Owen, who challenged bantamweight champion Lupe Pintor for the world title at Grand Olympic Auditorium in Los Angeles. Owen was known as the "Merthyr match-stick man" because he lived in Merthyr Tydfil, Wales, and possessed a very slight build. "Charles Dickens would have loved Johnny Owen," wrote Jim Murray. "He looks as if he has just walked out of 'the Christmas Carol.' Tiny Tim without the crutches."[61] When he was 10 years old, Owen concealed lead in his pants in order to weigh enough to be allowed to box.[62] He entered the ring with a record of 25–1–1. Despite his slight build, he had never tasted the canvas in his professional career. He ran 15 miles a day and dedicated his life to winning a world championship.

The champion, Lupe Pintor, was tough as nails. A Mexican slugger, Pintor had captured the title in June 1979, with a controversial split decision over the legendary Carlos Zarate, a countryman. Owen boxed well in the early going, and the fight was close through 8 rounds. Owen had opened cuts over both of Pintor's eyes. Owen had a badly cut lip as early as the 3rd round. Pintor began to impose his strength, dropping Owen in the 9th round. "I knocked him down in the ninth and they should have stopped the fight," Pintor said years later.[63] Instead, Owen soldiered on, showing great perseverance. Finally, Pintor dropped him twice in the 12th round. Pintor knocked Owen out cold on the second knockdown. Owen did not regain consciousness in the ring and had to be removed by stretcher. Doctors performed emergency brain surgery to remove a blood clot. He showed slight improvement in late September 1980 but never awoke from his coma. He died 45 days later.

In November 1982, popular lightweight champion Ray "Boom Boom" Mancini defended his title against South Korean challenger Duk Koo Kim. The challenger entered the ring with a record of 17–1–1 but had not faced much world-class opposition. Kim fought surprisingly well early in the bout, giving as good as he was taking. But Mancini gradually imposed his will on Kim, who finally succumbed in the 14th round. Doctors tried to revive Kim in the ring but to no avail. Emergency brain surgery was performed. "He's just about dead," said the surgeon who operated on him, Lonnie Hammargren. "There are no signs of any brain function. There are no reflexes, no movement, nothing."[64]

Only a month later, the World Boxing Council (WBC) voted to eliminate 15-round title bouts, shortening them to 12 rounds. The WBC also instituted a standing eight-count to give the referee more discretion to look out for clearly harmed fighters.[65] A spokesman for the organization said the change to 12-round title bouts "will change boxing history because it will prevent boxers from suffering irreparable injuries."[66]

While the move from 15 rounds to 12 rounds seems logical from a safety perspective, it has not eliminated deaths in the ring. In May 1995, challenger Jimmy Garcia succumbed to WBC lightweight champion Gabriel Ruelas in the 11th round. Two weeks later, Garcia died from injuries in the ring.

DEATHS IN THE 21ST CENTURY

Sadly, boxers still die in the ring. In March 2001, light heavyweight Beethavean Scotland died six days after his nationally televised match against George Jones. Scotland moved up in weight to fight Jones, a prospect. Scotland took tremendous punishment during the bout, leaving the ESPN commentators calling for a stop to the bout. The referee, Arthur Mercante Jr., did not stop the contest until 37 seconds were left in the 10-round bout. Scotland died six days later.

In September 2005, former world champion Leavander Johnson died five days after losing his International Boxing Federation world lightweight title to Jesus Chavez. Johnson walked under his own power from the ring but showed signs of significant injury as he was walking to the dressing room. Chavez landed more than 400 blows during the bout, but he showed tremendous heart. Referee Tony Weeks stopped the bout 38 seconds into the 11th round. He fought like a warrior when he was on death's door," weeping promoter Lou DiBella said. He added, "There will be all these people who will come out and say this is the brutality of our sport." "It is, but this was also something where you can't blame people. Nobody blames auto racing when guys die hitting walls driving 200 miles per hour because it's not poor kids who race cars."[67]

In March 2006, Kevin Payne of Evansville, Indiana, died from injuries suffered during an eight-round bout that he won over Ryan Maraldo. In July 2009, heavyweight Francisco Montivais died after losing a four-round bout to Bobby O'Bannon in a bout held in Bay Saint Louis, Mississippi.

SAFETY OF BOXING

The American Medical Association (AMA) called for the abolition of boxing in 1983. Dr. George D. Lundsberg, editor of the *Journal of the American Medical Association,* called on civilized nations to ban boxing as "an obscenity."[68] He added in an editorial: "No caring person could have observed the events in professional prizefighting in the past few months and not have been revolted. No prudent physician could have watched the most recent debacle/ mismatch on Nov. 26, 1982, between Larry Holmes and Randall 'Tex' Cobb and believe that the current boxing control system is functioning."[69]

Numerous medical studies in the early 1980s found evidence of serious brain injuries in boxers. "The only way to prevent brain injuries is to disqualify blows to the head," concluded one study from Great Britain.[70] The British Medical Association also called for a ban on boxing and continues to do so.[71]

Boxing supporters often contend that there are more injuries in other sports. Carl Rowan, the former syndicated columnist, excoriated the AMA for its call to ban boxing, calling it a "class-action joke."[72] He accused the AMA of a double-standard, as the violent sport of football is not banned. Rowan suggested that a reason for the possible disparate treatment of the two sports was "because a different class of kids—college graduates—plays football, and a different class of businessmen profits from football."[73]

Richard N. Weinstein, a prominent ringside physician in New York, notes that other sports have more injuries without any calls for bans. "There are deaths in other sports like football," he told the *New York Times.* "It's the nature of the beast. I see more injuries in football and hockey. Percentage-wise, I see more in cheerleading than boxing."[74] Weinstein also makes the point that there are ways to make more boxing safer, including the presence of qualified ring physicians and emergency ambulance personnel at ringside.

Chapter 10

PRISON BOXERS

March 10, 1979, featured a different sort of live audience for a nationally televised boxing match. There were no celebrities in the front row. Viewers may have noticed that the members in the crowd exhibited similar sartorial choices. In fact, the faces in the crowd had no choice at all, as they were inmates at Rahway State Prison in Rahway, New Jersey. Most were there to cheer on inmate number 57735, better known as James Scott, light heavyweight contender.

GREAT SCOTT

Scott possessed a shaved head, a terrifying scowl, and enough boxing skill to nearly become the first world champion while incarcerated. Many of his opponents admitted they were intimidated of Scott, particularly when they had to fight him inside the prison walls.

That day in March, Scott faced former world light heavyweight challenger Richie Kates in a 10-round bout. Scott, a self-described "relentless brute force," wore down the contender, stopping him in the final round.

Scott became acquainted with the penal system at the age of 13, serving in a juvenile detention center. He grew up in a rough neighborhood in Newark, New Jersey. He later was convicted for armed robbery, earning him his first stint in Rahway. As a young man, he first took an interest in boxing when he was the only inmate to last three rounds with former middleweight contender Rubin "Hurricane" Carter. Scott claimed that an older inmate named Albert Dickens turned his life around by convincing him to focus on boxing. "I was in the prison yard boxing and Dickens came over and showed me how to jab. He then encouraged me to stay in school. He was my teacher and philosopher and changed my entire outlook on life."[1]

Released from prison in 1974, Scott turned professional in Miami, Florida. He won 10 of his first 11 bouts—his only blemish a draw. In his fifth pro bout, he stopped Baby Boy Rolle—a veteran of more than 50 professional bouts. Scott's early performances created a buzz. Trainer Lou Gross said: "He's the best prospect I've seen in all my life, and I saw Joe Louis in his first fight."[2]

However, back in New Jersey, he allegedly violated his parole and was accused of first-degree murder. Scott claimed he merely loaned his car to some friends who then committed an armed robbery.

In May 1978, Scott resumed his professional career behind bars. He stopped Diego Roberson in two rounds. After another victory over a non-descript opponent, he received the opportunity of a lifetime—a fight against number-one contender Eddie Gregory in October 1978. Scott battered Gregory around the ring for 12 rounds, earning a unanimous decision. Despite the lack of top-notch sparring, Scott stayed in shape with a daily regimen of pushups, running, and boxing drills. "As far as being in isolation here, prison is the best thing that happened to me," he told Beth Schenerman of the *New York Times.* "Forced isolation permits no distractions. It gives you a chance to think about what you're doing."[3]

Scott continued his climb up the light heavyweight ladder, with a unanimous-decision win over Jerry Celestine in March 1979—who once fought as an inmate in the New Orleans Parish boxing program. Scott later earned the moniker the "uncrowned champion" after he defeated the tough Alvaro "Yaqui" Lopez over 10 rounds in Rahway in December 1979. Scott moved forward with his powerful left jab, opening several cuts on Lopez's face. Scott proclaimed his status as the number-one contender and the best in the division after this victory. Many in the boxing public clamored for Scott to be given a shot at the title. He had defeated three top-10 contenders in Gregory (later Eddie Mustafa Muhammad), Celestine, and Lopez. But he never received that coveted chance.

Instead, Scott's trek to stardom took a serious hit from lightly regarded Jerry "the Bull" Martin from Philadelphia. A native of Antigua, Martin dropped Scott in the first two rounds and built a big lead with his aggressive style. Scott rallied in the middle rounds but lost a unanimous 10-round decision. He graciously told the press: "I got beat. I just want to say that Jerry Martin was the best fighter today."[4] Boxing experts still regard Martin's victory as a major upset. Martin's promoter, J. Russell Peltz of Philadelphia, told expert boxing scribe Bernard Fernandez in 2011 on the eve of Martin's induction into the Pennsylvania Boxing Hall of Fame: "For Martin to go in there and be the first guy to take that monster down was just an amazing thing. Nobody knew who Martin was outside of Philly."[5]

Martin himself admitted that he was intimidated by Scott. "People thought of him as Superman," Martin said. "Everyone was afraid to fight him. I was, too."[6] Scott's career seemed to be over, as he didn't fight for more than a year. He suffered a more serious defeat in February 1981, when a jury convicted him of the murder of Everett Russ outside a Newark public housing project in 1975. Previously, a jury had found Scott guilty of armed robbery but not the murder charge. Prosecutors had alleged that Scott killed Russ to cover up his robbery of a drug dealer. Represented by famed attorney William Kuntsler, Scott showed little emotion when the verdict was read.[7]

While his appeals were underway, Scott returned to the ring for the first time in 15 months in August 1981, against Lee Royster. Scott showed his characteristic sharp punching and body attack, stopping an overmatched Royster in the seventh round. Now 33 years old, Scott looked to regain his lofty perch in the division by facing the tough Dwight Braxton—another former Rahway inmate.

Braxton—a future world champion as Dwight Muhammad Qawi—had served two and half years of a five-year sentence in Rahway in the 1970s. He showed no fear of Scott and took the fight to his opponent. Braxton won most of the early rounds over Scott, who did show some good boxing skills from the outside. Referee Larry Hazzard scored the bout five rounds to Braxton, four to Scott, and one even. Judges Charles Spina and Frank Burnett saw it 6–3–1 for Braxton.

Scott felt he had won the bout. Afterward, he showed his characteristic sharp wit when polling reporters their opinion of the scoring. When one member of press row said he scored it for Scott, the inmate quipped: "Well, there's one smart guy at least."[8]

Scott never fought another professional bout, retiring with a record of 19–2–1. He served 28 years in prison before his eventual release in 2005.

While Scott may be the most noteworthy example of a prison boxer, since his most high-profile bouts were fought behind bars, he is not alone in boxing history. In 1961, Thomas Dejarnette, serving a life sentence for murder in a West Virginia prison, fought Tunney Hunsaker, a former police chief from Fayetteville, West Virginia. Hunsaker is best known as the fighter against whom Cassius Clay made his professional debut. Hunsaker lost a six-round decision to Clay in 1960. He fared even worse against convicted murderer Dejarnette, who stopped Hunsaker in the eighth and final round in the bout, which was held at the West Virginia State Penitentiary in Moundsville.[9]

Scott was also not the first New Jersey–based inmate to fight with the permission of authorities. In 1927, Timothy J. Murphy introduced a new proposal for keeping the peace and instituting discipline in his prison—allowing inmates to settle minor differences in the boxing ring. "Hereinafter, if any two fellows think they do not like each other, we will send them to the doctor Friday night to be examined," he explained. "The next day, after three or four two-minute rounds, under strict supervision, they will have all of the fight taken out of them."[10]

Many other famed pugilists learned their craft in prison. Unlike James Scott, however, these fighters left prison and made their mark in free society as top boxers. A classic case in point was heavyweight contender Ron Lyle.

RON LYLE

Lyle served seven and half years in a Colorado prison for second-degree murder. One of 19 children born to a religious family, Lyle rebelled as a youngster. He landed in reform school at age 16 and then at age 19 allegedly shot a 21-year-old man. He received a 25- to 30-year sentence.

During his incarceration, Lyle nearly died after being stabbed by another inmate. Once he survived, Lyle's attitude changed and he looked for any positive lights around him. He saw boxing as a potential avenue for improving his life.

He approached Lt. Clifford Mattox, recreation director at the Colorado State Penitentiary and asked for instruction on boxing. Mattox says Lyle was a natural athlete who starred on the prison's basketball, baseball, and football teams. But boxing was his number-one choice. "Right from the start I knew I had something to teach," Mattox said. "I'm no ex-boxer, but a lot of good teachers never fought."[11] Mattox told him: "When you wake up to your potential, what you're capable of doing, it's going to scare you."[12]

Once released from prison, Lyle boxed briefly as an amateur, winning 25 of 29 bouts. Backed by businessman Bill Daniels—former owner of the Utah Stars of the American Basketball Association—Lyle turned professional in 1971. He won his first 19 professional bouts—nearly all of them by knockout. He stopped the durable George "Scrap Iron" Johnson in the third round. In his 20th bout, Lyle faced prospect Jerry Quarry, who outboxed him over 12 rounds. Lyle returned to the ring with a vengeance and continued to pile up victories, including wins over former champion Jimmy Ellis and the tough Oscar Bonavena.

Lyle then lost a decision to the clever Jimmy Young in February 1975, presumably ending his title hopes. However, Lyle received the opportunity of a lifetime when he faced the great Muhammad Ali in May 1975. Lyle won many of the early rounds over the great champion before Ali stopped him in the 11th round. Only four months after facing Ali, Lyle defeated perhaps the hardest puncher in heavyweight history: the powerful Earnie Shavers. Surviving an early knockout, Lyle came back to stop Shavers in the sixth round. Lyle still says that Shaver was the hardest puncher he ever faced. "The ground came up and met me," he says when reflecting on battling "the Acorn."[13] That earned Lyle a date with the powerful George Foreman, who also hoped to earn a return match with Ali. Lyle and Foreman engaged in an epic brawl—

one of the greatest in the history of boxing. Both men hit the canvas multiple times, with Foreman prevailing in the fifth round.

Lyle kept fighting until he suffered a brutal first-round knockout at the hands of vicious puncher Gerry Cooney. Lyle made a brief return to the ring in 1995 in his 50s, winning four bouts against nondescript opposition.

Lyle still fervently insists that boxing in prison saved his life. It gave him a second chance and an opportunity to succeed. He spoke about the impact of boxing on his life in March 2011, as he was inducted into the Colorado Golden Gloves Hall of Fame. "I had to prove my worth," he says. "But I had to prove my worth to me. I believe I have. When they bury me, maybe they'll say, 'He wasn't too bad, after all.'"[14]

For several years, Lyle worked with young boxers at the Red Shield Community Center in Denver. He cherished every moment, hoping that boxing could give the youngsters a second chance or a different outlook on life—just like it had done for him many years earlier. Lyle died at the age of 70 in November 2011. The boxing community expressed great sadness at the passing of this warrior who learned the art of boxing in prison.[15]

SONNY LISTON

Ron Lyle put fear into the heart of many opponents with his scowl and powerful punch. But he was a pussycat compared to Charles "Sonny" Liston, a man who allegedly broke heavy bags with his powerful punches. Liston's glowering at opponents literally sent shivers down men's spines. He often won fights before having to throw a punch, because his opponents were overcome with trepidation—often for good reason.

Similar to Scott and Lyle, Sonny Liston learned to box in prison. Unlike Scott and Lyle, Liston won a world boxing championship. He devastated Floyd Patterson in 1962 to win the world heavyweight title. Many believed Liston to be invincible, a dark destroyer bent on wreaking havoc in and outside the ring.

Born in May 1932 (or earlier) to Tobe and Helen Liston, Liston was the 25th child of his brutal father. Living in the cotton fields of Arkansas, Liston had a hard life. Though Tobe was 5' 5" and Helen 5' 1", Sonny grew to be more than six feet tall with massive hands. He survived frequent beatings from his father.

Liston didn't go to school and receive an education. Years later, when he was questioned by Congress—the Kefauver Commission named after U.S. senator Estes Kefauver—Liston admitted as much. "How much education did you get," Senator Kefauver asked. Liston replied: "I didn't get any."[16] Liston explained to a reporter later: "I never went to school regularly. . . . I never had the opportunity to attend school more than two months in succession. I had to help out around the little plot of ground we grew cotton on. They didn't force kids to go to school in Arkansas, especially colored kids."[17]

Liston later moved to St. Louis, where he worked construction and drifted into crime. At age 16, he participated in robbing a restaurant. He faced arrest at least six times for muggings. Then, at age 18, he was arrested for armed robbery and sentenced to the Missouri State Penitentiary in Jefferson City in June 1950. "We were always looking for trouble," Liston admitted. "Someone says, 'Let's stick up the restaurant' and we did. We never got a chance to count the loot. . . . We just did the job like the stupid, crazy, bad kids we were."[18]

Liston earned a reputation as an inmate to respect. He allegedly whipped three leaders of various white prison gangs for beating black inmates. In prison, Liston earned the nickname "Mr. Big" for his powerful physique, huge hands, and overall toughness.

Liston's life changed forever due to the efforts of Father Adois Stevens, a Catholic chaplain in charge of the prison boxing program. "Sonny was the most perfect-looking specimen of manhood," Stevens recalled. "His hands were so large. Astonishing. Boxing kept him out of trouble."[19] Liston listened intently to Father Stevens's teaching. Liston proved to be a natural and proved to be too strong for his fellow inmates. After 10 prison bouts, Stevens reached out to his friend Bob Burns, a local sportswriter. Burns then told Monroe Harrison, a former sparring partner of Joe Louis, to come down to the prison and take a look at this young fighter that Father Stevens kept touting.

Harrison brought with him a professional heavyweight named Thurman Wilson. Liston sparred four rounds with Wilson. At the end of the fourth round, Wilson yelled out to Harrison to get him out of the ring before this guy killed him.[20] Legend has it that Liston ripped the headgear off Wilson with his powerful punches.

Father Stevens persisted on trying to persuade officials to give Liston an early release. His efforts worked, as Liston was paroled in October 1952—halfway through his original sentence. Frank Mitchell, publisher of the *St. Louis Argus,* and Harrison served as Liston's first managers and helped him line up several amateur bouts. Liston won a local Golden Gloves tournament in St. Louis before moving to the Midwestern championships in Chicago. He beat Ed Saunders, the future Olympic champion, in the finals.

A St. Louis police officer said that without Father Stevens, Sonny Liston would never have become heavyweight champion, but likely would be dead. "If he hadn't gone to the can, he never would have met Father Stevens and if he never met Father Stevens, he never would have learned how to box, and if he hadn't learned how to box, he'd be dead of a bullet in the back."[21]

In September 1953, Liston turned pro by stopping Don Smith in just more than 30 seconds of the first round. Mitchell needed cash to further the career of his heavyweight prospect. He turned to John Vitale, an alleged figure in organized crime and an associate of Frankie Carbo. Vitale gave Liston a job at his concrete manufacturing company as a favor to Mitchell. Vitale really employed Liston as a bill collector.

Meanwhile, Liston won his first seven fights before dropping a decision to the clever Marty Marshall, who managed to break Liston's jaw in the second round. He battered Marshall around the ring in the rematch and later defeated him over 10 rounds a second time. After defeating Marshall a second time in March 1956, Liston ran afoul of law enforcement. He allegedly beat up a police officer who was giving a cab driver a ticket. Liston apparently believed the white police officer was unfairly targeting the black driver and voiced his opposition. Liston claimed that the officer tried to pull his gun on him.

The judicial system believed the police officer, earning Liston a nine-month stay in the city workhouse. He had no professional bouts in 1957, as the Missouri State Athletic Commissioner suspended his boxing license. St. Louis police officers apparently began targeting Liston for roughing up their brother in blue. Liston knew the cops were after him. He told one sportswriter: "If I went into a store and asked for a stick of gum, they'd say it was a stick-up."[22]

In January 1958, Liston resumed his professional career with a second-round knockout of Billy Hunter. In the meantime, Vitale, Carbo, and Joseph "Pep" Barone became Liston's managers, moving Mitchell out of the picture. These organized crime figures believed they had the next heavyweight champion of the world.

Liston gave them optimism as he mowed through stiffer opposition, including veterans Bert Whitehurst and Julio Mederos. That landed him a date in August 1958 against Wayne Bethea—supposedly his toughest test to date. Liston passed the test with flying colors, toppling Bethea in the first round. He broke seven of Bethea's teeth in the process.

Liston paid a steep price for the associations of his management. Several states, most notably New York, refused to grant him a boxing license because of the connection with Blinky Palermo and his ilk. Liston defiantly said he would fight somewhere else and would never fight in New York.[23]

Liston climbed the professional ladder in 1959 with wins over Mike De John and contender Cleveland "Big Cat" Williams in Miami Beach. Williams, a fearsome puncher, was no match for Liston, falling in the third round. Former world heavyweight champion Rocky Marciano touted Liston as the future champ: "His left jab is the best of any fighter I've seen since Louis. . . . He's great, just great."[24]

In 1960, Liston earned the number-one ranking in the heavyweight division after he destroyed Williams in a rematch in the second round and then topped once-beaten Roy Harris in the first round. Harris emphatically said that Liston was a better puncher than Floyd Patterson after tasting Liston's power.

Liston left St. Louis for Philadelphia, partly to remove himself from further situations with the police there and to come closer to his manager of record, Pep Barone. Unfortunately, trouble followed Liston in Pennsylvania, too, as he was charged with impersonating an officer, disorderly conduct, and other charges. A jury later acquitted Liston of the charges.

Liston moved away from Philadelphia to Denver, Colorado. In the Mile-High City, he met Father Edward Murphy, a local Jesuit priest, who became a spiritual mentor to the heavyweight contender. Murphy persistently defended Liston to the press, saying "this man has overcome more obstacles and difficulties than 90 percent of us ever would be able to conquer."[25]

In the ring, Liston kept winning, dispatching the talented Zora Folley in three rounds and the tough Eddie Machen over 12 rounds. In December 1960, Liston faced a potentially much tougher foe in the United States Senate Subcommittee on Antitrust and Monopoly, which was investigating the influence of the mob in the fight game. Liston answered questions with his characteristically blunt replies. He told the Senate that the cure for the fight game was a new heavyweight champion like Joe Louis, who would fight all comers, and not someone who would "just sit on the title." Liston's testimony apparently impressed Republican senator Everett Dirksen, who said Liston was "short on words but long on clout."[26] Blinky Palermo also appeared before the subcommittee but invoked his Fifth Amendment privilege against self-incrimination when asked about his connections with different boxers.

Floyd Patterson and his manager, Cus D'Amato, the future manager of Mike Tyson, avoided Liston for as long as they could. Finally, the inevitable happened in September 1962 at Comiskey Park in Chicago. Patterson, a former Olympic middleweight champion, was youngest man to ever win the heavyweight championship. He also was the first heavyweight fighter to regain the championship, as he defeated Ingemar Johannson in a rematch to regain his title.

But many boxing experts believed that the former inmate Liston was simply too strong for Patterson. Others worried that Liston was not the proper person to hold sport's most prestigious crown. President John F. Kennedy reportedly implored Patterson to retain his title and keep it out of the hands of Liston. The civil rights organization, the National Association for the Advancement of Colored People, urged Patterson to not defend his title against Liston, who would make a bad role model for African Americans.

Liston accepted the fact that he was the bad guy. He famously said: "I'm the bad guy. Okay, peoples want to think that, let them. Only—bad guys are supposed to lose. I change that. I win."[27]

The crowd lustily booed Liston as he entered the ring. They sounded like a "convention of foghorn blowers."[28] At the opening bell, Patterson rushed forward and threw a quick left hook. Liston then landed his powerful left jab and began to pound Patterson with wide body shots. Liston then landed a devastating left hook that felled the champion. Patterson struggled to his feet seemingly at the count of 9, but the referee had counted to 10. The fight lasted only 125 seconds.

Liston told the press he hoped they would give him a chance. "I want to prove to the public that I can be a good and decent champion," he said.[29] But some in the press mocked his former inmate status. Larry Merchant, then a writer for the *Philadelphia Daily News,* wrote that when they give Liston a parade, they should use shredded arrest warrants as confetti.[30]

Liston eventually left Philadelphia for good for Denver in early 1963, famously stating: "I'd rather be a lamppost in Denver than Mayor of Philadelphia."[31]

The next year, Liston gave Patterson a rematch. The result was a near-mirror of the first bout. Liston simply had too much power for Patterson, who lasted only four seconds longer than the first fight. Liston had defended his title with a first-round knockout. He had convinced the public of his invincibility.

Liston did not defend his title for seven months. His opponent was another former Olympic gold medalist—a loud-mouthed braggart named Cassius Marcellus Clay. The man who would become known as Muhammad Ali stalked Liston around the country, derisively calling him the "Big Ugly Bear." Boxing experts believed that Liston would destroy Clay, who had struggled mightily against the English fighter Henry Cooper. If Henry Cooper's left hook nearly kayoed Clay, how could he survive the left hook of Liston?

Liston entered the ring as the overwhelming favorite. But Clay's superior speed proved the decisive factor. The aging Liston simply couldn't handle the superior speed. At the end of the fourth round, an agitated Clay wanted to quit in his corner because of a horrible burning sensation in his eyes. Clay's trainer, Angelo Dundee, surmised that some substance on Liston had gotten in his fighter's eyes. He pushed his young pupil out into the ring and told him to stay away from Liston. Clay managed to survive the fifth round. At the end of the sixth, Liston claimed that his shoulder was injured and he couldn't lift his arm up anymore. The world now had to deal with the emergence of

Muhammad Ali, who exclaimed "I shook up the world" to the press that had disrespected and underestimated him.

Amazingly, the fight was a draw through six rounds, as one judge had Liston ahead 58 to 56, another judge had Clay ahead 59 to 56, while referee Barney Felix had it even at 57 to 57. A doctor examining Liston after the bout said that he had suffered an injury to his bicep tendon muscle of his left shoulder.

Liston trained diligently for the rematch, originally scheduled for November 1964. Unfortunately, Ali suffered a hernia that forced the postponement of the bout. The two then fought on May 25, 1965, in Lewiston, Maine— virtually the only place that would hold the bout. Ali was mired in controversy as a member of the Black Muslims. The second bout ended controversially in the first round, as Ali landed a short right hand that sometimes is called the phantom punch. Many people believed that Liston had taken a dive and yelled cries of "Fix." Boxing expert Nigel Collins, in his book *Boxing Babylon,* writes that a "careful examination of the films indicates, Liston had been hit, though certainly not hard enough to cause a one-punch knockout."[32] Collins recounts the theory that Liston had been threatened by Black Muslims who said that if won the title from Clay, he would be killed.[33] It remains a mystery to this day.

Liston never really recovered from those two bouts with Cassius Clay and Muhammad Ali. Liston took a year off and returned to the ring in 1966 overseas. Over the next several years, Liston won 14 straight bouts, including an impressive win over contender Henry Clark. There was talk of Liston facing Joe Frazier and other top fighters. In 1969, Liston faced a young contender named Leotis Martin. Liston dominated the bout with his still-potent left jab. However, Martin knocked him out flush with a powerful right hand in the ninth round.

Liston returned to the ring a year later and stopped the courageous Chuck Wepner in the fifth round. Unfortunately, Liston never fought again. His wife Geraldine found him dead in their Las Vegas home in late December 1970. Authorities ruled the death a drug overdose, but to this day many believe that Liston was the victim of foul play. Collins accurately writes that Liston "carried countless secrets to his grave."[34]

BOBBY LEE HUNTER

Scott, Lyle, and Liston are just three of the more colorful, better known fighters who learned to box in prison. Other fighters honed their craft behind bars as well. One of the more fascinating human-interest stories involved a young amateur boxer from South Carolina named Bobby Lee Hunter. This flyweight nearly made the 1972 U.S. Olympic boxing team—while incarcerated in prison.

Hunter grew up poor in Charleston, South Carolina. As a youngster, he learned to fight with his fists. He lived with his grandmother and became adept at learning to survive—and fight. In 1967, he got into a fight with an older man. "The man swung and hit me," Hunter told Will Grimsley. "I got mad and pulled a knife."[35] The man died, leading to a manslaughter conviction for Hunter and a 16-year prison term.

Behind bars, Hunter found a prison boxing program. It gave him an outlet for his aggression and his natural talent. He became the best flyweight boxer in the state prison program. This enabled him to fight on the traveling prison team. He kept winning and earned a shot at the Amateur Athletic Union (AAU) championship in 1970. He lost that year but then won the AAU title the next year in New Orleans.

When he traveled to national competitions, Hunter had to be accompanied by a prison guard named Ray Satterfield. In New Orleans, Hunter had to sleep on papers in a New Orleans jail every night.[36] "When Bobby Lee fought, Satterfield was always at ringside, Grimsley reported. A prison official said that the two were "like father and son."[37]

Hunter and Satterfield traveled to the 1971 Pan American Games in Cali, Colombia. Hunter became an international star. He lost a disputed decision in the semifinals and earned a bronze medal. "I am a different person now than I was when I went to prison," Hunter said in an interview. "There was a time when I thought I'd never have a chance in this world."[38]

Hunter continued to have international success in amateur boxing in 1972. In February, he defeated British boxer Paw Cowdell to help the U.S. team defeat the British 6–4 in an international, head-to-head matchup.[39] Later that month, Hunter traveled with a U.S. team to the Soviet Union, where he defeated Russian boxer Eduard Dubovski, as the U.S. split with its superpower rival 3–3.[40] Hunter's performances caught the eye of international boxing officials. A German official expressed his opposition to Hunter's participation in the upcoming Olympic Games in Munich, West Germany. Willi Daume, an Olympic organizer in Germany, said that Hunter did not represent the ideals of an Olympic athlete.[41] However, some U.S. politicians—including Democratic U.S. senators Edward Kennedy and Ernest Hollings—formally asked that Olympic officials give Hunter the opportunity to compete if he made the U.S. team. "All the talking today is about prison reform and rehabilitation of inmates," Hollings said. "Here is a young man who proves every day that he takes rehabilitation seriously."[42]

Hunter nearly made the 1972 Olympic team, which would have earned him a trip to Munich. However, he lost a decision at the Olympic trials before a hostile crowd in Fort Worth, Texas, who cheered mightily for his opponent, Tim Dement, a much taller fighter from nearby Louisiana.[43] Hunter's coach, Red Johnson, was heartbroken. "I lost the fight, not Bobby. I overtrained him. Three years of preparation and I blew it."[44]

The 21-year-old Hunter had to return to prison in South Carolina and serve several more years. He obtained his release in 1974, after serving six years. Hunter turned professional later that year and won his first six bouts. However, he dropped a few fights and then ran into some legal trouble in 1977. He fought professionally again a few years later but could not recapture the magic of his amateur days. Still, a prison boxing program gave Hunter international fame, however fleeting.

VALUE OF PRISON BOXING PROGRAMS

The story of Bobby Lee Hunter shows the value of prison boxing programs. Another person who benefited from a prison boxing program later—unlike Hunter—went on to achieve incredible professional success. When one thinks of the term *executioner* and prisons, one naturally thinks of the death penalty and whether it constitutes cruel and unusual punishment. But in boxing parlance, "the Executioner" refers to Bernard Hopkins—the longtime middleweight kingpin who made history in 2011, when he won the world light heavyweight championship at age 46 to become the oldest world champion in boxing.

Hopkins rediscovered boxing in prison, when he served nearly five years in Graterford Prison in Pennsylvania for armed robbery. Hopkins had boxing as a young teen in the amateurs but soon delved deeply into criminal activity. Fortunately, Graterford Prison had a boxing program. "If they didn't have that program, then you wouldn't be talking to Bernard Hopkins right now," Hopkins said. "I ran into the best trainers, the best boxers. It wasn't easy."[45] When Pennsylvania eliminated boxing in the 1990s, Hopkins was not happy.

DECLINE OF PRISON BOXING PROGRAMS

Sadly, the chance for an inmate to rehabilitate himself or herself through a prison boxing program has declined, as more and more state departments of corrections have eliminated boxing programs either for fear of liability or as part of a new get-tough, no-frills-for-prisoners mentality. Montana eliminated its boxing program in 2004, and several other states—including New York and Connecticut—had eliminated their programs in the 1990s.[46] "Organized boxing is virtually non-existent in U.S. prisons, a startling decline for the sport that has produced more post-prison success stories than any other," Michael Dobie reported for *Newsday* in 2004.[47]

Prison boxing programs give inmates an outlet for their aggression. Louisiana had an excellent boxing program that gave many young people a chance to turn their lives around. Sheriff Charles Foti told the Associated Press in 1975 that he had never seen a better rehabilitation tool than the prison boxing program. "They've become better inmates, better men," he explained. "They're more receptive to other rehabilitation programs. Several of them have started working on getting high school diplomas. They've started believing they can win in life."[48]

One seemingly great success story was heavyweight boxer Clifford Etienne. In 1997, Clifford Etienne was a high school football star who had the chance to play college football. Sadly, he made a poor choice and participated in an armed robbery. It led him to a 40-year prison sentence and 10 years behind bars in Louisiana prisons. However, he participated in the state's prison boxing program and became the prison heavyweight champion. He showed great promise and upon his early release embarked on a professional boxing career.

Called "the Black Rhino," Etienne won his first 19 professional bouts. He upset Lawrence Clay-Bey and future world champion Lamon Brewster in action-packed bouts. Many believed Etienne might become a top contender. He certainly made for exciting bouts with his aggressive, swarming style. However, Etienne possessed a suspect chin that was exposed by Fres Oquendo, who knocked him down seven times and stopped him. He won several fights over suspect opposition before landing a bout against Francois "the White Buffalo" Botha. The two fought a highly competitive, 10-round draw.

Then, in 2003, Etienne hit a financial jackpot when he was selected as Mike Tyson's opponent. Tyson destroyed Etienne in the first round. At that time, many believed that Etienne was a great success story. One reporter wrote that Etienne had "already won his biggest fight" by coming out of prison as a "changed man."[49]

That proved to be an overly optimistic assessment, as in August 2005, Etienne robbed a check-cashing business and carjacked a woman with two kids. He pled not guilty by reason of insanity. His wife testified that he was not the same after the punches he took from the Fres Oquendo bout in 2001.[50] Etienne received a 150-year prison sentence.

To this day, prison boxing remains strong in Louisiana. The Louisiana Institutional Boxing Association holds matches for inmates and gives these men a chance to better themselves. Angola—a very tough prison—still maintains an amateur boxing program for inmates.

Frank McMains photographed the Angola boxing program in 2010 and found the experience exhilarating. "So, if you remove the fact that it is boxing from the equation then I think that an approach to incarceration that does something other than let people rot away in a cell is a good thing," said Mc-Mains. "Boxing is a commitment to rehabilitation."[51]

Without prison boxing, there would never have been a Sonny Liston, a Bernard Hopkins, or any number of great world champions. Prison boxing programs provide inmates with an outlet for aggression and something to look forward to in an otherwise bleak existence. Prison officials should consider reimplementing or starting boxing programs. It might just turn lives around in a positive direction.

Chapter 11

THE FUTURE OF BOXING AND THE THREAT OF MIXED MARTIAL ARTS

This book features the subtitle "An Autopsy"—a serious choice of diction for those who love the "Sweet Science." Aficionados of boxing sometimes wonder whether the sport is healthy, on life support, or virtually dead on arrival.

DECLINING COVERAGE

In earlier parts of the 20th century, boxing was one of the three most popular sports in the United States—along with baseball and horse racing. Many sportswriters had a double beat, covering boxing and horse racing. In those days, boxing ruled the radio airwaves and the television sets. People listened to fight broadcasts or watched fights on television with some regularity. Today, boxing is largely dominated by pay-per-view and cable channels. In earlier times, people cared who won the local club fight. Now, the club show is dead in many states. In earlier times, local fighters were well-known sports figures. Now, boxers struggle to receive consistent media coverage—other than from some excellent online reporting.

Boxing is no longer one of the leading sports in the United States. Professional and college football, college basketball, professional baseball, and many others sports receive more coverage. Many major news outlets do not have a scribe for the boxing beat. Some newspapers avoid boxing like it is the plague.

"On a world level I think the sport is doing okay but in the United States I think the sport has lost some popularity with the masses," says Mike Fitzgerald, a boxing historian and world class boxing judge. "When I got hooked on the sport in the '80s, boxing was televised on network television and the networks did a terrific job of building their fighters. I remember following great boxers like Larry Holmes, Aaron Pryor, Alexis Arguello, and Ray "Boom Boom" Mancini."[1]

A related problem is the almost complete lack of coverage and respect given to amateur boxing. Olympic boxing used to be one of the most highly anticipated sports of the great athletic contest. Cassius Clay won Olympic gold in the 1960 Rome Olympics, Joe Frazier won in the 1964 Tokyo Games, and George Foreman in the 1968 Mexico City Games. People knew boxers' names when they made their professional debuts and followed their careers. The same thing happened with the vaunted 1976 Olympic class of Leon and Michael Spinks, Leo Randolph, Howard Davis Jr., and the great Sugar Ray Leonard. "Coverage from the Olympics for boxing has all but evaporated," Fitzgerald explains. "I started following Sugar Ray Leonard, Oscar De La Hoya [in 1992], and the all-star class of 1984 in the Olympics. For the most recent Olympic Games, I didn't see one live fight on television or advertised, and I'm only vaguely familiar with the names of some of the most recent Olympians."[2]

But, at its best, boxing remains the most entertaining, exhilarating, and engaging sport in the world. No sport can match the adrenaline rush of a major, competitive world championship bout—particularly in the heavyweight division, where the bout can end with a single punch.

Some vital signs are still strong. Boxing in the United States still commands major audiences for select bouts. When current pound-for-pound greats Floyd "Money" Mayweather and Filipino sensation Manny Pacquiao engage in championship fights, the general public takes notice. Home Box Office (HBO) has promoted the two star's bouts with an intriguing show called *24/7* that examines the fighters' training camps and personal lives before the bouts.

For the past several years, Mayweather and Pacquiao have been circling each other but have yet to meet in the ring. Even though each fighter reportedly could command $40 million—making it the highest-grossing fight in boxing history—the fight still has not happened at the time of this writing. Instead of fighting in a boxing ring, the two have engaged in legal battles, with Pacquiao suing Mayweather for defamation, claiming that Mayweather falsely stated that Pacquiao was taking steroids. Speculation abounds that the two may finally get together in May 2012.

A Pacquiao–Mayweather bout needs to happen. Other top fighters need to face the other top fighters. Sometimes rival promoters fail to reach agreement or do not want to risk their fighter losing a title belt or prestige in the boxing world. In 1997, the sport's two top promoters, Don King and Bob Arum, managed to co-promote a bout between the two top welterweights of the day—Felix Trinidad and Oscar De La Hoya. But, as Bernard Fernandez explains, "for every De La Hoya–Trinidad, you can point to a half-dozen other incidents in which the top promoters did not come together because they want to protect their share of the turf."[3]

Boxing needs a compelling heavyweight champion. Consider that boxing history largely revolves around dominant champions. John L. Sullivan, Jack Johnson, Joe Louis, Rocky Marciano, Muhammad Ali, and—yes, Mike Tyson—represent defining, significant eras of boxing history. When Ali and Tyson ruled the heavyweight division, boxing was popular. People may have bought tickets or pay-per-view shows to watch Ali lose or Tyson knock out an opponent, but at least people were talking about the sport. People genuinely cared about boxing.

The current heavyweight division lacks such a forceful American heavyweight. Instead, the talented Ukrainian brothers Vitali and Wladimir Klitschko rule the division with iron fists. They are great fighters, intelligent men, and fine champions, but they don't sell tickets and engage the American public. "Boxing needs a superstar in the United States and some new heavyweights to challenge the Klitschkos," says Harold Lederman, HBO's official ringside scorer, former world-class boxing judge, and one of the genuine good guys in the sport of boxing.[4]

Lederman explains that, as the heavyweight division goes, so goes boxing. "It all depends on who the heavyweight champion is. When Joe Louis was at the top of his game, when Rocky Marciano was at the top his game, when Ali was in his prime, boxing did great. In the last several years the Eastern bloc fighters have dominated the heavyweight division, especially the Klitschkos. They are incredible athletes and great boxers. But they are not the most exciting guys the sport has ever known."[5]

Lederman says that boxing is in good shape, noting the high number of pay-per-view buys at some recent high-profile bouts. "There continues to be a lot of interest in Pacquiao–Mayweather," he says. Many agree that boxing needs that fight to happen.

However, others worry that the sport continues to be beset with numerous problems. Bernard Fernandez, one of the sport's great writers, says that many of the problems have beset the sport for years: "There are too many sanctioning bodies, too many alleged world titles so that people can't identify the real champions."[6]

Fernandez identifies a common complaint about the sport from many people—the dilution of world championships with more weight classes and a dizzying, alphabet-soup array of sanctioning bodies. There are five major sanctioning organizations: the World Boxing Council (WBC), the World Boxing Association (WBA), the International Boxing Federation (IBF), the World Boxing Organization, and the International Boxing Organization. Many people cannot name the champions of the different divisions. Some can't even identify the different divisions. Undisputed champions are a rare, dying breed. Unification bouts are difficult to make, because there are so many different interests—financial and otherwise—that must be accommodated.

While sanctioning bodies are a convenient target, they do provide championship bouts and promote the growth of the sport. Some of the sanctioning bodies do an excellent job of providing training for ring officials, providing education about medical aspects of the sport, and facilitating championship-level fight cards. I can personally attest that Lindsey Tucker and Daryl Peoples of the IBF and Ed Levine of the IBO are excellent ambassadors for the sport and are conscientious in ensuring professionally run world title bouts. Still, the sheer number of champions and belts can dilute the sport and confuse the public.

FEDERAL CONTROL

Some question whether a national commission would solve various problems with the sport. Currently, state commissions regulate the sport of boxing with no overarching federal or national czar to regulate the sport. "I've always said we need a national boxing commission," says former Indiana boxing commissioner Jake Hall. "If you have a national commission, you can assess and deal more effectively with the sanctioning bodies. You could have better control over the ranking of boxers."[7]

Others question whether a national commissioner is the right answer. Tim Lueckenhoff, president of the Association of Boxing Commissions (ABC) and who oversees boxing in the state of Missouri, says that a national commission is not needed, but more federal enforcement of current laws is needed. "I don't think we need a federal commission, but we need a higher authority to dictate the rules of the sport, and in the event one of the commissions or participants in boxing violates those rules, there has to be an agency that will enforce the rules," explains Lueckenhoff. "That is the entire problem right now, the federal law is not being enforced. When the U.S. attorney has been sent complaints of obvious violations, they have either declined prosecution or ignored the complaint."[8]

Calls for federal control for boxing are nothing new. Rep. Ambrose Kennedy of Maryland threatened federal investigation and control over boxing after the widely unpopular decision in the 1939 world featherweight title bout between Joey Archibald and Harry Jeffra. The bout, held in the District of Columbia, led to one of the great outcries that an injustice was done in the scoring of the bout. Archibald received a split-decision victory, but virtually everyone in attendance felt that Jeffra deserved the verdict. "I feel that rank injustice was done to Contestant Jeffra in the Archibald–Jeffra contest," Kennedy said. "When such things as the Archibald–Jeffra decision can happen, no matter how honest the mistake is, and steps cannot be taken to immediately correct such gross errors, there's something wrong with the conduct of the ring sport."[9] The National Boxing Association agreed that boxing needed some federal oversight. However, some members disagreed with one memorable retort: "A Judge Landis [referring to baseball commissioner Kenesaw Mountain Landis] of boxing is a pipe dream."[10] Kennedy's voice was heard loud and clear, as Archibald and Jeffra fought again in May 1940 in Baltimore, Maryland, with Jeffra winning this bout by unanimous decision.

Kennedy also expressed outrage over the virtual monopoly of big-time boxing held by promoter Mike Jacobs in New York City. Kennedy introduced a measure for federal oversight in April 1940, after he saw the heavyweight title mismatch between Joe Louis and Johnny Paycheck. "It appears that it's up to Congress to take action to save a sport that's definitely worth saving," he said.[11]

U.S. senator Estes Kefauver of Tennessee called for a federal commission and investigated boxing vigorously into the 1960s amid reports of mob control of the fight game and other problems. Kefauver said that congressional hearings showed that mob figures wield "monopoly control over most of the major boxing contests."[12] Kefauver's plan was to create a federal commission for three years with power to license all bouts in "interstate matches."[13] A few years later, the Boxing Writers Association of New York urged passage of Kefauver's proposed legislation.[14]

Speculation abounded in the mid-1960s that former heavyweight champion Jack Dempsey might serve as the head or czar of a new federal commission.[15] Others indicated that another former heavyweight champ—Rocky Marciano—would be the likely federal czar. "We are on the threshold of boxing dying or living right here," Marciano told a House committee in 1965. "Boxing has cancer and a good doctor wouldn't kill the patient to cure him."[16] Around this time, nearly half of the public thought the sport should be banned. The four major reasons given for its abolition were: "1. The sport is too brutal, too violent. 2. It's crooked, a racket, it's fixed. 3. References to Clay–Liston fight. 4. The whole idea is morally wrong."[17]

Federal legislation was proposed and cleared the House, but the Senate never voted on it. Other calls for greater federal control continued. In October 1970, Rep. Lester L. Wolff called for a federal investigation of boxing for a sport that was "riddled with inequities."[18]

In 1979, the House Subcommittee on Labor Standards held hearings to determine whether a federal commission was a good idea. Rep. Edward Beard from Rhode Island said that federal control was necessary, including a passport for boxers that would enable officials in one state to identify the status of a fighter from bouts in other states. "In some ways boxing is on its deathbed,"

Beard said. "We have a chance now to do something constructive and set some standards by which it can continue to live."[19] Beard introduced legislation for federal control—a plan that was supported by ring announcer Howard Cosell and former boxers Willie Pep, Tony Zale, Carmen Basilio, and Chuck Davey. Cosell said that Beard's measure would give the federal commission "the clout to deal with the desire of international boxing organizations to dominate the sport."[20] Floyd Patterson, the former two-time heavyweight champion, urged Congress to create a federal commission that would help the "desperately sick sport" of professional boxing.[21] Sportswriter Richard Hoffer bluntly stated: "So without some sort of federal commission to establish procedures for the ranking, matchmaking and safety of fighters, the business remains a chaotic enterprise, with each individual entrepreneur, hardly answerable to the joke governing bodies (the WBC and WBA), making the rules as he goes."[22]

Fresh calls for federal control of the sport ensued after a highly unpopular decision in a title fight between IBF middleweight champion James Toney and challenger Dave Tiberi. Toney earned a highly unpopular split-decision victory that caused William Roth, a U.S. senator from Tiberi's home state of Delaware, to call for federal legislation to control the sport. "For too long, professional boxing has not taken any meaningful steps to get its house in order," Roth said in a statement upon introduction of his bill. "The time has come for something to be done to protect the boxers and the fans."[23] Rep. Bill Richardson from New Mexico introduced a similar bill in the House.

Congress did pass the Professional Boxing Safety Act of 1996 and the Muhammad Ali Boxing Reform Act of 2000. The Professional Boxing Safety Act of 1996 provided for some minimum safety standards that had to be implemented at fight cards in the United States. Each boxer must have a physical examination before fighting that evening, and each boxing event must have in place either an ambulance or other medical personnel available to treat injured boxers. The law also provided that there must be a ringside physician and a minimum level of health insurance to cover fighters injured at the event. The law also provided for a boxer identification card with the fighter's name, photograph, and social security number. This was designed to prevent fighters from fighting under fake names or while they were under suspension in other jurisdictions.

While the measure didn't create a national commission, it at least got the federal government involved with trying to improve the safety of the sport. Dave Anderson of the *New York Times* spoke for many in his column: "So without diligent enforcement, the new Federal law won't mean much. But after all of these years, a Federal law exists that boxing people must obey or face the consequences. Finally!"[24]

The Muhammad Ali Boxing Reform Act of 2000 provided some controls on contracts that boxers may be required to sign to participate in boxing matches. It also required the sanctioning bodies to disclose fees and other requirements to the state commissions. A stated purpose of the law was "to protect the rights and welfare of professional boxers on an interstate basis by preventing certain exploitive, oppressive, and unethical business practices." Ali had testified before Congress in support of the bill.

Congress—including U.S. senators John McCain and Byron Dorgan—attempted to do more by introducing the Professional Boxing Amendments Act of 2002, which would have created a federal commission. Numerous members of the boxing community supported the measure. "A new national boxing law must be written and a national boxing commission established," testified boxing promoter Lou DiBella. Many panelists urged for some regulation of the judging of bouts, citing several bad decisions in recent memory. Others called for greater federal control to require greater uniformity of rules and standards from different states.[25]

To date, there still is no national, federal commission in boxing. State commissions still control much of boxing, though they work more closely together.

Currently, the Association of Boxing Commissioners works hard to improve the sport and establish greater connectivity between the different state commissions. "The ABC ultimately has brought commissions together to share information with one another," says Lueckenhoff. "We have also continued to work on adhering to each other's medical and administrative suspensions on contestants and others involved in the sport. Over the last ten years the ABC has grown by leaps and bounds simply because technology has changed and the ABC has been able to adapt."[26]

Some believe that the federal safety standards may have had an adverse impact on the club shows by making it too expensive for small promoters to put on fight cards. The required health tests, insurance, and other requirements make it prohibitively expensive for some. "They killed boxing and the club shows," says former fighter Rob Bleakley, who fought frequently in the Midwest. "Baseball has the minor leagues. We have lost that in boxing in part because of these federal laws."[27]

Still others wonder whether a national commission would have a major impact on a worldwide, global sport. "Boxing is so dependent on its global market," says Jake Donovan, a boxing writer and former boxing promoter. "A federal commission would be irrelevant beyond U.S. borders."[28]

THE MIXED MARTIAL ARTS THREAT

In some people's eyes, boxing faces a serious threat in terms of its long-term survival from another combat sport: mixed martial arts (MMA). As boxing has suffered some loss of popular appeal, mixed martial arts has escalated in popularity. Dominated by a private organization known as the Ultimate Fighting Championships (UFC), mixed martial artists have replaced boxers in the public consciousness. The UFC has done a better job than major boxing promoters in providing fans with thrilling fight cards. The result is highly competitive cards from top to bottom.

Many boxing experts say that boxing can learn many things from MMA. "One world champion in each weight division fighting the best available contender increases fan interest," says boxing matchmaker Eric Bottjer. "Having one organization run the business—at least at the higher level—makes for a much more profitable business model (at least for the promoters). Reinvesting money into marketing the sport itself would be wise."[29]

In some states, mixed martial arts dominates boxing in terms of events. In the state of Indiana, there were only nine professional boxing cards in the state in 2009, but there were more than 150 mixed martial arts shows. "In my opinion the state of boxing is down," says former Indiana boxing commissioner Jake Hall. "The number of events have been declining for some time."[30]

Others say that mixed martial arts is not a long-term threat to boxing. They point out that the sports have different audiences. "The popularity of MMA has only risen this past decade," long after boxing already started to decline in terms of television coverage, says Bottjer, "Major networks dropped boxing well before the rise of MMA, and the absence of prime-time national TV exposure eventually regulated boxing to a niche sport. MMA also is a niche sport, but as a business, it is controlled at the top level by one entity and therefore has much greater financial success, even though it does not, as a sport, gross as much as boxing overall. Also, the audience is decidedly different: the MMA audience is younger, predominately white and also, compared with boxing, a much higher women-to-men ratio."[31]

Jake Donovan, managing editor of *Boxing Scene,* says that boxing has learned lessons from mixed martial arts. "MMA succeeded by learning from the mistakes of boxing," he explains. "Now, boxing is learning from its own mistakes and learning from MMA."[32] He notes that boxing is appealing to a younger audience and that many promoters are making events more entertaining.

GREAT APPEAL

Boxing may have its share of problems—questionable judging, too many champions, lack of federal control, loss of club shows, too much politics, and others. It may still be a seedy sport in the eyes of some. Jimmy Cannon years ago called it "the red light district of sports." Jack Newfield famously called it his "guilty pleasure" and proceeded to eloquently describe its many woes in his classic piece "The Shame of Boxing."[33] Yes, boxing has its flaws and its fissures.

But it remains the most exciting of sports, the purest of athletic contests. It enthralls, entertains, titillates, and repulses. It provides what boxing analyst Larry Merchant called the "theater of the unexpected." Donovan explains that no sport can match its "sudden endings," and no sport provides "greater drama" than an excellent fight.[34] It is a sport that requires the most rigid discipline, the most exacting demands, and the clearest courage. Anyone who has ever punched the heavy bag, sparred with another human, or tried to hit the speed bag understands its magnetic allure and appeal. It represents the beauty and cruelty of life. It depicts culture at its highest and lowest.

Notes

Introduction

1. Dave Brady, "Fighters' Egos Bruised," *Washington Post*, March 26, 1980, p. D4.

Chapter 1

1. Michael T. Isenberg. *John L. Sullivan and His America.* Urbana: University of Illinois Press, 1988, at p. 77.
2. Ibid. at p. 81.
3. Nat Fleischer. *John L. Sullivan.* New York: G. P. Putnam Son's, 1951, at p. xi.
4. John L. Sullivan. *Reminiscences of a 19th Century Gladiator: The Autobiography of John L. Sullivan.* Frisco, TX: Promethean Press, 2008, at p. 11 (edited by James Bishop).
5. Fleischer at p. 10.
6. Sullivan at p. 13.
7. Fleischer at p. 10.
8. Ibid. at p. 15.
9. Ibid. at p. 16.
10. Sullivan at p. 16.
11. Ibid. at p. 16.
12. Fleischer at p. 20.
13. Sullivan at p. 24.
14. Fleischer at pp. 28–29.
15. Isenberg at pp. 88–89.
16. Fleischer at p. 35.
17. Ibid. at p. 36.
18. "Sullivan Wins the Fight," *New York Times,* February 8, 1882, at p. 2.
19. Ibid.
20. Ibid.
21. Isenberg at pp. 108–9.
22. Quoted in Sullivan at p. 48.
23. Sullivan at p. 57.
24. Quoted in Sullivan at p. 59.
25. "Tug Takes the Stakes," *Washington Post,* July 18, 1882, at p. 1.

26. Sullivan at p. 63.
27. Fleischer at p. 66.
28. Quoted in Fleischer at pp. 67–68.
29. Quoted in Fleischer at p. 69.
30. Sullivan at p. 77.
31. "Knocked Out in Court," *New York Times,* November 16, 1884, at p. 14.
32. "Both Pugilists Arrested," *New York Times,* November 19, 1884, at p. 1.
33. Fleisher at p. 82.
34. Ibid. at p. 88.
35. "Peter Declines with Thanks," *Chicago Daily Tribune,* February 12, 1890, at p. 5.
36. Fleischer at pp. 88, 151.
37. Ibid. at p. 92.
38. "A Day with Sullivan," *Washington Post,* April 5, 1887, at p. 2.
39. Fleischer at p. 102.
40. "After the Great Fight," *Chicago Daily Tribune,* March 12, 1888, at p. 1.
41. Fleischer at p. 117.
42. "Planning for the Fight," *Chicago Daily Tribune,* July 2, 1889, at p. 6.
43. Sullivan at p. 131.
44. Ibid. at p. 135.
45. Ibid. at p. 137.
46. Fleischer at p. 136.
47. "John L. Sullivan for Congress," *Chicago Daily Tribune,* September 8, 1889, at p. 9.
48. Fleischer at p. 139.
49. Ibid. at p. 155.
50. "Jake Kilrain Favors Sullivan," *Chicago Daily Tribune,* August 22, 1892, at p. 7.
51. "Corbett Now Is Champion," *New York Times,* September 8, 1892, at p. 3.
52. Ibid.
53. Fleischer at p. 171.
54. Isenberg at p. 323.
55. "Madden on Sullivan," *Washington Post,* January 17, 1898, at p. 8.
56. "John L. Sullivan Punishes Talk," *Chicago Daily Tribune,* January 17, 1905, at p. 5.
57. "John L. Sullivan Fatally Stricken," *New York Times,* February 3, 1918, at p. 23.
58. Isenberg at p. 384.
59. "The Manly Art," *Chicago Daily Tribune,* October 21, 1883, at p. 21.
60. Fleischer at p. ix.
61. "John L. Sullivan Fatally Stricken," at p. 23.

CHAPTER 2

1. W.E.B. Du Bois. *The Souls of Black Folk.* Chicago: A. C. McClurg, 1903.
2. Cornel West. *Race Matters.* Boston: Beacon Press, 2001.
3. "Bill Richmond," International Boxing Hall of Fame, at http://www.ibhof.com/pages/about/inductees/pioneer/richmond.html

4. Bill Calogero, "Tom Molineaux: From Slave to American Heavyweight Champion," in *The First Black Boxing Champions.* Jefferson, NC: McFarland, 2011 (edited by Colleen Aycock and Mark Scott), 9–21, at p. 9.

5. Ibid. at p. 10.

6. Ibid. at p. 11.

7. Ibid. at p. 11.

8. Ibid. at p. 14.

9. Ibid. at p. 16.

10. Ibid. at p. 16.

11. Ibid. at p. 17.

12. Quoted in Calogero at p. 17.

13. Calogero at p. 21.

14. Monte D. Cox, "George Dixon, Little Chocolate . . . A Fighter Without a Flaw," Cox's Corner Profiles, at http://coxscorner.tripod.com/dixon.html

15. Mike Glenn, "George Dixon: World Bantamweight and Featherweight Champion," in *The First Black Boxing Champions.* Jefferson, NC: McFarland, 2011 (edited by Colleen Aycock and Mark Scott), 48–59, at p. 48.

16. Ibid. at p. 49.

17. Ibid. at p. 51.

18. Ibid. at p. 52.

19. Ibid. at p. 56.

20. Colleen Aycock, "Joes Gans: World Lightweight Champion," in *The First Black Boxing Champions.* Jefferson, NC: McFarland, 2011 (edited by Colleen Aycock and Mark Scott), 79–101, at p. 79.

21. Ibid. at p. 81.

22. Ibid. at p. 87.

23. Ibid. at p. 99.

24. *Plessy v. Ferguson,* 163 U.S. 537 (1896).

25. Ibid. at 552.

26. Ibid. at 559 (J. Harlan, dissenting).

27. Geoffrey C. Ward. *Unforgiveable Blackness: The Rise and Fall of Jack Johnson.* New York: Alfred A. Knopf, 2004, at p. 3.

28. Finis Farr. *Black Champion: The Life and Times of Jack Johnson.* New York: Charles Scribner's Sons, 1964, at p. 7.

29. Quoted in Farr at p. 21.

30. "Looks Black for Jeffries," *Los Angeles Times,* December 4, 1903, at p. 12.

31. "Hart Is Winner in Hard Battle," *Los Angeles Times,* March 29, 1905, at p. 29.

32. Randy Roberts. *Papa Jack: Jack Johnson and the Era of White Hopes.* New York: Free Press, 1983, at p. 37.

33. Arthur Ashe. *Hard Road to Glory: Boxing: The African-American Athlete in Boxing.* New York: Amistad, 1993, at p. 18.

34. Ward at p. 136.

35. Quoted in Thomas R. Hietala. *The Fight of the Century: Jack Johnson, Joe Louis and the Struggle for Racial Equality.* New York: M. E. Sharpe, 2002, at p. 30.

36. "Facts Regarding Jack Johnson's Ring Career," *Washington Post,* February 7, 1909, at p. S4.

37. "Jeffries Refuses $50,000 for Fight with Johnson," *Atlanta Journal Constitution,* January 1, 1909, at p. 4

38. James J. Corbett, "Corbett Makes Known His Stand," *Chicago Daily Tribune,* January 3, 1909, at p. B1.

39. James J. Corbett, "Jeff Is Not Sure He Will Battle," *Chicago Daily Tribune,* May 21, 1909, at p. C1.

40. Ibid.

41. "Jeffries Declines to Meet Jack Johnson," *Atlanta Journal Constitution,* July 13, 1909, at p. 4.

42. Jack Earl of Dublin, "Jack Johnson," *New York Times,* November 3, 1909, at p. 10.

43. Jack Johnson, "Final Statement of Jack Johnson," *Chicago Daily Tribune,* July 4, 1910, at p. 10.

44. Quoted in Hietala at p. 38.

45. John L. Sullivan, "Jack Johnson and Tools Which Brought Him Pugilistic Victory," *Chicago Daily Tribune,* July 5, 1910, at p. 25.

46. Ibid.

47. Quoted in Kent at p. 88.

48. Ward at p. 217.

49. "Racial Clashes Follow Victory of Jack Johnson," *Atlanta Journal Constitution,* July 5, 1910, at p. 1.

50. "Mob Menaced Jack Johnson," *Atlanta Journal Constitution,* July 6, 2010, at p. 2.

51. Quoted in Ward at p. 235–236.

52. Nat Fleischer. *50 Years at Ringside.* New York: Fleet Publishing, 1958, at p. 75.

53. Hietala at p. 44.

54. "Fight-Picture Ban Is Now Widespread," *New York Times,* July 7, 1910, at p. 3.

55. Farr at p. 134.

56. Graeme Kent. *The Great White Hopes: The Quest to Defeat Jack Johnson.* Gloucestershire, UK: Sutton, 2005, at p. 87.

57. James J. Corbett, "Two Big Upsets in Pugilistic World," *Chicago Daily Tribune,* January 1, 1911, at p. C1.

58. Kent at p. 8.

59. Quoted in Kent at p. 233.

60. *Loving v. Virginia,* 388 U.S. 1 (1967).

61. "Place Johnson under Arrest," *Washington Post,* November 8, 1912, at p. 9.

62. "Color Line in Chicago Jail," *Washington Post,* November 10, 1912, at p. S1.

63. "U.S. Jury Finds Johnson Guilty; May Go to Prison," *Chicago Daily Tribune,* May 14, 1913, at p. 1.

64. Ward at p. 346.

65. M. A. Majors, "Jack Johnson Is Crucified for His Race," *Chicago Defender,* July 5, 1913, at p. 1.

66. Fleischer at p. 83.

67. Ibid. at p. 87.

68. Robert Edgren, "Defeated Champ Says Good-By to Jess Willard," *Los Angeles Times,* April 8, 1915, at p. III1.

69. Westbrook Pegler, "Jack Johnson Says He Dove for Willard," *Atlanta Journal Constitution,* 8August 14, 1927, at p. A5.

70. "Jack Johnson Is No. 15,461," *New York Times,* September 21, 1920.

71. Quoted in Ward at p. 448.

72. H. Con. Res. 52 (112th Cong.) (introduced May 24, 2011).

73. Ibid.

74. "Senator McCain and Congressman King Are Reintroducing Legislation to Pardon Boxing Legend Jack Johnson," May 24, 2011, at http://mccain.senate.gov/public/index.cfm?FuseAction=PressOffice.PressReleases&ContentRecord_id=23fc279c-802a-23ad-4939–51f7e4dd0a85

75. Fleischer at p. 84.

76. Ray Pearson, "Negro's Reign May End with Havana Bout," *Chicago Daily Tribune,* April 4, 1915, at p. B4.

CHAPTER 3

1. Joe Louis with Edna and Art Rust Jr. *Joe Louis: My Life.* New York: Harcourt Brace Jovanovich, 1978.

2. Richard Bak. *Joe Louis: The Great Black Hope.* New York: Da Capo Press, 1998 at p. 7.

3. Louis at p. 4.

4. Ibid. at p. 10.

5. Bak at p. 13.

6. Louis at p. 16.

7. Bak at p. 21.

8. Louis at p. 23.

9. Bak at p. 24.

10. Louis at p. 20.

11. Jerry P. Gallagher, "Joe Louis Hailed as Another Jack Johnson," *Los Angeles Times,* December 17, 1934, at p. 9.

12. Louis at p. 25.

13. Bak at p. 30.

14. Ibid. at pp. 33–34.

15. Associated Press, "Joe Louis Is Ring Champion," *Chicago Defender,* April 14, 1934, at p. 16.

16. Quoted in Budd Schulberg. *Budd Schulberg's Ringside: A Treasury of Boxing Reportage.* Chicago: Ivan R. Dee, 2006, at p. 52.

17. Bak at pp. 74–75.

18. Ringside Pete, "Joe Louis Wins Start as Pro Fighter Here," *Chicago Defender,* July 14, 1934, at p. 17.

19. Ibid.

20. "Joe Louis Beats Jack Kranz for Fourth in Row," *Chicago Daily Tribune,* August 14, 1934, at p. 21.

21. Bak at p. 78.

22. Biff Davis, "Baer Sees Joe Louis K.O. Massacre," *Chicago Defender,* December 8, 1934, at p. 17.

23. Gallagher at p. 9.

24. Bill Potts, "Joe Louis Would Knock Out Max Baer, Lasky, Levinsky, Says Lee Ramage," *Los Angeles Times,* December 26, 1934, at p. 7.

25. "Joe Louis K.O.'s Ramage in 2 Rounds," *Chicago Defender,* March 2, 1935, at p. 17.

26. Quoted in Bak at p. 82.

27. Bak at p. 105.

28. Quoted in "'Save Joe Louis For Me,' Says Max Baer," *Chicago Defender,* March 23, 1935, at p. 17.

29. Ibid.

30. "Rise of Joe Louis Is Biggest Sensation in Sport's History," *Chicago Defender,* May 4, 1935, at p. 9.

31. Paul Gallico, "Joe Louis Is Utterly Vicious, Pitiless in Ring, Says Gallico," *Washington Post,* June 20, 1935, at p. 19.

32. Ibid.

33. Randy Roberts. *Joe Louis: Hard Times Man.* New Haven, CT: Yale University Press, 2010, at p. 74.

34. Braven Dyer, "Managers of Joe Louis May Have Overstepped Themselves in Matching Boy with Primo," *Los Angeles Times,* June 23, 1935, at p. 18.

35. Wilfrid Smith, "57,000 See Louis Stop Carnera in 6th," *Chicago Daily Tribune,* June 26, 1935, at p. 1.

36. Ibid.

37. Grantland Rice, "Joe Louis Stops Levinsky in First Round," *Los Angeles Times,* August 8, 1935, at p. A9.

38. "CBS Announcer Calls Joe Louis 'Nigger' in Talk," *Chicago Defender,* August 17, 1935, at p. 2.

39. Associated Press, "Roosevelt Greets Joe Louis," *New York Times,* August 28, 1935, at p. 23.

40. "Dempsey Tabs Baer to Knock Out Joe Louis," *Los Angeles Times,* September 10, 1935, at p. A9.

41. Rice at p. A9.

42. Grantland Rice, "Joe Louis Knocks Out Max Baer in Fourth," *Los Angeles Times,* September 25, 1935, at p. A9.

43. Quoted in Roberts at p. 95.

44. Roberts at p. 97.

45. Associated Press, "Louis Voted Year's Best Athlete," *Washington Post,* December 17, 1935, at p. 22.

46. Quoted in Earl J. Hilligan, "Max Schmeling Is Easy Target, Says Joe Louis," *Atlanta Journal Constitution,* October 17, 1935, at p. 11.

47. Max Schmeling. *Max Schmeling: An Autobiography* (translated and edited by George Von Der Lippe). Chicago: Bonus Books, 1998, at p. 114.

48. Alan Gould, "Joe Louis Expected to Flatten Max Schmeling in Five Rounds," *Atlanta Journal Constitution,* June 14, 1935, at p. 5B.

49. Louis at p. 87.

50. Roberts at p. 119.

51. Bill Henry, "Schmeling Knocks Out Joe Louis," *Los Angeles Times,* June 20, 1936, at p. 1.

52. Roberts at p. 124.

53. Wilfrid Smith, "Schmeling Whips Joe Louis," *Chicago Daily Tribune,* June 20, 1936, at p. 1.

54. Bak at p. 122.

55. Schmeling at p. 140.

56. Bak at p. 131.

57. Quoted in Bak at p. 149.

58. Quoted in Patrick Myler. *Ring of Hate.* New York: Arcade Publishing, 2005, at p. 109.

59. Quoted in Bak at p. 150.

60. Quoted in Myler at p. 117.

61. Louis at p. 127.

62. Quoted in Louis at p. 137.

63. Myler at p. 134.

64. Louis at p. 137.

65. Quoted in Wilfrid Smith, "Tunney Praises Power Behind Joe Louis' Right," *Chicago Daily Tribune,* June 15, 1938, at p. 21.

66. Schmeling at p. 155.

67. Quoted in Bak at p. 171.

68. Louis at p. 143.

69. Schmeling at p. 156.

70. Associated Press, "Joe Louis Wins on Technical K.O. in First," *Washington Post,* January 26, 1939, at p. 18.

71. Damon Runyon, "Joe Louis Knocks Out Roper in First Round," *Washington Post,* April 18, 1939, at p. 17.

72. Frank Young, "Is Joe Louis the Greatest Fighter of All Time?" *Chicago Defender,* March 25, 1939, at p. 13.

73. Joseph Monninger. *Two Ton.* Hanover, NH: Steerforth Press, 2006, at p. 78.

74. Bak at p. 178.

75. Monninger at p. 2.

76. Louis at p. 151.

77. "Joe Louis Aims a Verbal Hook at Mr. Galento," *Chicago Daily Tribune,* January 28, 1939, at p. 15.

78. James P. Dawson, "Louis Knocks Out Galento in 4th after Challenger Drops Him in 3d," *New York Times,* June 29, 1939, at p. 1.

79. Quoted in Bak at p. 179.

80. Monninger at p. 96.

81. Louis at p. 152.

82. Quoted in Bak at p. 181.

83. Jack Cuddy, "Joe Louis Wins; Decision Booed," *Atlanta Journal Constitution,* February 10, 1940, at p. 1.

84. Jack Blackburn, "Tells Why Joe Louis Didn't Kayo Godoy," *Chicago Defender,* February 17, 1940, at p. 1.

85. United Press International, "Would Investigate Bout," *New York Times,* February 19, 1941, at p. 27.

86. Associated Press, "Billy Conn Wins Writers' Award over Joe Louis," *Chicago Daily Tribune,* November 25, 1939, at p. 16.

87. James P. Dawson, "Conn Named No. 1 Boxer of Year; Joe Louis Rated 5th," *New York Times,* December 27, 1940, at p. 24.

88. Quoted in Roberts at p. 194.

89. Quoted in Roberts at p. 195.

90. Roberts at p. 196.

91. Sid Feder, "Joe Louis Stops Conn in 13th to Retain Championship," *Los Angeles Times,* June 19, 1941, at p. 19.

92. Quoted in Roberts at p. 196.

93. Roberts at p. 197.

94. Quoted in Bak at p. 207.

95. Bak at p. 209.

96. Quoted in Bak at p. 231.

97. Louis at p. 203.

98. Fay Young, "Fay Says Walcott Whipped Louis," *Chicago Defender,* December 13, 1947, at p. 11.

99. Wilfrid Smith, "Joe Louis Beats Walcott, Keeps Title," *Chicago Daily Tribune,* December 6, 1947, at p. 21.

100. James P. Dawson, "Joe Louis Rallies to Stop Walcott in the 11th," *New York Times,* June 26, 1948, at p. 1.

101. Russ J. Cowans, "Charles Takes Title; Joe Louis Weeps," *Chicago Defender,* October 7, 1950, at p. 16.

102. Ibid.

103. Louis at p. 223.

104. Schulberg at p. 61.

105. Ted Thackrey Jr., "Boxing Great Joe Louis Dies," *Los Angeles Times,* April 13, 1981, at p. A7.

106. Quoted in Schulberg at p. 62.

Chapter 4

1. Russell Sullivan. *Rocky Marciano: The Rock of His Times.* Urbana: University of Illinois Press, 2005, at p. 12.

2. Ibid. at p. 21.

3. Ibid. at pp. 24–25.

4. Ibid. at p. 34.

5. Quoted in Sullivan at p. 34.

6. James P. Dawson, "Bronx Boxer Placed on Critical List in Hospital after Knockout at Garden," *New York Times,* December 31, 1949, at p. 11.

7. Joseph C. Nichols, "La Starza at 5–6 to Beat Marciano," *New York Times,* March 24, 1950, at p. 32.

8. "Marciano Wins Split Decision over La Starza," *Chicago Daily Tribune,* March 25, 1950, at p. A1.

9. Ibid. at p. 48, quoting Jesse Abramson of the *New York Herald Tribune.*

10. Ibid. at 49.

11. "Layne Rated 8–5 over Rocky Marciano," *Washington Post,* July 1, 1951, at p. C5.

12. James P. Dawson, "Layne is 5–9 Choice to Beat Marciano," *New York Times,* July 12, 1951, at p. 29.

13. James P. Dawson, "Marciano Knocks Out Layne for His 36th Victory in Row," *New York Times,* July 13, 1951, at p. 15.

14. Whitney Martin, "Fight Future Is Bright for Marciano," *Washington Post,* July 14, 1951, at p. 9.

15. Gene Ward, "Unbeaten Marciano Stops Louis in 8th," *Chicago Daily Tribune,* October 27, 1951, at p. B1.

16. Joseph M. Sheehan, " 'Better Man Won,' Admits the Loser," *New York Times,* October 27, 1951, at p. 27.

17. Ibid.

18. Ibid.

19. Jack Hand, "Marciano Kayoes Matthews in 2nd," *Los Angeles Times,* July 29, 1952, at p. C1.

20. Frank Finch, "Marciano 5–7 over Walcott," *Los Angeles Times,* September 23, 1952, at p. C1.

21. Ibid.

22. "Marciano Will Be New Champ, Tunney Claims," *Chicago Defender,* August 5, 1952, at p. B3.

23. Frank Finch, "Marciano KO'S Walcott to Win Title," *Los Angeles Times,* September 24, 1952, at p. C1.

24. Wilfrid Smith, "Meet the New Champion: Marciano, First Unconquered Heavyweight King, Can't Believe It's True," *Chicago Daily Tribune,* September 28, 1952, at p. C1.

25. Ibid.

26. Dave Brady, "Right Hand Uppercut Ends Fight after 2:35," *Washington Post,* May 16, 1953, at p. 1.

27. Al Wolf, "Marciano TKO's La Starza in Eleventh," *Los Angeles Times,* September 25, 1953, at p. C1.

28. "La Starza Sees No Knockout of Marciano," *Chicago Daily Tribune,* June 8, 1954, at p. E6.

29. Sullivan at p. 254.

Chapter 5

1. Quoted in Thomas Hauser. *Muhammad Ali: His Life and Times.* New York: Simon & Schuster, 1991, at p. 14.

2. Quoted in Hauser at p. 18.

3. Quoted in Hauser at p. 19.

4. "Amos Johnson Victor," *New York Times,* May 1, 1959, at p. 21.

5. "Clay–Shomo Take NAAU Ring Titles," *Chicago Daily Defender,* April 11, 1960, at p. A22.

6. Wilfrid Smith, "Clay, Two Other Yanks Win Olympic Ring Titles," *Chicago Daily Tribune,* September 6, 1960, at p. C6.

7. Quoted in Mike Marqusee. *Redemption Song: Muhammad Ali and the Spirit of the Sixties.* London: Verso, 1999, at p. 47.

8. Quoted in Marqusee at p. 48.

9. Jim Murray, "Cassius on Clay," *Los Angeles Times,* April 20, 1962, at p. B1.

10. Angelo Dundee (with Mike Winters). *I Only Talk Winning.* Contemporary Books: Chicago, 1985, at p. 167.

11. Ibid. at p. 168.

12. "I'll Spank the Brat, Moore Says of Cassius Clay, His October 25th Foe," *Chicago Daily Defender,* August 20, 1962, at p. 24.

13. Bob Roy, "Liston Tells Shortcomings of Foes," *Chicago Daily Defender,* August 27, 1962, at p. 21.

14. John Hall, "Moore Will Be Easiest, Says Clay," *Los Angeles Times,* October 9, 1962, at p. B7.

15. John Hall, "Clay Calls Shot, Kayoes Moore in Four," *Los Angeles Times,* November 16, 1962, at p. C11.

16. Quoted in Frank Finch, "'I'll Fix You in Eight'—Cassius," *Los Angeles Times,* November 16, 1962, at p. C1.

17. Associated Press, "Clay Calls Shot, Kayos Powell in Third," *Chicago Daily Tribune,* January 25, 1963, at p. C1.

18. Quoted in Hauser at p. 51.

19. Ibid.

20. United Press International, "Doug Jones in Chin Talk for Clay, 'the Lip,'" *Chicago Daily Defender,* January 29, 1963, at p. 24.

21. United Press International, "Careful Clay, Jones May Be Hard to Stop," *Chicago Daily Defender,* March 4, 1963, at p. 24.

22. United Press International, "Brash Clay Has Volumes to Say," *Washington Post,* March 7, 1963, at p. D1.

23. Gene Ward, "Clay Gets Unpopular Decision over Jones," *Chicago Daily Tribune,* March 14, 1963, at p. F1.

24. Ibid.

25. Quoted in Lincoln A. Werden, "Spectators Boo Official Verdict," *New York Times,* March 15, 1963, at p. 16.

26. Quoted in Frank Finch, "Heavyweight Champ Unimpressed," *Los Angeles Times,* March 14, 1963, at p. B1.

27. Quoted in United Press International, "Clay Nixes Hush, Says Cooper Goes in Five," *Chicago Daily Defender,* May 27, 1963, at p. A28.

28. Quoted in United Press International, "Cassius Clay's Claim of Greatness Irks Trainer," *Chicago Daily Defender,* June 12, 1963, at p. 22.

29. Quoted in Hauser at p. 54.

30. Quoted in Stephen Brunt. *Facing Ali.* Guilford, CT: Lyons Press, 2002, at p. 37.

31. Quoted in Dundee at p. 189.

32. Quoted in Dundee at p. 189.

33. United Press International, "As Predicted: Clay Wins in Five," *Chicago Daily Defender,* June 19, 1963, at p. 24.

34. Al Monroe, "Liston's Afraid but Not of Cassius Clay," *Chicago Daily Defender,* August 8, 1963, at p. A29.

35. Oscar Fraley, "Says Its Murder Just Thinking of Cassius in Ring with Liston," *Chicago Daily Defender,* December 11, 1963, at p. 25.

36. Steve Snyder, "Thinks Young Clay in for Lesson Shouldn't Have Agreed to Learn," *Chicago Daily Defender,* February 15, 1964, at p. 20.

37. Sid Ziff, "Better Be Early," *Los Angeles Times,* February 24, 1964, at p. B1.

38. Arthur Daley, "The Big Bear," *New York Times,* February 24, 1964, at p. 30.

39. Ibid.

40. Hauser at p. 69.

41. Leonard Koppel, "The Plot," *New York Times,* February 23, 1964, at p. S1.

42. Hauser at p. 67.

43. Quoted in Hauser at p. 71.

44. Quoted in Hauser at p. 74.

45. Sid Ziff, "'I've Upset the World,' Cries Cassius," *Los Angeles Times,* February 26, 1964, at p. B1.

46. Associated Press, "Clay Proclaims Legal Name Is Muhammad Ali," *Washington Post,* February 11, 1967, at p. C1.

47. Marqusee at p. 59.

48. United Press International, "Cassius Clay Speaks at Muslim's Meeting," *Washington Post,* January 24, 1964, at p. B1.

49. William Juneau, "Black Muslim Chief Claims Cassius Clay Is in Sect," *Chicago Tribune,* February 27, 1964, at p. 8.

50. "Army Rejects Cassius Clay for Service," *Chicago Tribune,* March 21, 1964, at p. C21.

51. Associated Press, "Army Rules Cassius 4-F," March 21, 1964, at p. A1.

52. Robert Lipsyte, "Cassius Clay, Cassius X, Muhammad Ali," *New York Times,* October 25, 1964, at p. SM29.

53. Dundee at p. 204.

54. Nicholas Von Hoffman, "Clay Refuses Induction, Stripped of World Title," *Washington Post,* April 29, 1967, at p. A1.

55. Dave Anderson, "Clay Prefers Jail to Army," *New York Times,* March 17, 1967, at p. 50.

56. Ibid.

57. Jackie Robinson, "Heroism, Tragedy of Muhammad Ali," *Chicago Daily Defender,* October 21, 1967, at p. 10.

58. 403 U.S. 698, 704 (1971).

59. Bob Woodward and Scott Armstrong, "Ali and Draft: He Nearly Went to Jail," *Chicago Tribune,* December 4, 1979, at p. 1 (excerpt from *The Brethren*).

60. "Ali Wins Reversal of Draft Sentence," *Los Angeles Times,* June 29, 1971, at p. 1.

61. Robert Lipsyte, "Clay Knocks Out Liston in One Minute; Bout, Like First, Ends in Controversy," *New York Times,* May 26, 1965, at p. 1.

62. Associated Press, "Didn't Hear the Count, Says Sonny," *Chicago Tribune,* May 26, 1965, at p. C1.

63. Dick Young, "It Was Short but Not Sweet," *Chicago Tribune,* May 26, 1965, at p. C1.

64. John Hall, "It Only Takes One Minute to Kill Boxing," *Los Angeles Times,* May 26, 1965, at p. B1.

65. Associated Press, "WBA Legal Chief Calls Title KO, 'Farce and Fraud,'" *Los Angeles Times,* May 26, 1965, at p. B4.

66. Jim Murray, "The Greatest?" *Los Angeles Times,* May 26, 1965, at p. B1.

67. Paul Zimmerman, "Floyd Attempts Crusader Role in Fight with Clay," *Los Angeles Times,* November 21, 1965, at p. H3.

68. Robert Lipsyte, "Clay Knocks Out Patterson in the 12th and Keeps Heavyweight Title," *New York Times,* November 23, 1965, at p. 1.

69. Arthur Daley, "Clay Mocks Foe in Word and Deed," *New York Times,* November 23, 1965, at p. 54.

70. Paul Zimmerman, "Clay Ends Patterson's Misery in 12th," *Los Angeles Times,* November 23, 1965, at p. B1.

71. Cooper Rollow, "Patterson Hurt Me Once, Says Clay," *Chicago Tribune,* November 23, 1965, at p. C1.

72. Daley, "Clay Mocks Foe," at p. 54.

73. Sid Ziff, "Clay Tried, Couldn't Humiliate Foe," *Los Angeles Times,* November 23, 1965, at p. B1.

74. Shirley Povich, "Clay Gores Cooper into Submission," *Washington Post,* May 22, 1966, at p. G1.

75. Arthur Daley, "Right Ends Bout," *New York Times,* August 7, 1966, at p. 161.

76. United Press International, "Clay 'Fastest I've Ever Seen,' Says Disgusted London after Bout," *Washington Post,* August 7, 1966, at p. C6.

77. Quoted in Sid Ziff, "Clay Faces Real Test," *Los Angeles Times,* September 6, 1966, at p. B3.

78. Quoted in Lloyd E. Milligan, "Louis Sees Trouble for Clay Against German Southpaw," *New York Times,* September 2, 1966, at p. 53.

79. Quoted in Hauser at p. 160.

80. Robert Lipsyte, "Muhammad Ali Slaps at Terrell after Name-Calling Exchange at Garden," *New York Times,* December 29, 1966, at p. 38.

81. Ibid.

82. Quoted in Hauser at p. 164.

83. Dave Anderson, "Victor Consoles Aging Rival," *New York Times,* March 23, 1967, at p. 40.

84. Hauser at p. 192.

85. Ibid. at p. 194.

86. Ibid. at p. 203.

87. Steve Cady, "A Black Fighter Wins a Big One," *New York Times,* July 4, 1971, at p. E3.

88. "Muhammad Ali Vows He'll Return to Ring," *Chicago Daily Defender,* November 25, 1967, at p. 15.

89. John Hall, "Champ's Back; Ali TKOs Quarry in 3," *Los Angeles Times,* October 27, 1970, at p. D1.

90. Quoted in Dave Anderson, "Frazier Responds to Ali's Taunts: 'He Talks Loud Because He's Scared,'" *New York Times,* November 20, 1970, at p. 68.

91. Quoted in Dave Anderson, "Lunch Crowd Eats Up Ali's Punching, Poetry and Put-On," *New York Times,* December 1, 1970, at p. 79.

92. Norman O. Unger, "Ali Kayos Oscar, It Wasn't Easy," *Chicago Daily Defender,* December 8, 1970, at p. 24.

93. Gerald Eskenazi, "Bonavena Predicts Ali Will Defeat Frazier for Title," *New York Times,* December 8, 1970, at p. 64.

94. "Garden Wins Out as Site of Ali–Frazier Heavyweight Title Bout March 8," *New York Times,* December 28, 1970, at p. 60.

95. Quoted in Dave Anderson, "Frazier and Ali: Morality Drama Unfolds," *New York Times,* March 7, 1971, at p. S1.

96. Quoted in Stanley O. Williford, "Cocksure Ali Says Frazier Will Be Easy," *Los Angeles Times,* December 23, 1970, at p. E3.

97. Quoted in Red Smith, "Frazier Labels Ali 'Silly Little Kid,'" *Washington Post,* January 11, 1971, at p. D3.

98. Dan Hafner, "Frazier Says He Will KO Ali by 10th Round," *Los Angeles Times,* February 23, 1971, at p. G5.

99. United Press International, "Frazier Calls Ali 'Phony' and 'a Clown,'" *Washington Post,* January 1, 1971, at p. D6.

100. Quoted in Hauser at p. 231.

101. Neil Milbert, "Our Sunday Punch: Ali to Take Frazier in 15," *Chicago Tribune,* January 16, 1971, at p. B5.

102. Dave Brady, "Oddsmakers Disagree on Ali-Frazier," *Washington Post,* February 7, 1971, at p. 98.

103. United Press International, "Joe Louis Tabs Frazier to Beat Ali on Monday," *Los Angeles Times,* March 4, 1971, at p. D9.

104. Quoted in Charles Maher, "Frazier Wins, Decks Ali in 15th Round," *Los Angeles Times,* March 9, 1971, at p. C1.

105. Dave Anderson, "Frazier Outpoints Ali and Keeps Title," *New York Times,* March 9, 1971, at p. 1.

106. Quoted in Maher at p. C1.

107. Ibid.

108. Anderson, "Frazier Outpoints Ali," at p. 1.

109. Dave Brady, "Frazier Awarded Decision, as Ali Goes Down in 15th," *Washington Post,* March 9, 1971, at p. A1.

110. United Press International, "Ali Wins Latest TV Round as Frazier Fails to Show," *Washington Post,* March 14, 1971, at p. 101.

111. Quoted in United Press International, "Ali Blasts Frazier," *Chicago Daily Defender,* November 13, 1971, at p. 33.

112. Quoted in United Press International, "Muhammad Ali Vows Win over Frazier Next Time," *Chicago Daily Defender,* February 19, 1972, at p. 31.

113. Reuters, "Ali–Frazier Fight Fixed, British Doctor Charges," *Los Angeles Times,* March 22, 1971, at p. C1.

114. Ibid.

115. Howard L. Bingham and Max Wallace. *Muhammad Ali's Greatest Fight: Cassius Clay vs. The United States of America.* New York: M. Evans, 2000.

116. Quoted in Cooper Rollow, "Frazier Jabs Ali; Spars for Fight," *Chicago Tribune,* January 13, 1972, at p. E5.

117. William N. Wallace, "Norton, a 5–1 Underdog, Breaks Ali's Jaw, Wins Split Decision," *New York Times,* April 1, 1973, at p. 247.

118. Quoted in Hauser at p. 253.

119. Quoted in Dave Brady, "Norton Breaks Ali's Jaw, Captures Decision," *Washington Post,* April 1, 1973, at p. D1.

120. Dave Anderson, "Ali Beats Norton on 12-Round Rally," *New York Times,* September 11, 1973, at p. 57.

121. Quoted in Associated Press, "Frazier Loss No Surprise to Ali," *Los Angeles Times,* January 23, 1971, at p. E4.

122. United Press International, "Ali Mocks Frazier, Decked 'Six' Times," *Chicago Daily Defender,* February 26, 1971, at p. 26.

123. Bill Lyons, "Ali Decisions Frazier; Both Want Third Match," *Los Angeles Times,* January 29, 1974, at p. C1.

124. Quoted in David Condon, "Frazier Won Ali's Respect," *Chicago Tribune,* January 29, 1974, at p. B1.

125. Quoted in Mikal Gilmore, "How Muhammad Ali Conquered Fear and Changed the World," *Men's Journal,* November 2011, at p. 132.

126. Quoted in "Morning Briefing: Foreman Looks Big and Mean . . . Like Liston, Says Ali's Mother," *Los Angeles Times,* October 28, 1974, at p. D2.

127. Tony Blackwell, "Ali Will Triumph over Foreman," *Chicago Daily Defender,* October 29, 1974, at p. 24.

128. Quoted in Skip Mylenski, "Ali Flattens Foreman in 8th to Retain Title," *Los Angeles Times,* October 30, 1974, at p. E1.

129. Dave Anderson, "Ali Regains Title, Flooring Foreman," *New York Times,* October 30, 1974, at p. 93.

130. "Ali, Frazier May Battle Once Again, in Iran," *Chicago Daily Defender,* December 20, 1974, at p. 26.

131. William Barry Furlong, "Frazier Sharpens Jab of Verbal Nature for Ali," *Washington Post,* August 15, 1975, at p. D1.

132. Quoted in Dave Anderson, "Ali Retains Title as Fight Is Stopped after 14th," *New York Times,* October 1, 1975, at p. 93.

133. Quoted in Associated Press, "Frazier Saluted by Weary Ali," *Los Angeles Times,* October 1, 1975, at p. E1.

134. Quoted in Anderson, "Ali Retains Title," at p. 93.

135. Quoted in Cooper Rollow, "Young Scares Ali, but Champ Hangs On," *Chicago Tribune,* May 1, 1976, at p. I1.

136. Quoted in Dave Anderson, "Ali Outpoints Norton and Retains His Heavyweight Crown," *New York Times,* September 29, 1976, at p. 89.

137. Quoted in Associated Press, "Norton Can't KO Ali So Ali Retains Title," *New York Times,* September 29, 1976, at p. E1.

138. Quoted in David Condon, "Ali Just Good Enough to Win," *Chicago Tribune,* September 30, 1977, at p. E1.

139. Quoted in Jack Hawn, "Ali Finally Taps Out in Las Vegas," *Los Angeles Times,* February 16, 1978, at p. E1.

140. Jack Hawn, "Ali Turns Back Clock and Wins Title Again," *Los Angeles Times,* September 16, 1978, at p. C1.

141. Jim Murray, "Ali Shell Enough to Topple Spinks," *Washington Post,* September 17, 1978, at p. F4.

142. Dave Kindred, "Ali Errs on Choice of a Foe," *Washington Post,* April 18, 1980, at p. D1.

143. Bob Verdi, "Holmes Batters Ali from Start to Finish," *Chicago Tribune,* October 3, 1980, at p. C1.

144. Ibid.

145. Bill Pennington, "Tears, Cheers as Ali Takes Stage, the Greatest Lights Up World," *The Record,* July 21, 1996, at p. S03.

146. Robert Lipsyte, "'I Don't Have To Be What You Want Me To Be,'" *New York Times,* March 7, 1971, at p. SM24.

147. David Maraniss, "Ali's Amazing Grace: Still Preaching, Teaching, Now He Contemplates His 'House in Heaven,' in *The Muhammad Ali Reader.* Hopewell, NJ: Ecco Press, 1998 (edited by Gerard Early), 287–297, at p. 293.

148. Quoted in Bingham and Wallace.

149. Office of the White House, "President Honors Recipients of the Presidential Medal of Freedom," November 9, 2005, at http://www.whitehouse.gov/news/releases/2005/11/20051109–2.html

150. Quoted in Mark Collings (ed.). *Muhammad Ali: Through the Eyes of the World.* New York: Skyhorse Publishing, 2007, at p. 47.

CHAPTER 6

1. George Foreman and Joel Engel. *By George.* New York: Villard Books, 1995, at p. 4.

2. Neil Amdurs, "Foreman, U.S. Olympic Heavyweight Candidate, Displays Pro Potential," *New York Times,* October 2, 1968, at p. 46.

3. "Foreman's Not the Same," *Chicago Daily Defender,* January 27, 1973, at p. 29.

4. Greg Gallo and Darrell Mack, "Life in Ghetto: Foreman Tells It Like It Happened," *Los Angeles Times,* March 12, 1973, at p. D1.

5. Foreman and Engel at p. 42.

6. Earl Gustkey, "Foreman Ranks Gold Medal as Favorite Boxing Moment," *Los Angeles Times,* July 26, 1984, at p. 123.

7. John Hall, "Foreman's Fan Club," *Los Angeles Times,* November 6, 1968, at p. H3.

8. Dave Zirin, "An Interview with George Foreman," *Counterpunch,* November 7, 2003, at http://www.counterpunch.org/2003/11/07/an-interview-with-george-oreman/

9. Quoted in "Olympic Heavy Champ Turns Pro," *Chicago Daily Defender,* November 9, 1968, at p. 16.

10. Zirin.

11. "Olympic Heavy Champ Turns Pro," *Chicago Daily Defender,* November 9, 1968, at p. 16.

12. Quoted in Deane McGowen, "Foreman Takes 16th in a Row, Beating Peralta; Verdict Booed," *New York Times,* February 17, 1970, at p. 46.

13. Associated Press, "Glare Helps Foreman in Easy Victory," *Washington Post,* July 22, 1970, at p. D7.

14. United Press International, "Foreman KO's Mystery Opponent, Crowd Boos," *Chicago Daily Defender,* February 11, 1970, at p. 38.

15. Sandra Haggerty, "Boxer George Foreman Is Keeping Himself 'Hungry,'" *Los Angeles Times,* August 22, 1972, at p. C7.

16. Quoted in Dan Hafner, "Foreman Comes Alive Vocally for Frazier," *Los Angeles Times,* January 8, 1973, at p. E7.

17. Cooper Rollow, "Foreman Stops Frazier in 2d," *Chicago Tribune,* January 23, 1973, at p. C1.

18. Quoted in Rollow at p. C1.

19. Will Grimsley, "Foreman: Champ Straight, Genuine," *Los Angeles Times,* January 24, 1973, at p. E1.

20. "Norton Confident, Calls Foreman 'Slow,'" *Chicago Daily Defender,* February 16, 1974, at p. 29.

21. David Condon, "Foreman Mauls Norton in 2d for TKO: Decks Foe Three Times; Battles Ali Next," *Chicago Tribune,* March 27, 1973, at p. E1.

22. Charles Maher, "The Foreman Camp: Perspiration: But No Sweat," *Los Angeles Times,* August 28, 1974, at p. E1.

23. Associated Press, "Foreman Left Unhurt after Auto Mishap," *Washington Post,* October 6, 1974, at p. D11.

24. Tony Blackwell, "Ali Will Triumph over Foreman," *Chicago Daily Defender,* October 29, 1974, at p. 24.

25. United Press International, "Foreman Demands Inquiry on Fight," *New York Times,* November 5, 1974, at p. 44.

26. Zirin.

27. "Foreman, in Playful Mood, Defeats 5 Foes Handily," *New York Times,* April 27, 1975, at p. 207.

28. Quoted in Norman O. Unger, "Foreman to End 'Good Guy' Image," *Chicago Daily Defender,* April 29, 1975, at p. 34.

29. A. S. Doc Young, "George Foreman, Part I . . ." *Chicago Daily Defender,* May 5, 1975, at p. 73.

30. Leonard Koppett, "Foreman, Down Twice, Knocks Out Lyle in 5th," *New York Times,* January 25, 1976, at p. 225.

31. Jack Hawn, "Foreman Rallies, KOs Lyle in 5," *Los Angeles Times,* January 25, 1976, at p. B1.

32. Quoted in Dave Anderson, "Young Floors Foreman in 12th and Wins Unanimous Decision," *New York Times,* March 18, 1977, at p. 46.

33. Foreman and Engel at p. 147.

34. George Foreman with Ken Abraham. *God in My Corner.* Nashville, TN: Thomas Nelson, 2007, at p. 30.

35. Associated Press, "Foreman's Future: 'Fighting for God,'" *Washington Post,* May 7, 1977, at p. D4.

36. George Vecsey, "Foreman Fights from Pulpit," *New York Times,* November 17, 1981, at p. C13.

37. United Press International, "Preacher Foreman's Broke but Happy," *Chicago Tribune,* March 27, 1979, at p. C4.

38. Ibid.

39. David Maraniss, "The Coming of Age of George Foreman," *Washington Post,* July 16, 1989, at p. C1.

40. "Hey, Foreman! Fat Chance," *Chicago Tribune,* November 11, 1986, at p. C2.

41. Shirley Povich, "Foreman: A Punchy, Paunchy Comeback," *Washington Post,* January 25, 1988, at p. B3.

42. Ibid.

43. Earl Gustkey, "George Foreman Joins Comeback Parade," *Los Angeles Times,* August 30, 1986, at p. OC_B15.

44. Dave Anderson, "Foreman's Second Wind," *New York Times*, February 26, 1987, at p. B10.

45. Ibid.

46. Maraniss at p. C1.

47. Phil Berger, "A Step for Foreman Despite the Flab," *New York Times,* March 11, 1987, at p. B9.

48. Ibid.

49. Phil Berger, "Foreman Is Fighting Waistline and Critics," *New York Times,* February 3, 1988, at p. A26.

50. Phil Berger, "Foreman Wins in 2d Round and Sends Cooney into Retirement," *New York Times,* January 16, 1990, at p. B7.

51. Ed Schuyler Jr. and Tim Dahlberg, "Tyson, Foreman Triumph," *Washington Post,* June 17, 1990, at p. B1.

52. Karl Hente, "At 42, Foreman Hero Even in Defeat," *Washington Post,* April 20, 1991, at p. G8.

53. Tim Dahlberg, "Morrison Decisions Foreman," *Washington Post,* June 8, 1993, at p. E1.

54. Gerald Eskenazi, "Foreman Flattens Moorer with Blast from the Past," *New York Times,* November 6, 1994, at p. S1.

55. Andrew Pollack, "Morrison and Foreman Prevail," *New York Times,* November 3, 1996, at p. S11.

56. Bob Raissman, "Foreman's Charge a Low Blow," *Daily News,* September 16, 2003, at p. 67.

57. Quoted in Don Steinberg, "HBO Ready for Life without Foreman," *Philadelphia Inquirer,* March 12, 2004, at p. D2.

58. "George Foreman: Marketing Champ of the World," *Business Week,* December 20, 2004, at http://www.businessweek.com/magazine/content/04_51/b3913093.htm

CHAPTER 7

1. Jose Torres. *Fire and Fear: The Inside Story of Mike Tyson.* New York: Warner Books, 1989, at p. 8.

2. Ibid. at p. 10.

3. Ibid. at 32.

4. Phil Berger, "Tyson, at Age 19, Rushes to Fulfill D'Amato Vision," *New York Times,* December 2, 1985, at p. C1.

5. Sam Smith, "Tyson: 'Nobody Will Stand in the Way," *Chicago Tribune,* March 23, 1986, at p. C6.

6. Phil Berger, "Tyson Beats Toughest Foe: Himself," *New York Times,* November 21, 1986, at p. D23.

7. Berger, "Tyson at Age 19."

8. Quoted in Sam Smith, "Tyson's fists leave Ferguson in a daze," *Chicago Tribune,* February 17, 1986, at p. B5.

9. Dave Anderson, "Another Knockout for Tyson," *New York Times,* February 17, 1986, at p. C3.

10. Richard Hoffer, "Tyson Knocks Out Berbick in Second to Earn WBC Title," *Los Angeles Times,* November 23, 1986, at p. SD_B1.

11. Quoted in Bob Verdi, "The Ripple Effect of Tyson's Fists," *Chicago Tribune,* November 24, 1986, at p. B1.

12. William Golea, "Awakened Holmes Calls Tyson 'a True Champion,'" *Washington Post,* January 24, 1988, at p. D1.

13. Ellis Cashmore. *Tyson: Nurture of the Beast.* Cambridge, UK: Polity Press, 2005, at p. 202.

14. Jon Saraceno, "Tyson's Prowess Proclaimed," *USA Today,* February 23, 1989, at p. 3C.

15. Phil Berger, "Tyson's Turbulent Rounds: Conflict, Crisis, Street Fight," *New York Times,* August 25, 1988, at p. D23.

16. "Givens: 'Pure Hell' Living with Tyson," *Miami Herald,* September 30, 1988, at p. D3.

17. Wallace Matthews, "Words Sink Rooney as Tyson's Trainer," *Newsday,* December 10, 1988, at p. 26.

18. Jon Saraceno, "And in This Corner: Tyson and Novices," *USA Today,* February 21, 1989, at p. 3C.

19. Joe Layden. *The Last Great Fight: The Extraordinary Tale of Two Men and How One Fight Changed Their Lives Forever.* New York: St. Martin's Press, 2007, at p. 32.

20. *Tyson v. State,* 619 N.E.2d 276,300 (Ind. App. 1993).

21. Scott Horner, "Boxer Mike Tyson Gets Six Years for Rape," *United Press International,* March 26, 1992.

22. Wallace Matthews, "He Was Robbed: Doubts Persist about Tyson's Conviction," *Newsday,* July 18, 1993, at p. 7.

23. *Tyson v. State,* 619 N.E.2d 276,300 (Ind. App. 1993).

24. *Tyson v. State,* 619 N.Ed.2d 276, 301 (Ind. App. 1993) (J. Sullivan dissenting).

25. Alan Dershowitz, "Tyson Shouldn't Apologize," *Times-Union,* August 14, 1995, at p. A6.

26. "Mike Tyson Apologizes Video," Oprah.com, October 16, 2009, at http://www.oprah.com/oprahshow/Mike-Tyson-Apologizes-to-Evander-Holyfield-Video

27. Quoted in Cashmore at p. 33.

28. Quoted in Cashmore at p. 34.

29. David Williams, "Some Fancy Footwork Took Fight to Pyramid," *Commercial Appeal,* March 31, 2002, at p. A1.

30. Dave Anderson, "Tyson Sent Tumbling into the Tomb of Doom," *New York Times,* June 9, 2002, at p. G9.

31. Quoted in Jack Chevalier, "Tyson's Loss to Lewis Lets Down His Followers," *Philadelphia Tribune,* June 11, 2002, at p. 1C.

32. Bud Shaw, " 'Nice' Tyson? Now That's Nuts," *Plain Dealer,* June 11, 2002, at p. D1.

33. Dan Rafael, "Tyson Punches Ticket for Rematch with Lewis, but Ex-champ Acts Hesitant," *USA Today,* February 2003, at p. 7C.

34. Ibid.

35. Quoted in "In Interview, Tyson Makes Rape Remark," *New York Times,* May 29, 2003, at p. D7.

36. Quoted in Richard Sandomir, "Good and Bad Tyson on Display," *New York Times,* July 14, 2003, at p. D4.

37. Sandomir at p. D4.

38. Ira Berkow, "Money Is the Least of Tyson's Problems," *New York Times,* August 5, 2003, at p. D1.

39. Richard Sandomir, "Tyson's Bankruptcy Is a Lesson in Ways to Squander a Fortune," *New York Times,* August 5, 2003, at p. A1.

40. Quoted in William Glaberson, "Tyson Agrees to Plea Deal in Hotel Fight," *New York Times,* February 27, 2004, at p. B2.

41. Quoted in Viv Bernstein, "Tyson's Free Fall Continues with Knockout Loss in 4th," *New York Times,* July 31, 2004, at p. D1.

42. Quoted in Clifton Brown, "Tyson Quits Fight and May Quit Boxing Next," *New York Times,* June 12, 2005, at p. G1.

43. Bob Mee. *The Heavyweights: The Definitive History of the Heavyweight Fighters.* Stroud, UK: Tempus, 2006, at p. 294.

44. J. B. Alderman, "'Tyson' Is Riveting Look at Troubled Champion," *Contra Costa Times,* November 24, 2009.

45. Roger Ebert, "The Champ Battles Back; 'Tyson' Examines Fighter's Psychic Wounds and Scars," *Chicago Sun-Times,* May 1, 2009, at p. B6.

46. "Muhammad Ali and Mike Tyson Chosen as Cover Athletes for EA Sports Fight Night Round 4," *Business Wire,* March 9, 2009.

47. Larry King, "Interview with Mike Tyson," CNN, December 2, 2010.

48. Bert Randolph Sugar. *Boxing's Greatest Fighters.* Guilford, CT: Lyons Press, 2006, at pp. 344–49.

49. Admittedly, Holmes was past his prime when he fought Tyson.

50. Quoted in Mike Waters, "Tyson Chokes Up During His Speech, the Former Champion Can't Finish When He Talks about Cus D'Amato," *Post Standard,* June 13, 2011, at p. B1.

CHAPTER 8

1. Ted Kluck. *Facing Tyson.* Guilford, CT: Lyons Press, 2006, at p. 23.

2. Michael Murray. *The Journeyman.* Edinburgh, Scotland: Mainstream Publishing, 2002.

3. Ibid. at p. 11.

4. Quoted in David L. Hudson Jr., "Emanuel Augustus: Seeking Respect, Belts," Fightnews.com, May 21, 2002.

5. Daniel Lane, "Meet the Man Who Can't Stop Dancing," *Sun Herald* (Sydney, Australia), January 18, 2009, at p. 65.

6. Quoted in Hudson, "Emanuel Augustus."

7. Quoted in Shelley Lewellen, "Taunt, Rattle, Win," *Tucson Citizen,* April 3, 2004, at p. 1C.

8. Quoted in David L. Hudson Jr., "Interview: Marion Wilson," Fightnews. com, April 15, 2002.

9. Ibid.

10. Ibid.

11. Personal interview with Eric Bottjer, October 15, 2011.

12. Quoted in Geoffrey Gray, "This Job Includes a One-way Ticket to Palookaville," *International Herald Tribune,* May 12, 2004, at p. 20.

13. Personal interview with Tim Lueckenhoff, July 14, 2011.

14. Ibid.

15. George Diaz. "Meet Reggie Strickland, Professional Loser," *Orlando Sentinel,* August 11, 2003, at p. D1.

16. Jay Rotz, "A Tough Career in the Ring," *Patriot News* (Harrisburg, PA), May 11, 2010, at p. T2.

17. Kirk Johnson, "Boxing in the Shadows," *New York Times,* June 1, 1998, at p. A1.

18. Personal interview with Jake Hall, May 2010.

19. Quoted in Mark Alesia, "Local Man Makes a Living as Boxing's Biggest Loser," *Indianapolis Star,* 10/17/2004, at p. 10C.

20. Personal interview with Jake Hall, May 2010.

21. Personal interview with Tim Lueckenhoff, July 2011.

22. The author respectfully acknowledges that he was one of the three judges that night. I scored the bout for Strickland 39–37.

23. Quoted in Diaz, supra n. 15.

24. Personal interview with Fred Berns, October 2011.

25. Personal interview with Rob Bleakley, November 16, 2011.

26. Ibid.

27. Personal interview with Fred Berns, October 2011.

28. Quoted in David L. Hudson Jr., "Reggie Strickland: Elusive Journeyman Nears 300 Pro Bouts," Fightnews.com, December 15, 2001.

29. Quoted in Hudson, "Reggie Strickland."

30. Quoted in Greg Logan, "Meet Mouse, World Class KO Victim," *Newsday,* February 11, 1997, at p. A59.

31. Rick Reilly, "Palookas, Tomato Cans, Opponents. Whatever They're Called, These Are the Fighters Who Go Down So That the Hometown Heroes Can Get Up," *Sports Illustrated,* October 16, 1989, at http://sportsillustrated.cnn.com/vault/article/magazine/MAG1068923/5/index.htm

32. Ibid.

33. Ibid.

34. Philip Wuntch, "The Mouse: In This Corner, the Winning Tale of a Losing Boxer," *Dallas Morning News,* December 5, 1997, at p. 1C.

35. Wallace Matthews, "It's Quite an Honor to Be a Knucklehead," *Newsday,* September 10, 1993, at p. 189.

36. Personal interview with Mike Glenn, August 29, 2011.

37. Ibid.

38. Ibid.

39. Ibid.

40. John Allen, "Scrap Iron Tests Quarry's Punch," *Los Angeles Times,* April 3, 1966, at p. C10.

41. Jim Murray, "King of the Palookas," *Los Angeles Times,* March 27, 1979, at p. D1.

42. Dan Hafner, "Machen Beats Scrap Iron in Rugged Fight," *Los Angeles Times,* September 30, 1966, at p. C4.

43. Dan Hafner, "Quarry Gets Decision, Johnson Gets Cheers," *Los Angeles Times,* March 20, 1970, at p. E1.

44. Dan Hafner, "Foreman Scores KO; Rose Loses," *Los Angeles Times,* May 17, 1970, at p. C2.

45. Nat Fleischer. *50 Years at Ringside.* New York: Fleet Publishing, 1958, at p. 172.

46. Ibid. at p. 173.

47. "Grim Not Hurt by Lanky Bob," *Atlanta Journal Constitution,* October 15, 1903, at p. A4.

48. "Failed to Knock Grim Out," *Washington Post,* October 15, 1903, at p. 3.

49. Quoted in John J. Daly, "Joe Grim Is Here; Puzzled Fighters and Medical Men," *Washington Post,* July 26, 1925, at p. 12

50. Quoted in Mike Casey, "Hit Me with Your Rhythm Stick: Joe Grim and George Chuvalo," Cyber Boxing Zone, at http://cyberboxingzone.com/boxing/casey/MC_GrimChuvalo.htm

51. "Gans 'Outfought' Joe Grim," *New York Times,* October 20, 1903, at p. 7.

52. George Siler, "Grim Makes a Poor Showing," *Chicago Daily Tribune,* December 4, 1903, at p. 8.

53. Ibid.

54. "Thomas Swats Iron Man Grim," *Los Angeles Times,* July 15, 1906, at p. III1.

55. Associated Press, "Joe Grim, Noted Iron Man Prize Fighter, Dies at 58," *Chicago Tribune,* August 20, 1939, at p. B5.

56. Daly at p. 12.

57. Personal interview with Eric Bottjer, October 15, 2011.

CHAPTER 9

1. "Fourteen Boxers Die: 1906 Fatalities Greater Than Previous Two Years," *Washington Post,* December 23, 1906, at p. S2.

2. "Boxer Dies; Fake Is Cried," *Chicago Daily Tribune,* September 25, 1906, at p. 6.

3. Ibid.

4. "Chicago Boxer Dies of Injury in Ring Battle," *Chicago Daily Tribune,* November 4, 1919, at p. 15.

5. "Injured Boxer Dies," *New York Times,* September 30, 1922, at p. 28.

6. "Negro Boxer Dies from Ring Injury," *New York Times,* March 18, 1927, at p. 18.

7. "Boxer Dies after Bout and Opponent Is Held," *New York Times,* August 21, 1929, at p. 20.

8. Associated Press, "Boxer Dies of Injury after Refusing Early KO Victory," *Washington Post,* December 12, 1954, at p. C1.

9. Associated Press, "Boxer Dies, Another Injured in Same Ring," *Washington Post,* November 1, 1930, at p. 19.

10. "German Boxer Dies in His First Bout Here; His Opponent at a Harlem Club Arrested," *New York Times,* October 21, 1930, at p. 1.

11. Ibid.

12. "Boxer Dies of Blow Received in Battle," *Atlanta Journal Constitution,* June 2, 1927, at p. 19.

13. "Mandell Blow Kills Boxer," *Chicago Daily Tribune,* June 2, 1927, at p. 1.

14. See, e.g., "Boxer Dies from Injuries," *New York Times,* August 26, 1928, at p. 14.

15. "Jury Clears Boxer after Opponent Dies in the Ring," *Chicago Daily Tribune,* January 13, 1922, at p. 14.

16. "Boxer Dies from Injuries," *New York Times,* January 25, 1922, at p. 2.

17. "Boxer Jimmy Costello, Knocked Out in El Monte Bout, Dies of His Injuries," *Los Angeles Times,* July 8, 1934, at p. 16.

18. Associated Press, "Boxer Stricken in Ring, Dies of Heart Failure," *Chicago Daily Tribune,* June 16, 1935, at p. A5.

19. "Scarpati Dies from Injuries in Ambers Bout," *Chicago Daily Tribune,* March 21, 1936, at p. 24.

20. "Sandusky Boxer Dies One Hour after Bout," *New York Times,* November 29, 1928, at p. 38.

21. Associated Press, "Hines, Boxer, Dies of Ring Injuries," *New York Times,* March 5, 1946, at p. 30.

22. "Tony Azzera, Boxer, Dies," *New York Times,* March 30, 1929, at p. 15.

23. Ted Sares, "My First One: Lavern Roach vs. George Small, 1950," Bad Left Hook, November 17, 2010, at http://www.badlefthook.com/2010/11/17/1820872/my-first-one-lavern-roach-v-georgie-small-1950

24. Associated Press, "West, 21 Year Old Boxer, Dies from Injuries in Ring," *Chicago Daily Tribune,* December 22, 1950, at p. B1.

25. Michael Weinrub, "The Tragic Story of Charlie Mohr," Sports Illustrated.com, April 16, 2010, at http://sportsillustrated.cnn.com/2010/writers/the_bonus/04/16/mohr/index.html

26. Ibid.

27. Howard A. Rusk, M.D., "Paret: A Prognosis," *New York Times,* April 1, 1962, at p. 52.

28. Ibid.

29. "Benny Paret Dies of Fight Injuries," *New York Times,* April 3, 1962, at p. 1.

30. Associated Press, "Brown Asks Review of Ring Rules," *Los Angeles Times,* April 4, 1962, at p. B5.

31. Jerry Gillam, "Bills Designed to Make Boxing Less Dangerous," *Los Angeles Times,* March 11, 1963, at p. 29.

32. United Press International, "Paret Referee 'Blows Up' at Inquiry," *Chicago Daily Defender,* May 22, 1962, at p. 22.

33. United Press International, "Memory of Paret Keeps Ruby Away from Ring," *Chicago Tribune,* December 7, 1967, at p. E1.

34. Michael Shapiro, "Paret Tragedy: A Shared Burden," *New York Times,* March 23, 1983, at p. B9.

35. Associated Press, "Elite Ring Referee Corps Urged Here," *New York Times,* November 28, 1962, at p. 49.

36. Ibid.

37. Jim Murray, "No Rose for Benny," *Los Angeles Times,* April 5, 1962, at p. B1.

38. John Hall, "Moore's Death Saddens Ring World," *Los Angeles Times,* March 26, 1963, at p. B1.

39. Quoted in Gladwin Hill, "Demands for Boxing Ban Grow as Davey Moore Dies of Injury," *New York Times,* March 26, 1963, at p. 1.

40. Herald Tribune News Service, "Vatican Says Boxing 'Immoral, Barbarous,'" *Washington Post,* March 26, 1963, at p. A22.

41. Ibid.

42. Quoted in John Hall, "Davey Moore in Coma, Fights for Life," *Los Angeles Times,* March 23, 1963, at p. A1.

43. "Boxing: Moore's Death Prompts New Attacks," *Los Angeles Times,* March 31, 1963, at p. M5.

44. John Hall, "10,000 View Moore's Body Lying in State," *Los Angeles Times,* March 27, 1963, at p. B1.

45. Associated Press, "N.Y. Group Says Boxing Worthwhile," *Chicago Tribune,* March 31, 1963, at p. B6.

46. "Ban Boxing? Opinion Split," *Chicago Tribune,* March 26, 1963, at p. B1.

47. Oscar Fraley, " 'Officials at Fault' Al Weill Says after Run of Ring Deaths," *Chicago Daily Defender,* March 27, 1963, at p. 24.

48. George Gallup, "Poll Even on Banning of Boxing," *Washington Post,* May 9, 1963, at p. D6.

49. Jim Murray, "Dracula of Sport," *Los Angeles Times,* March 26, 1963, at p. B1.

50. Harry Golden, "Boxing's Last Round," *Chicago Daily Defender,* May 16, 1964, at p. 8.

51. Ibid.

52. "Ban Boxing?" at p. B1.

53. Quoted in United Press International, "Abolish Boxing?—Here Are Pros and Cons," *Chicago Daily Defender,* March 30, 1963, at p. 11.

54. United Press International, "New York Bans 6-Oz. Gloves in Title Fights," *Los Angeles Times,* April 3, 1963, at p. B7.

55. Don Page, "Boxing on Ropes? Not So, Say TV Ratings," *Los Angeles Times,* April 27, 1963, at p. B3.

56. Robert Lipsyte, "Countdown in Boxing," *New York Times,* April 2, 1964, at p. 38.

57. Robert H. Boyle, "No Man Was His Keeper," *Sports Illustrated,* March 24, 1980, at http://sportsillustrated.cnn.com/vault/article/magazine/MAG1123302/index.htm

58. Ibid.

59. Ibid.

60. Quoted in Dave Anderson, "The Burden of the Haunted Boxers," *New York Times,* December 2, 1979, at p. S4.

61. Jim Murray, "Thin Man of Wales," *Los Angeles Times,* September 18, 1980, at p. F1.

62. Richard Hoffer, "Owen Has Heard All the Jokes," *Los Angeles Times,* September 14, 1980, at p. C17.

63. Quoted in Rick Broadbent. *The Big If: The Life and Death of Johnny Owen.* London: Macmillan, 2007, at p. 198.

64. Quoted in "Mancini Foe Suffers Brain Damage," *Chicago Tribune,* November 14, 1982, at p. C2.

65. Angus Phillips, "WBC Limits Title Fights to 12 Rounds," *Washington Post,* December 10, 1982, at p. C1.

66. Ibid.

67. Quoted in Dan Rafael, "Johnson Dies from Brain Injury Sustained in Title Fight," ESPN.com, November 27, 2005, at http://sports.espn.go.com/sports/box ing/news/story?id=2169415

68. Quoted in Victor Cohn, "AMA Editor Urges Boxing Ban, Cites Brain Injuries," *Washington Post,* January 14, 1983, at p. A16.

69. Quoted in John Noble Wilford, "Physicians' Journal Calls for a Ban on Boxing," *New York Times,* January 14, 1983, at p. A1.

70. Ibid.

71. British Medical Association, "Boxing—The BMA's Position," January 16, 2009.

72. Carl T. Rowan, "AMA Bid to Ban Boxing a Class-Action Joke," *Los Angeles Times,* December 11, 1984, at p. C5.

73. Ibid.

74. Quoted in Marek Fuchs, "For the Record: Fight Doctor Battles Injuries, and Skeptics," *New York Times,* January 11, 2004, at http://www.nytimes.com/2004/01/11/nyregion/for-the-record-fight-doctor-battles-injuries-and-skeptics.html

CHAPTER 10

1. Quoted in Associated Press, "Ex-Convict's Sights Set on World Title," *Los Angeles Times,* March 16, 1974, at p. OC_A4.

2. Quoted in Associated Press, "Ex-Convict's Sights Set."

3. Beth Schenerman, "Inmate Sets Sights on Boxing Title," *New York Times,* December 17, 1978, at p. NJ31.

4. Al Harvin, "Scott Is Floored in Defeat," *New York Times,* May 26, 1980, at p. C2.

5. Bernard Fernandez, "Jerry 'the Bull' Martin Going into Pa. Hall of Fame," *Philadelphia Daily News,* May 9, 2011, at p. 74.

6. Quoted in Fernandez at p. 74.

7. Associated Press, "Scott Is Found Guilty of Murder, Faces Life," *New York Times,* February 5, 1981, at p. B7.

8. Quoted in Michael Katz, "Braxton Outpoints Scott in Prison Bout," *New York Times,* September 6, 1981, at p. S11.

9. Associated Press, "Convict Gains Knockout over Ex-Police Chief," *New York Times,* September 29, 1961, at p. 43.

10. Quoted in "Convicts Use Boxing Gloves to End Rows in Jersey Prison," *New York Times,* May 25, 1927, at p. 25.

11. Quoted in David Condon, "Boxing, Knifing Changed Lyle," *Chicago Tribune,* January 23, 1976, at p. C3.

12. Quoted in John Henderson, "Ex-boxer Ron Lyle Muscling up on Life," *Denver Post,* June 7, 2009, at http://www.denverpost.com/sports/ci_12537544

13. Quoted in Henderson.

14. Quoted in Tina Griego, "Redeemed Boxer Ron Lyle Now Living His Dream," *Denver Post,* March 1, 2011, at p. B1

15. See International Boxing Hall of Fame, "Remembering Heavyweight Star Ron Lyle," November 27, 2011, at http://www.ibhof.com/pages/news/ron_lyle.html

16. Quoted in A. S. "Doc" Young. *Sonny Liston: The Champ Nobody Wanted.* Chicago: Johnson Publishing, 1963, at p. 40.

17. Quoted in Young at p. 46.

18. Quoted in Young at p. 55.

19. Quoted in Rob Steen. *Sonny Boy: The Life and Strife of Sonny Liston.* London: Methuen, 1993, at p. 31.

20. Tommy Picou, "He Was 'Mr. Big' in Prison," *Chicago Daily Defender,* September 6, 1962, at p. 1.

21. Quoted in Young at p. 56.

22. Quoted in Steen at p. 59.

23. Sam Heckart, "The Black Gulliver: Sonny Liston's Story," *Chicago Daily Defender,* June 22, 1964, at p. 21.

24. Quoted in Steen at p. 65.

25. "Give Liston Chance, Asks Priest Who Knows Champ," *Chicago Daily Defender,* July 25, 1963, at p. A32.

26. Tom Wicker, "Boxer Describes Rise from Prison," *New York Times,* December 14, 1960, at p. 54.

27. Quoted in Young at p. 3.

28. Young at p. 1.

29. Quoted at Steen at p. 119.

30. Quoted in Steen at p. 128.

31. Quoted in Steen at p. 129

32. Nigel Collins. *Boxing Babylon: Behind the Shadowy World of the Prize Ring.* New York: Citadel Press, 1990, at p. 133.

33. Ibid. at pp. 133–34.

34. Collins at p. 138.

35. Will Grimsley, "A Con and a Guard . . . Their Story," *Washington Post,* November 28, 1971, at p. C1.

36. Ibid.

37. Quoted in Grimsley.

38. Quoted in "Young Inmate Gets Chance in Pan-Am Games Boxing," *Jet,* August 26, 1971, at p. 48.

39. Associated Press, "U.S. Boxer on Prison Leave Helps U.S. Beat British," *New York Times,* February 4, 1972, at p. 22.

40. Associated Press, "Soviet Boxers Held to a 3–3 Deadlock by American Team," *New York Times,* February 12, 1972, at p. 23.

41. United Press International, "Convict Hunter Not Wanted by Munich Official," *Chicago Tribune,* June 13, 1972, at p. C4.

42. Quoted in Reuters, "2 Senators Fight for Boxer-Convict," *New York Times,* June 20, 1972, at p. 48.

43. Neil Milbert, "Hostile Fans Boo as Tearful Hunter Loses," *Chicago Tribune,* July 21, 1972, at p. C1.

44. Quoted in Dan Levin, "A Couple of Hit and Miss Propositions," *Sports Illustrated,* July 31, 1972, at http://sportsillustrated.cnn.com/vault/article/magazine/MAG1086358/2/index.htm

45. Quoted in Michael Dobie, "Sports in Prison, Boxing Is Getting Punched Out of the System," *Newsday,* August 8, 2004, at p. B7.

46. Dobie at p. B7.

47. Ibid.

48. Austin Wilson, "Boxing Gives Prisoners 'Escape,'" *Los Angeles Times,* December 4, 1975, at p. F8.

49. David Williams, "Etienne Already Has Won His Biggest Fight—Emerged from Prison a Changed Man," *Commercial Appeal,* February 20, 2003, at p. D1.

50. Emily Kern, "Testimony: Etienne Changed after Beatings," *The Advocate,* March 23, 2006, at p. B2.

51. Pete Brook, "Exclusive: Photos of the Angola Amateur Boxing Association, Louisiana State Penitentiary," August 10, 2010 at http://prisonphotography.wordpress.com/2011/08/10/exclusive-photos-of-the-angola-amateur-boxing-association louisiana-state-penitentiary/

CHAPTER 11

1. Personal interview with Mike Fitzgerald, November 2011.

2. Ibid.

3. Personal interview with Bernard Fernandez, June 2011.

4. Personal interview with Harold Lederman, May 2011.

5. Ibid.

6. Personal interview with Bernard Fernandez, June 2011.

7. Personal interview with Jake Hall, May 2011.

8. Personal interview with Tim Lueckenhoff, July 2011.

9. Quoted in Associated Press, "Return Archibald–Jeffra Bout Urged by Rep. Kennedy," *Washington Post,* October 4, 1939, at p. 21.

10. Quoted in Associated Press, "N.B.A. Agrees That Ring Sport Needs Thorough House-cleaning," *Los Angeles Times,* December 13, 1939, at p. A14.

11. Quoted in Al Hailey, "Kennedy to Introduce Fight Bill Tomorrow," *Washington Post,* April 7, 1940, at p. 2.

12. Quoted in Associated Press, "Asks U.S. to Police Pro Boxing Game," *Chicago Tribune,* December 15, 1960, at p. E1.

13. Tom Wicker, "Licensing Power Is Core of Plan," *New York Times,* December 15, 1960, at p. 65.

14. "Boxing Writers Endorse Federal Control of the Sport," *New York Times,* April 2, 1964, at p. 38.

15. United Press International, "Dempsey Ring Czar?" *Chicago Daily Defender,* July 1, 1965, at p. 40.

16. George Minot, "Marciano Looks Like Solid Bet as Federal Boxing Commissioner," *Washington Post,* July 11, 1965, at p. C4.

17. "Survey Shows Public Divided on Boxing Plan," *Washington Post,* July 11, 1965, at p. C3.

18. Thomas Rogers, "U.S. Commission Urged for Sport," *New York Times,* October 20, 1970, at p. 57.

19. Quoted in Michael Katz, "Is Federal Commission for Boxing Feasible?" *New York Times,* March 21, 1979, at p. B10.

20. Quoted in Dave Brady, "Cosell Favors Boxing Council," *Washington Post,* April 4, 1979, at p. D3.

21. Quoted in Associated Press, "Patterson Urges Federal Boxing Control," *New York Times,* February 16, 1983.

22. Richard Hoffer, "It's a Sport That's Courting Disaster," *Los Angeles Times,* June 18, 18983, at p. SD_B11.

23. Quoted in Bill Brubaker, "Lawmakers to Introduce Bills to Regulate Boxing," *Washington Post,* June 16, 1992, at p. D1.

24. Dave Anderson, "Finally! Federal Law for Boxing," *New York Times,* February 29, 1997, at p. S1.

25. David L. Hudson Jr., "Senators, Panelists Discuss National Commissioner and Other Woes of Boxing!" Fightnews.com, May 25, 2002.

26. Personal interview with Tim Lueckenhoff, July 2011.

27. Personal interview with Rob Bleakley, November 2011.

28. Personal interview with Jake Donovan, December 2011.

29. Personal interview with Eric Bottjer, November 2011.

30. Personal interview with Jake Hall, May 2011.

31. Personal interview with Eric Bottjer, November 2011.

32. Personal interview with Jake Donovan, December 2011.

33. Jack Newfield, "The Shame of Boxing," *The Nation,* October 25, 2001, at http://www.thenation.com/print/article/shame-boxing

34. Personal interview with Jake Donovan, December 2011.

BIBLIOGRAPHY

Ali, Muhammad, with Richard Duncan. *The Greatest: My Own Story.* New York: Random House, 1975.

Allen, David Rayvern. *Punches on the Page: A Boxing Anthology.* Edinburgh, Scotland: Mainstream Publishing, 1998.

Anderson, Dave. *In the Corner: Boxing's Greatest Trainers Talk about Their Art.* New York: William Morrow, 1991.

Armstrong, Henry. *Gloves, Glory and God.* Westwood, NJ: Fleming H. Revell, 1956.

Ashe, Arthur, Jr. *A Hard Road to Glory: A History of the African-American Athlete: Boxing.* New York: Amistad Press, 1993.

Atlas, Teddy, and Peter Alson. *Atlas: From the Streets to the Ring: A Son's Struggle to Become a Man.* New York: Ecco, 2006.

Aycock, Colleen, and Mark Scott, eds. *The First Black Boxing Champions.* Jefferson, NC: McFarland, 2011.

Bak, Richard. *Joe Louis: The Great Black Hope.* New York: Da Capo Press, 1997.

Berger, Phil. *Punchlines: Berger on Boxing.* New York: Four Walls Eight Windows, 1993.

Bingham, Howard L., and Max Wallace. *Muhammad Ali's Greatest Fight.* London: Robson Books, 2004.

Blewitt, Bert. *The A–Z of World Boxing: Authoritative and Entertaining Compendium of the Fight Game from Its Origins to the Present Day.* London: Robson Books, 1996.

Bodner, Allen. *When Boxing Was a Jewish Sport.* Westport, CT: Praeger Trade, 1997.

Boyd, Herb, with Ray Robinson II. *Pound for Pound: A Biography of Sugar Ray Robinson.* New York: Amistad Press, 2006.

Brenner, Teddy, and Barney Nagler. *Only the Ring Was Square.* Englewood Cliffs, NJ: Prentice Hall, 1981.

Broadbent, Rick. *The Big If: The Life and Death of Johnny Owen.* London: Pan Books, 2006.

Bromberg, Lester. *Boxing's Unforgettable Fights.* New York: Ronald Press, 1962.

Bromberg, Lester. *World Champs.* New York: Retail Distributors, 1958.

Brunt, Stephen. *Facing Ali: Fifteen Fighters, Fifteen Stories.* Guilford, CT: Lyons Press, 2004.

Buchanan, Ken. *Buchanan: High Life and Hard Times*. London: Mainstream Publishing, 1986.

Buchanan, Ken. *The Tartan Legend*. London: Headline Book Publishing, 2000.

Cantwell, Robert. *The Real McCoy: The Life and Times of Norman Selby*. New York: Auerbach, 1971.

Carpentier, Georges. *The Art of Boxing*. New York: George H. Doran, 1926.

Carter, Rubin. *The Sixteenth Round: From Number 1 Contender to #45472*. New York: Penguin Global, 1991.

Cashill, Jack. *Sucker Punch: The Hard Left Hook That Dazed Ali and Killed King's Dream*. Nashville, TN: Nelson Current, 2006.

Cashmore, Ellis. *Tyson: Nurture of the Beast*. Cambridge, UK: Polity Press, 2005.

Cavanaugh, Jack. *Tunney: Boxing's Brainiest Champ and His Upset of the Great Jack Dempsey*. New York: Ballantine Books, 2006.

Century, Douglas. *Barney Ross*. New York: Schocken, 2006.

Chaiton, Sam, and Terry Swinton. *Lazarus and the Hurricane: The Freeing of Rubin "Hurricane" Carter*. New York: St Martin's Press, 2000.

Collins, Mark. *The 100 Greatest Boxers: The Ultimate Boxing Who's Who to Settle Every Argument and Start 100 More!* London: Generation Publications, 1999.

Collins, Nigel. *Boxing Babylon: Behind the Shadowy World of the Prize Ring*. New York: Citadel Press, 1990.

Cottrell, John. *Man of Destiny: The Story of Muhammad Ali/Cassius Clay*. London: Muller, 1967.

Couture, Randy, with Loretta Hunt. *Becoming the Natural: My Life In and Out of the Cage*. New York: Simon Spotlight Entertainment, 2008.

Crigger, Kelly. *Title Shot: Into the Shark Tank of Mixed Martial Arts*. Auberry, CA: Victory Belt, 2008.

De La Hoya, Oscar, with Steve Springer. *American Son: My Story*. New York: It Books, 2008.

DeLisa, Michael C. *Cinderella Man*. London: Milo Books, 2005.

Dibble, Roy F. *John L. Sullivan: An Intimate Narrative*. Boston: Little, Brown, 1925.

Dundee, Angelo. *My View from the Corner*. New York: McGraw-Hill, 2007.

Dundee, Angelo, with Mike Winters. *I Only Talk Winning*. Chicago: Contemporary Books, 1985.

Early, Gerald, ed. *The Muhammad Ali Reader*. New York: Harper Perennial, 1999.

Edwards, Robert. *Henry Cooper: The Authorized Biography of Britain's Greatest Boxing Hero*. London: Chivers, Windsor, Paragon and Camden, 2003.

Ercole, Andy, and Ed Oconowicz. *Tiberi: The Uncrowned Champion*. Wilmington, DE: Jared, 1992.

Erenberg, Lewis. *The Greatest Fight of Our Generation: Louis v. Schmeling*. New York: Oxford University Press, 2005.

Evans, Gavin. *Prince of the Ring: The Naseem Hamed Story*. London: Robson Books, 1998.

Fair, James. *Give Him to the Angels: Story of Harry Greb*. New York: Smith and Durrell, 1946.

Farr, Finis. *Black Champion: The Life and Times of Jack Johnson.* New York: Charles Scribner's Sons, 1964.

Fields, Armond. *James J. Corbett: A Biography of the Heavyweight Boxing Champion and Popular Theater Headliner.* Jefferson, NC: McFarland, 2001.

Fitzgerald, Mike. *The Ageless Warrior: The Life of Boxing Legend Archie Moore.* Champaign, IL: Sports Publishing, 2004.

Fitzgerald, Mike. *Tale of the Gator: The Craig Bodzianowski Story.* Milwaukee, WI: Lemieux International, 2000.

Fleischer, Nat. *50 Years at Ringside.* New York: Fleet Publishing, 1958.

Fleischer, Nat. *The Heavyweight Championship: An Informal History of Heavyweight Boxing from 1719 to the Present Day,* rev. ed. New York: G. P Putnam's Sons, 1961.

Fleischer, Nat. *Max Baer: The Glamour Boy of the Ring.* New York: C. J. O'Brien, 1942.

Foreman, George, and Joel Engel. *By George: The Autobiography of George Foreman.* New York: Simon & Schuster, 2000.

Franklin, Rich, and Jon F. Merz. *The Complete Idiot's Guide to Ultimate Fighting.* New York: Alpha Books, 2007.

Fraser, George McDonald. *Black Ajax.* New York: Carroll & Graf, 1999.

Frazier, Joe, and Phil Berger. *Smokin' Joe: The Autobiography of a Heavyweight Champion of the World, Smokin' Joe Frazier.* New York: Macmillan General Reference, 1996.

Fried, Ronald K. *Corner Men: Great Boxing Trainers.* New York: Four Walls Eight Windows, 1991.

Fullerton, Hugh. *Two Fisted Jeff: Life Story of James J. Jeffries World's Greatest Heavyweight Champion.* Chicago: Consolidated Book Publishers, 1929.

Giudice, Christian. *Hands of Stone: The Life and Legend of Roberto Duran.* London: Milo Books, 2006.

Goldstein, Alan. *A Fistful of Sugar: The Sugar Ray Leonard Story.* New York: Coward, McCann & Geoghegan, 1981.

Graziano, Rocky, with Ralph Corsel. *Somebody Down Here Likes Me Too.* New York: Stein & Day, 1981.

Hague, Jim. *Braddock: The Rise of the Cinderella Man.* New York: Chamberlain Brothers, 2005.

Hales, A. G. *Black Prince Peter: The Romantic Career of Peter Jackson.* New York: Wright & Brown, 1931.

Harrison, Audley. *Audley Harrison: Realising the Dream.* London: Andre Deutsch, 2001.

Haskins, James. *Sugar Ray Leonard.* London: Robson Books, 1989.

Hatton, Ricky. *The Hitman: My Story.* London: Ebury Press, 2007.

Hauser, Thomas. *The Black Lights: Inside the World of Professional Boxing.* Fayetteville: University of Arkansas Press, 2000.

Hauser, Thomas. *The Lost Legacy of Muhammad Ali.* Toronto: Sport Media Publishing, 2005.

Hauser, Thomas. *Muhammad Ali: His Life and Times.* New York: Simon & Schuster, 1992.

Heinz, W. C. *What a Time It Was.* New York: Da Capo Press, 2001.

Heinz, W. C., ed. *The Fireside Book of Boxing.* New York: Simon & Schuster, 1961.

Heller, Peter. *Bad Intentions: The Mike Tyson Story.* New York: Da Capo Press, 1995.

Hietala, Thomas. *Jack Johnson, Joe Louis and the Struggle for Racial Equality.* New York: M. E. Sharpe, 2002.

Hirsh, James S. *Hurricane: The Miraculous Journey of Rubin Carter.* Boston: Houghton Mifflin, 2000.

Holmes, Larry, with Phil Berger. *Larry Holmes: Against the Odds.* New York: St. Martin's Press, 1998.

Holyfield, Evander, and Bernard Holyfield. *Holyfield: The Humble Warrior.* Nashville, TN: Thomas Nelson, 1996.

Holyfield, Evander, with Lee Guenfeld. *Becoming Holyfield: A Fighter's Journey.* New York: Simon & Schuster, 2008.

Hudson, David L., Jr. *Combat Sports: An Encyclopedia of Wrestling, Fighting, and Mixed Martial Arts.* Westport, CT: Greenwood Press, 2009.

Hudson, David L., Jr., and Mike Fitzgerald Jr. *Boxing's Most Wanted: The Top Ten Book of Champs, Chumps and Punch-Drunk Palookas.* Washington, DC: Brassey's, 2004.

Hughes, Brian. *Willie Pep: The Will o' the Wisp.* Manchester, UK: Collyhurst and Hughes, 1997.

Hughes, Brian, and Damian Hughes. *Hit Man: The Thomas Hearns Story.* Preston, UK: Milo Books, 2010.

Isenberg, Michael. *John L. Sullivan and His America.* Urbana: University of Illinois Press, 1988.

Jarrett, John. *The Champ in the Corner: The Ray Arcel Story.* London: Tempus, 2007.

Jarrett, John. *Dynamite Gloves: The Fighting Lives of Boxing's Big Punchers.* London: Robson Books, 2002.

Jarrett, John. *Gene Tunney: The Golden Guy Who Licked Jack Dempsey Twice.* London: Robson Books, 2003.

Johannson, Ingemar. *Seconds Out of the Ring.* London: Sportsmens Book Club, 1961.

Johnson, Jack. *My Life and Battles.* Edited by Chris Rivers. Westport, CT: Praeger, 2007.

Johnston, Alexander. *Ten and Out! The Complete Story of the Prize Ring in America.* New York: Ives Washburn, 1943.

Kaye, Andrew M. *The Pussycat of Prizefighting: Tiger Flowers and the Politics of Black Celebrity.* Athens: University of Georgia Press, 2004.

Kearns, Jack "Doc", and Oscar Fraley. *The Million Dollar Gate.* New York: Macmillan, 1966.

Kennedy, Paul. *Billy Conn: Pittsburgh Kid.* Bloomington, IN: AuthorHouse, 2007.

Kent, Graeme. *The Great White Hopes: The Quest to Defeat Jack Johnson.* Gloucester, UK: Sutton Publishing, 2005.

Kimball, George. *Four Kings: Leonard, Hagler, Hearns, Duran and the Last Great Era of Boxing.* Ithaca, NY: McBooks Press, 2008.

Kimball, George, ed. *At the Fights: American Writers on Boxing.* Des Moines, IA: Library of America, 2011.

Kram, Mark. *Ghosts of Manila: The Fateful Blood Feud between Muhammad Ali and Joe Frazier.* New York: HarperCollins, 2001.

LaMotta, Jake, with Joseph Carter and Peter Savage. *Raging Bull: My Story.* New York: Da Capo Press, 1997.

Lane, Mills, with Jedwin Smith. *Let's Get It On.* New York: Crown Publications, 1998.

Larnder, Rex. *The Legendary Champions.* New York: American Heritage Press, 1972.

Layden, Tim. *The Last Great Fight: The Extraordinary Tale of Two Men and How One Fight Changed Their Lives.* New York: St. Martin's Press, 2007.

Leonard, Sugar Ray, with Michael Axelrod. *The Big Fight: My Life In and Out of the Ring.* New York: Viking Press, 2011.

Lewis, Lennox. *Lennox Lewis: The Autobiography of the WBC Heavyweight Champion of the World.* London: Faber & Faber, 1994.

Liebling, A. J. *The Sweet Science.* New York: Grove Press, 1956.

Lipsyte, Robert. *An Accidental Sportswriter.* New York: HarperCollins, 2011.

Lipsyte, Robert, and Peter Levine. *Idols of the Game: A Sporting History of the American Game.* Atlanta, GA: Turner Publishing, 1998.

Lois, George, ed. *Ali Rap.* New York: ESPN Books, 2006.

Loiseau, Jean Claude. *Marcel Cerdan.* Paris: Flammarion, 1989.

Long, Bill, and John Johnson. *Tyson–Douglas: The Inside Story of the Upset of the Century.* Alexandria, VA: Potomac Books, 2006.

Magriel, Paul, ed. *The Memoirs of the Life of Daniel Mendoza.* London: B. T. Batsford, 1951.

Makinde, Adeyinka. *Dick Tiger: The Life and Times of a Boxing Immortal.* Tarentum, PA: Word Association Publishers, 2005.

Margolick, David. *Beyond Glory: Joe Louis v. Max Schmeling, and a World on the Brink.* New York: Vintage Books, 2005.

Marqusee, Mike. *Redemption Song: Muhammad Ali and the Spirit of the 60s,* 2nd ed. London: Verso, 1995.

Mayes, Harold. *Rocky Marciano.* London: Panther Books, 1956.

McCaffery, Dan. *Tommy Burns: Canada's Unknown World Heavyweight Champion.* Toronto, Ontario: Lorimer, 2001.

McCallum, John. *World Heavyweight Boxing Championship: A History.* Philadelphia: Chilton Book, 1974.

McCullough, Wayne. *Pocket Rocket: Don't Quit, The Autobiography of Wayne McCullough.* London: Mainstream Publishing, 2005.

McGuigan, Barry, Gerry Callan, and Harry Mullan. *Barry McGuigan: The Untold Story.* London: Arrow Books, 1992.

McIlvaney, Hugh. *The Hardest Game: McIlvaney on Boxing.* New York: McGraw-Hill, 2001.

McRae, Donald. *Dark Trade: Lost in Boxing.* Edinburgh, Scotland: Mainstream Publishing, 1996.

Mee, Bob. *Bare Fists.* Warwickshire, UK: Lodge Farm Books, 1998.

Mee, Bob. *Boxing: Heroes and Champions.* London: Book Sales, 1997.

Mee, Bob. *The Heavyweights: The Definitive History of the Heavyweight Fighters.* Stroud, UK: Tempus, 2006.

Moore, Archie. *Any Boy Can: The Archie Moore Story.* Englewood Cliffs, NJ: Prentice Hall, 1971.

Moyle, Clay. *Sam Langford: Boxing's Greatest Uncrowned Champion.* Seattle: Bennett & Hastings, 2008.

Mullaly, Frederic. *Primo: The Story of 'Man Mountain' Carnera.* London: Robson Books, 1999.

Mullan, Harry. *Boxing: Inside the Game.* London: Icon Books, 1998.

Mullan, Harry, with Bob Mee. *The Ultimate Encyclopedia of Boxing.* London: Carlton Books, 2007.

Murray, Michael. *The Journeyman.* Edinburgh, Scotland: Mainstream Publishing, 2002.

Myler, Patrick. *Gentleman Jim Corbett: The Truth behind a Boxing Legend.* London: Robson Books, 1998.

Myler, Patrick. *Ring of Hate: Joe Louis v. Max Schmeling: The Fight of the Century.* New York: Arcade Publishing, 2006.

Newfield, Jack. *Only in America: The Life and Crimes of Don King.* New York: William Morrow, 1995.

O'Connor, Daniel, ed. *Iron Mike: A Mike Tyson Reader.* New York: Da Capo Press, 2002.

Odd, Gilbert. *Boxing: The Great Champions.* London: Hamlyn Publishing Group, 1974.

Odd, Gilbert. *Debatable Decisions.* London: Nicholson & Watson, 1953.

Odd, Gilbert. *Encyclopedia of Boxing.* New York: Crescent Books, 1983.

O'Toole, Andrew. *Sweet William: The Life of Billy Conn.* Champaign: University of Illinois Press, 2007.

Otty, Harry. *Charley Burley and the Black Murderers Row.* n.p.: Exposure Publishing, 2006.

Patterson, Floyd, and Milton Gross. *Victory over Myself.* n.p.: Scholastic Book Services, 1966.

Pep, Willie, with Robert Sacchi. *Willie Pep Remembers.* Hollywood, FL: Frederick Fell Publishers, 1973.

Pepe, Phil. *Come Out Smokin': Joe Frazier, The Champ Nobody Knew.* New York: Coward McCann & Geoghegan, 1972.

Pitluck, Adam. *Standing Eight: The Inspiring Story of Jesus "El Matador" Chavez Who Became Lightweight Champion of the World.* New York: Da Capo Press, 2006.

Pitt, Nick. *The Prince and the Prophet: The Rise of Naseem Hamed.* London: Four Walls Eight Windows, 1999.

Pollack, Adam J. *John L. Sullivan: The Career of the First Gloved Heavyweight Champion.* Jefferson, NC: McFarland, 2006.

Remnick, David. *King of the World: Muhammad Ali and the Rise of an American Hero.* New York: Vintage Books, 1999.

Rendell, Jonathan. *This Bloody Mary Is the Last Thing I Own*. London: Faber & Faber, 1998.

Ribalow, Harold Uriel. *Fighter from Whitechapel: The Story of Daniel Mendoza*. London: Farrar, Straus and Cudahy, 1962.

Roberts, James B., and Alexander G. Skutt. *Boxing Register: International Boxing Hall of Fame Official Record Book*, 4th ed. Ithaca, NY: McBooks Press, 2006.

Roberts, Randy. *Joe Louis: Hard Times Man*. New Haven, CT: Yale University Press, 2012.

Roberts, Randy. *Papa Jack: Jack Johnson and the Era of White Hopes*. New York: Free Press, 1985.

Robinson, Sugar Ray, and Dave Anderson. *Sugar Ray*. New York: Viking Press, 1970.

Rosenfeld, Allen S. *Charley Burley: The Life and Hard Times of an Uncrowned Champion*. Bloomington, IN: AuthorHouse Publishing, 2007.

Ross, Barney, and Martin Abramson. *No Man Stands Alone: The True Story of Barney Ross*. New York: Lippincott, 1957.

Ross, Ron. *Bummy Davis vs. Murder Inc.: The Rise and Fall of the Jewish Mafia and an Ill-Fated Prizefighter*. New York: St. Martin's Press, 2003.

Rotella, Carlos. *Cut Time: An Education at the Fights*. New York: Houghton Mifflin, 2003.

Sammons, Jeffrey. *Beyond the Ring: The Role of Boxing in American Society*. Champaign: University of Illinois Press, 1988.

Samuels, Charles. *The Magnificent Rube: The Life and Gaudy Times of Tex Rickard*. New York: McGraw-Hill, 1957.

Schaap, Jeremy. *Cinderella Man: James J. Braddock, Max Baer and the Greatest Upset in Boxing History*. New York: Houghton Mifflin, 2005.

Schmeling, Max, and George Von Der Lippe. *Max Schmeling: An Autobiography*. Los Angeles: Bonus Books, 1998.

Shavers, Earnie, with Mike Fitzgerald and Marshall Terrill. *Welcome to the Big Time*. Champaign, IL: Sports Publishing, 2002.

Sheridan, Jim. *Leave the Fighting to McGuigan: The Official Biography of Barry McGuigan*. New York: Penguin Books, 1986.

Shropshire, Kenneth. *Being Sugar Ray: The Life of Sugar Ray Robinson, America's Greatest Boxer and First Celebrity Athlete*. New York: Basic Civitas Books, 2007.

Steen, Rob. *Sonny Boy: The Life and Strife of Sonny Liston*. London: Methuen, 1993.

Strauss, Darin. *The Real McCoy*. New York: Plume Books, 2002.

Sugar, Bert Randolph. *Boxing's Greatest Fighters*. Guilford, CT: Lyons Press, 2006.

Sugar, Bert Randolph, and the Editors of *Ring* Magazine. *The Great Fights: A Pictorial History of Boxing's Greatest Bouts*. New York: Rutledge Press, 1981.

Suster, Gerald. *Lighting Strikes: Lives and Times of Boxing's Lightweight Champions*. London: Robson Books, 1994.

Thomas, James J. *The Holyfield Way: What I Learned about Courage, Perseverance, and the Bizarre World of Boxing*. Champaign, IL: Sports Publishing, 2005.

Torres, Jose. *Fire and Fear: The Inside Story of Mike Tyson*. New York: Warner Books, 1989.

Torres, Jose. *Sting Like a Bee: The Muhammad Ali Story.* New York: McGraw-Hill, 2001.

Tsyzu, Kostya. *Kostya: My Story.* Sydney, Australia: ABC Books, 2003.

Walsh, Peter. *Men of Steel: The Lives and Times of Boxing's Middleweight Champions.* London: Robson Books, 1995.

Young, A. S. "Doc". *Sonny Liston: The Champ Nobody Wanted.* Chicago: Johnson Publishing, 1963.

INDEX

ABOUT THE AUTHOR

DAVID L. HUDSON, JR. is an attorney, author, and licensed boxing judge living in Nashville, Tennessee. He is the author or coauthor of more than 35 books, including ABC-CLIO's *Combat Sports: An Encyclopedia of Wrestling, Fighting, and Mixed Martial Arts.* He is also a feature writer for Fightnews .com (http://www.fightnews.com).